Harold
Lloyd
comedian

CHARLIE CHAPLIN

Charlie in *The Gold Rush*, 1925. Too often Chaplin's tramp is seen as a loser at love, as well as life in general. Yet this film finds him metaphorically striking gold with the heroine (played by Georgia Hale) after literally hitting paydirt with his mining partner. This success is especially pertinent in *The Gold Rush,* because this is the film Chaplin most wanted to be remembered by, as well as being probably his most acclaimed work. (Courtesy Museum of Modern Art/Film Stills Archive.)

CHARLIE CHAPLIN
A Bio-Bibliography

Wes D. Gehring

Popular Culture Bio-Bibliographies

Greenwood Press
Westport, Connecticut • London, England

Acknowledgments

All stills, with the exception of Fig. 4, were provided by the Museum of Modern Art/Film Stills Archive and the author's own collection. Fig. 4 came courtesy of the Franklin D. Roosevelt Library in Hyde Park, New York. The Rollin Kirby drawing (Fig. 5) was printed in the *New York World* in 1927 and appears in Gerald McDonald's *The Picture History of Charlie Chaplin* (Nostalgia Press, 1965). The John Held, Jr., drawings (Figs. 13-16) originally appeared in Konrad Bercovici's August 15, 1925, *Colliers* article, "Charlie Chaplin: An Authorized Interview." They were photographed for reproduction in this volume by Frank Foster and Mark Mattheis.

The poem "A Chaplin Celebration" by the author is reprinted with the permission of © *Ball State University Forum* 1981, Muncie, Indiana, where it appeared in the Autumn issue.

Library of Congress Cataloging in Publication Data

Gehring, Wes D.
 Charlie Chaplin, a bio-bibliography.

 (Popular culture bio-bibliographies, ISSN 0193-6891)
 Filmography: p.
 Discography: p.
 Includes index.
 1. Chaplin, Charlie, 1889-1977. 2. Chaplin, Charlie,
1889-1977—Bibliography. 3. Comedians—United States—
Biography. 4. Moving-picture actors and actresses—
United States—Biography. I. Title. II. Series.
PN2287.C5G38 1983   791.43'028'0924   82-20964
ISBN 0-313-23288-1 (lib. bdg.)

Library of Congress Catalog Card Number: 82-20964
ISBN: 0-313-23288-1
ISSN: 0193-6891

First published in 1983

Greenwood Press
A division of Congressional Information Service, Inc.
88 Post Road West
Westport, Connecticut 06881

Printed in the United States of America

10 9 8 7 6 5 4 3 2 1

To Eileen and Sarah, my family,
and Professors Richard D. MacCann
and Timothy J. Lyons

A CHAPLIN CELEBRATION
by
Wes D. Gehring

In 1914 a most unlikely hero appeared,
A lone ranger in comic garb,
Second cousin of Don Quixote,
Come to lighten a war torn world.

He wore baggy pants and a chocolate smudge
    mustache,
With a derby perched atop curly black hair,
And large gray eyes,
A stranger armed with a kick and a cane.

Like the classic cowboy he seldom spoke,
And because his shuffle tried for two directions
    at once,
It was fun to watch him walk,
And bedlam to see him run.

But this pint-sized hero was tough;
Who else kicked bullies in the behind,
Or, possessed a lariat-like cane,
Just right for tripping the troublesome?

And like the heroes of old—Achilles, Siegfried,
    and all the rest,
His armor too, had one weak spot,
Where he wore his heart on his sleeve,
For any fair thing to take.

But is this not expected of any romantic story,
Where good vanquishes evil,
And beauty kills the beast,
Especially if it stars little Sir Charles?

For he was a modern-day hero,
With a cane for a sword and a derby for a shield,
Who slayed the world's dragons with laughter,
Just as he captured our hearts.

CONTENTS

x   Contents

ILLUSTRATIONS

PREFACE

The goal of this work is to present a combined biographical, critical, and bibliographical estimate of the life and times of Charlie Chaplin in the field of cinema and the popular arts. With this in mind, the book is divided into five chapters. Chapter 1 is a biography of the artist that examines both his on-screen persona (hereafter to be designated as Charlie) and the man behind the screen (to be referred to as Charles and/or simply Chaplin). In the case of the comedian, it was often hard to distinguish one from the other, both for the person and the public.

Chapter 2 is a critique of the impact of his career on film comedy and film study in general, as well as upon contemporary culture and the popular arts. And to adequately understand his ongoing film comedy influence, it is necessary to examine his work in relation to basic traditions in American humor.

Because no examination of an artist would be complete without including some of his own observations, Chapter 3 is comprised of a reprinting of both an interview with the comedian, Konrad Bercovici's "Charlie Chaplin: An Authorized Interview" (*Colliers*, August 15, 1925), and an article by Chaplin, "In Defense of Myself" (*Colliers*, November 11, 1922). These inclusions were made because of the richness with which they demontrate basic characteristics of the man, and the world around him, during his most acclaimed decade of productivity, the 1920s.

Chapter 4 is a Chaplin bibliographic essay that assesses key published reference materials and locates research collections open to the student and/or scholar. The bulk of the chapter, however, is allocated to reference works and is divided into two sections. The first is devoted to book-length sources written about and/or by the comedian. These materials are then subdivided into four categories: Chaplin critical biographies, Chaplin on

Chaplin, Chaplin viewed by insiders, and Chaplin references. The second section of Chapter 4 is comprised of shorter works and includes articles, interviews, book chapters, and monographs. It also is subdivided into four parts: Chaplin critical analysis, Chaplin on Chaplin concerning comedy theory and pantomime, Chaplin's working style, and Chaplin's world view. To facilitate the use of both sections as a reference guide, Chapter 5 is a bibliographic checklist of all sources recommended in Chapter 4. (The checklist is meant to be a Chaplin research guide, not an all-encompassing bibliography on the comedian.)

The appendices contain a chronological biography, a filmography, musical compositions, and a discography, which includes recordings of Chaplin compositions by musicians outside the confines of his personal and/or movie supervision.

To say that this project was years in the making is not to exaggerate. Since childhood I have collected Chaplin films and books, as some youngsters collect baseball cards. In college at the University of Iowa (Iowa City), this Chaplin fascination was given guidance and inspiration by a number of teacher-scholars who often were Chaplin specialists themselves. In fact, I was able to capitalize on what might be called a "Chaplin connection" at the university. My first film teacher was Timothy J. Lyons, already a recognized Chaplin authority, who would go on to write the watershed *Charles Chaplin: A Guide to References and Resources*. Professor Lyons has encouraged my Chaplin interest through the years and was always quick to respond during the preparation of this volume whenever I queried him on a research problem.

In graduate school I had the distinct honor of taking a seminar with the celebrated French film historian-theorist-filmmaker Jean Mitry, who was a visiting professor at Iowa. Mitry, generally considered to be France's greatest Chaplin scholar, was both a joy and an inspiration as he directed discussion on the comedian and related areas in the seminar, which focused on American silent films.

Prof. J. Dudley Andrew, who heads the University of Iowa film program, introduced me to the writing of theorist André Bazin, whose work on Chaplin is central to a more complete appreciation of the comedian. And it was for an Andrew class that I first explored the "creative" manner in which several major film theorists utilized Chaplin in their work.

A fellow graduate student at Iowa, though he was well into the Ph.D. program when I was admitted, was Philip G. Rosen, who had already published the important essay "The Chaplin World View" and who was, needless to say, always available for discussions about the comedian.

Donald W. McCaffrey, who had completed his study at Iowa well before I arrived, was just establishing himself (early 1970s) as a major silent film historian. Though I was not to meet and discuss Chaplin with him until much later (nor was I always in agreement with his views), McCaffrey's work provided an ongoing forum for Chaplin discussion. And in *Focus on Chaplin* he compiled a still pivotal reference text that only seems marred in its view of Chaplin as a limited director.

A number of other individuals at Iowa, though not necessarily involved in Chaplin studies, have had an influence on my writing, and I would especially like to acknowledge three people. Humor scholar Dr. John Gerber helped give structure to my interest in American comedy. Prof. John Raeburn likewise provided direction in my study of American popular culture. And Prof. Richard Dyer MacCann guided and encouraged me through my graduate film years and, more than anyone else, has made projects like this possible for me.

Any "Chaplin connection" centering on the University of Iowa must also acknowledge the main library, which is recognized as one of the outstanding centers for Chaplin research. On that rare occasion when something was not available, no other library with which I was involved (and by the end of the study this had become a sizable number) responded so quickly to my needs.

Chapter 4 notes a number of outstanding libraries in which Chaplin research is possible, but I would like to add a special thank you to the following: the Academy of Motion Picture Arts and Sciences, the Library of Congress, the Museum of Modern Art (New York), the Franklin D. Roosevelt Library (Hyde Park, New York), the Ball State University Bracken Library (Muncie, Indiana), and both Indiana University's main library and its special collection, Lilly Library (Bloomington, Indiana).

I also wish to acknowledge the support and suggestions of friends, colleagues, and students (particularly members of my recent Chaplin seminar) for their contributions to this work and to my earlier *Charlie Chaplin's World of Comedy*. And I would especially like to recognize the support my past comedy writing (both on Chaplin and other subjects) has received from Prof. Larry Mintz, editor of *American Humor* (University of Maryland).

Finally, I would like to thank Prof. M. Thomas Inge for proposing this book, my family's patience and understanding while I actually performed the task, and Janet Warrner's typing and proofing of the various drafts. (My young daughter Sarah must now know more about Charlie Chaplin than any other little girl in the country, with the possible exception of Timothy J. Lyons's twin girls. And my wife Eileen could no doubt direct my next graduate seminar on Chaplin.)

I hope that this study of Chaplin represents not only further insight into his life and influence but also a general celebration of all that is comic.

Wes D. Gehring
Ball State University
Muncie, Indiana

CHARLIE CHAPLIN

1

BOTH SIDES
OF THE SCREEN:
CHAPLIN'S BIOGRAPHY

So many people have claimed to have given Chaplin his start that pioneer film historian Terry Ramsaye was moved to observe: "The original discoverers of Charlie Chaplin should form an association and hold a convention at the Polo Grounds, if the seating facilities are adequate."[1]

Charles Chaplin, the cinema's most celebrated figure, was born April 16, 1889, in East Lane, Walworth (London), though as biographer Denis Gifford has sardonically observed, earlier references also have listed Paris, Fontainebleau (France), Bermondsey, and a host of other London addresses.[2] Like Pan, the Greek god of fields and forests to whom Chaplin's comedy persona frequently is compared, mystery seems to have surrounded the creator of the tramp from the beginning.

His parents, Charles Sr. and Hannah Chaplin, were successful vaudeville performers; they would separate when Charles Jr. was still quite young. Charles Sr. was a well-known music hall baritone and comedian, whose picture often appeared on the covers of popular sheet music, which he sometimes also had written. Hannah, who went by the stage names of Lily Harley and Lily Chaplin, was a singer, dancer, and mimic. Her career never matched that of her husband.

Before her marriage to Charles, Hannah had eloped to Cape Town, South Africa, with Sydney Hawkes, a bookmaker passing himself off as a lord. The son born of this union, also named Sydney, would have a major influence on young Charles's life and career. Young Charles would have two other half brothers, Guy and Wheeler Dryden, born of his mother's post-Charles romance with music hall singer Leo Dryden. The Drydens, reared by their father, would have little contact with the future comedy great, though Wheeler would later hold numerous other positions at Chaplin's Studio.

Hannah's search for romance, a trait passed on to son Charles, was soon to go sour. With two boys to support and an ever-decreasing amount of aid from the elder Charles, who was already starting to display the signs of a losing battle with alcoholism, Hannah resumed her solo career.

For a time all went well, but eventually her voice, which had never been strong, was no longer dependable. Ironically her last performance, which was prematurely cut short when her voice failed, proved to be five-year-old Charles's entertainment debut. The theater manager merely explained the situation to the audience and then put the little boy on. In spite of the situation and because of the confidence of young Charles, who had long been entertaining family friends, his singing was an immediate hit. In fact, pathos turned to comedy when the now appreciative audience started throwing coins on stage and the boy stopped his own show to retrieve them.

One element of the child's impromptu but winning first performance would offer dark foreshadowing for his future career: he innocently imitated the cracking of Hannah's voice.[3] Though Charles could hardly be expected to realize the pain this would cause his mother, it seems a fitting beginning to a career that would always take precedence over family and other personal relationships.

Since Hannah's vaudeville days were finished, she attempted to earn a livelihood as a seamstress and part-time nurse. She pawned valuables and sometimes even altered her clothes to meet the needs of Sydney and Charles; this guaranteed them their fair share of fights with insensitive neighborhood boys. Yet Hannah constantly maintained a happy front for her children. She sang, danced, did scenes from plays, and most significantly in terms of Charles's future in silent film comedy, she provided invaluable lessons in pantomime.

> I learned from her everything I know. She was the most astound-
> ing mimic I ever saw. She would stay at the window for hours,
> gazing at the street and reproducing with her hands, eyes and
> expression all that was going on down there, and never stopped.
> It was in watching and observing her that I learned not only to
> translate motions with my hands and features, but also to study
> mankind.[4]

Chaplin was able to put his mother's lessons to use long before the movies or even his own music hall days, for as a child he often earned pennies dancing in the streets. Not surprisingly, the gamin in Chaplin's *Modern Times* (1936) is a street dancer, while his screen persona as a sometime street musician is seen from *The Vagabond* (1916) to *Limelight* (1952).

It has been suggested that the often vulnerable Chaplin heroine, be she the unwed mother of *The Kid* (1921) or the blind girl of *City Lights* (1931), was the comedian's way of footnoting his work with a reference to his mother. But a much more likely salute can be found in the battling heroine of *The Great Dictator* (1940), who just happens to be named Hannah.

Despite his mother's efforts, young Charles's dance pennies, and Sydney's paper selling, the family was forced in 1896 to enter Lambeth Borough workhouse, or "to use a crueler phrase better fitting the degrading situation. to enter the poorhouse."[5] Chaplin painfully notes in his autobiography that they were considered "inmates of the 'booby hatch,' the slang expression for workhouse."[6]

Chaplin's childhood now began to take on a Dickensian quality that the comedian himself often drew attention to in both his writing and his films. Separate housing requirements at Lambeth necessitated a traumatic family separation, and within a few weeks the boys were moved outside of London to the Hanwell School for Orphans and Destitute Children. This separation was the more difficult for Chaplin because at the workhouse he at least had felt physically near to his mother.

Living conditions at Hanwell were hardly pleasant, and the children were subjected to floggings for minor infractions, always with the whole school in attendance. Charles suffered one such punishment by impulsively confessing to something he had not done, burning scraps of paper in a bathroom. Chaplin later wrote of the incident as an "adventure," about which he felt "valiantly triumphant."[7] The theatrical setting, with the large audience of peers, had seemingly not been lost on the young boy. This incident would be consistent with a lifelong tendency to maximize the drama of his private life, both as it occurred and in his films.

Charles stayed at Hanwell over a year, losing even the companionship of Sydney who, at eleven years of age, exercised a poorhouse option of joining the Royal Navy as a trainee.

There would be a brief reuniting of the family as Hannah again tried to make a go of it and Sydney returned from the navy. But the boys would soon find themselves back at the workhouse. Then came the devastating news that their mother had gone insane and been institutionalized in the lunatic asylum at Cane Hill. This latest poverty-induced family breakup was too much to bear. Charles was too young to fully comprehend what had occurred, and preferred to see insanity as his mother's way of escaping their humiliating poverty. All this happened before he was nine.

These incidents would forever leave their mark on Chaplin. He had both a lifelong anxiety about going insane and a special need for the security of money. Not surprisingly, he would later remark that "the saddest thing I can imagine is to get used to luxury."[8] Moreover, his films would often reflect this orphan-like (outsider) situation, paralleling the Victorian Era trend in sentimental popular culture best exemplified by Dickens.

After the removal of Hannah, the courts placed Charles and Sydney in the home of Charles Sr. and his mistress, which was little home at all. The elder Chaplin was generally gone, or sleeping off the effects of his ever-increasing dependence on alcohol. His mistress, Louise, was resentful of the intrusion, since she and Charles Sr. already had a son of their own for whom she was responsible. As if in a male reversal of Cinderella, stepbrothers Charles and Sydney, destined for Hollywood fame and fortune, were made to do all the heavy work and often found themselves locked out by Louise when their father was gone.

The situation became serious enough to merit intervention by the Society for the Prevention of Cruelty to Children. Luckily, Hannah was discharged at this time, and her family of three could once again take up housekeeping, but her recovery was not to be permanent. Though Charles was hardly aware of it, his life was about to enter a new and exciting phase—that of a professional performer.

Cinema's greatest clown began with a clog-dancing troupe called Eight Lancashire Lads. One Christmas season found the troupe booked into the London Hippodrome as supporting players (cats and dogs) in a mime production of *Cinderella*. During this run Charles first displayed the gift for improvisation that would flower in silent film comedy. Like many of his later antics, such as using his cane to lift up dresses, the young comedian's spontaneity could be controversial. During one performance he upstaged the star by having his cat act like the most uncultured of pooches: both sniffing one dog's posterior, and then raising an outhouse-oriented leg at the corner of the stage. The laughter continued whenever Charles the cat turned to the audience and winked one of his large eyes, activated from the inside of the costume.[9] Everyone seemed to like it but the star and the stage manager, the latter unnecessarily concerned that his theater would be censored.

Even as a Lancashire Lads beginner, Charles dreamed of being more than one of eight, demonstrating early the drive that would eventually take him to ever more lucrative film contracts during the 1910s, before cofounding his own company (United Artists, 1919). As fate would have it, he planned to start a comedy team called the Millionaire Tramps. And though the team did not materialize, it nicely anticipated the irony of his later position—being a millionaire by way of his portrayal of a cinema tramp. (Paperback editions of his autobiography often carried the additional title: *Memoirs of a Millionaire Tramp*.)

The end of his Dickensian childhood came in 1901 with the close of *Cinderella*. The plot of this play seemed like a dark metaphor for Charles's almost nonexistent home life: his father died of alcoholism and his mother was readmitted to a mental institution. By the age of twelve he had survived "the most formative period in his life. . . . He had passed through virtually every strong experience which was to illuminate his art."[10]

In the ensuing years Chaplin found success both on the legitimate stage and in vaudeville. He played a street urchin in H. A. Saintsbury's *Jim: The Romance of a Cockney*, a melodrama being tested outside of London. Though it closed in a short time, Chaplin's reviews were excellent and he toured at length with Saintsbury in William Gillette's *Sherlock Holmes*, playing the detective's page boy Billy. Again there were good reviews, and Chaplin would repeat the role of Billy several times in subsequent years, even playing opposite author Gillette himself.

In 1906 he entered vaudeville in *Casey's Circus*, as part of a troupe which showcased young talent doing parodies of prominent people. Chaplin's routine included burlesques of both Dick Turpin, the robber, and "Doctor" Walford Bodie, a showman and hypnotist (sometimes called the "electrical wizard") who claimed to cure the handicapped with an application of electricity.

After his appearances in legitimate theater, Chaplin felt vaudeville a comedown. Thus he planned his burlesque of Bodie to be "such a marvelous character delineation that even the lowest music-hall audience would recognize it as great acting" and someone from the theater would rescue him from his vaudeville fate.[11] Such was not to be the case; instead he was to learn a painful but pertinent comedy lesson. Everything went wrong for Chaplin's Bodie, from a dropped cane to an unruly hat:

> The more serious I was, the funnier it struck the audience. I came off at last, pursued by howls of laughter and wild applause.
> . . . I had stumbled on the secret of being funny—unexpectedly.[12]

This comedy lesson, which would be one of the few articulated by Chaplin in print, could be labeled "mock dignity under duress," because the comic victim intensifies the humor by solemnly denying its existence.

The lesson would later be applied to all Chaplin's screen personas. Thus the comedian's "little fellow" often would have an aristocratic manner despite a tramp's station in life. And he would accent this class duality with such permanent accessories as the dandy's derby and cane. Interestingly enough, Chaplin's key artistic rival in silent comedy, Buster Keaton, would later relate a somewhat similar childhood performing story.[13] In Keaton's case, however, it was a discovery not of an aristocratic mask but of a stone face.

Chaplin's success in vaudeville weaned him from lofty theater ambitions. At the end of his tour with *Casey's Circus* he graduated to the Karno Company, pre-eminently an English pantomime troupe, though it also performed dialogue material. Brother Sydney, already a member of the group, had been the catalyst behind Charles's advancement, forever lobbying with troupe founder and leader Fred Karno about young Charles's talents.

Sydney, who had often played guardian angel to Charles when they were

Sydney

childhood partners in poverty, continued his parental role throughout their early careers. The significance of that guidance is reflected in the nonstop praise Chaplin showered on his brother throughout *My Autobiography*; he credited Sydney with everything from smuggling food to him at Hanwell to developing the original idea for United Artists.[14] Such praise is doubly impressive since Chaplin was never one to overindulge in compliments.

Showman Fred Karno was a major influence on Chaplin, a finishing school of slapstick. Stan Laurel, also a graduate of this school, has stated: "Fred Karno didn't teach Charlie and me all we know about comedy. He just taught us most of it."[15] But as historians Raoul Sobel and David Francis have observed, the degree of Chaplin indebtedness is difficult to judge, since little recorded evidence remains of Karno's material.[16]

As a general comedy inheritance, however, such later Chaplin trademarks as the mixing of humor and pathos, the perfectionist attitude about timing, and even a certain proclivity for cruel comedy (George De Coulteray's controversial *Sadism in the Movies* devotes nearly an entire chapter to Chaplin)[17] were all key elements in the Karno skits. Chaplin "borrowed" most specifically in his later film, *A Night in the Show* (1915), which was drawn directly from the Karno skit *Mumming Birds* (known in the United States as *A Night in an English Music Hall*). *Mumming Birds*, about a disruptive drunk at a show, also has the special distinction of being the skit in which film comedy pioneer Mack Sennett "discovered" Chaplin, while the young Englishman was on his first Karno tour of the United States, though Sennett did not have Chaplin signed until the Englishman's second American tour. Other more direct links between Karno skits and Chaplin films would include the latter's: *Work* (1915), in which Chaplin's screen persona, Charlie, is a challenging paperhanging assistant; *One A.M.* (1916), in which a drunken Charlie comes home to a nightmare of a house; and *The Rink* (1916), which showcased Charlie's skating skills and was originally partly written by Sydney Chaplin.[18]

Karno's signing of the young Chaplin, initially more a tribute to Sydney's persistence than to Karno's own confidence, immediately proved fruitful. Chaplin was a hit in his Karno debut on February 3, 1908. The skit was *The Football Match*, and the eighteen-year-old rookie had a small role as a comic villain trying to bribe the goalkeeper into throwing the event. Chaplin's success, however, was reminiscent of his earlier role as a dog-sniffing, leg-lifting cat; he again upstaged the star with his own ad-libbing expansion of an originally modest part.

Eventually Chaplin and jealous star Harry Weldon argued on tour, with their most celebrated verbal salvo clearly being in the upstart's favor. " 'I have more talent in my arse than you have in your whole body,' said Weldon. 'That's where your talent lies.' " fired back Chaplin.[19] Karno avoided teaming them in future skits.

Within a year Chaplin would be a featured Karno figure with an entirely new problem. He had fallen hopelessly in love with one of Bert Coutts's Yankee Doodle Girls, a troupe playing on the same bill as his *Mumming Birds*. Hetty Kelly was a fifteen-year-old beauty whose act preceded Chaplin's. But they would have only a handful of actual dates before the intensity of the comedian's romantic devotion would suffocate her interest.

Like the idealized Victorian child-woman with whom he would later populate his films and his marriages, Chaplin had already put poor Hetty on a pedestal and begun to worship her. Although their modest relationship was short-lived, her image was to stay with him all the rest of his days.[20] In fact, several sources have claimed that his sudden triumphant 1921 return to England was primarily to see her once again.[21] Tragically, she died shortly before his arrival. And in this death, as with the heroine of Coventry Patmore's Victorian poem celebrating womanhood, "The Angel in the House," their love would forever stay pure and otherworldly. Chaplin later wrote a song tribute to her entitled "There's Always Someone You Can't Forget."[22]

Beyond the romance Karno star Chaplin was experiencing and the advantage of professional training, there was also the opportunity for travel, no small item for a formerly impoverished youngster. In 1909 Chaplin's Karno troupe played Paris's Folies Bergère for a month. And between 1910 and 1913 there would be two extended tours of the United States.

While Paris was an adventure and possibly focused his attention on early cinema comedian Max Linder, whom Chaplin for a time would cite as a major influence, America was even more special. America represented opportunity for the comedian, a promised land not unlike the dream world his cinema tramp was often searching for at the end of the road. In his autobiography Chaplin relates that, much as he loved England, there was little chance for advancement there for someone with his limited background.[23] Like the little boy who had weathered the impoverished childhood, the adult Chaplin was a survivor fighting for more. Stan Laurel, Chaplin's understudy for the first American tour, has stated that as their ship approached shore, Chaplin ran to the rail and shouted, "America, I am coming to conquer you. Every man, woman and child shall have my name on their lips—Charles Spencer Chaplin!"[24]

His boast would be wrong only in its limited geography, for Chaplin was on the verge of conquering the world. The iron will that made this so would also serve him well when scandal and technological innovation (such as the coming of sound) later threatened to topple his career. Even at the time of his initial arrival in this country, Chaplin was gaining media attention. For example, a New York paper from autumn 1910 reported, "Charles Chaplin, leading comedian of Karno's Comedians, which are playing at the Orpheum Theatre, this week, is being extensively entertained by the British residents."[25] And *Variety* concluded its positive review with probably the biggest understatement of the decade: "Chaplin will do all right for America."[26]

During the Karno troupe's second American tour, in 1913, manager Alf Reeves (later general manager and vice-president of the Chaplin Film Corporation) received a short, vague, and unsigned telegram from Mack Sennett. It asked, "Is there a man named Chaffin in your company or something like that," and if so would he get in touch with the New York office of Kessel and Bauman (whose holdings included Sennett's Keystone Comedy Company.[27]

Sennett was losing his star comedian, Ford Sterling, and was anxious to find a replacement; though his memory was faulty as to the name, he remembered the Karno comedian who had so impressed him two years earlier. But while Sennett had hopes that Kessel and Bauman could sign the Englishman, Chaplin entered their New York office completely in the dark. Ironically, he even felt some disappointment when the nature of the visit was first explained: given the lawyer-dominated building complex where Kessel and Bauman had their office, Chaplin had been hoping he was about to come into an inheritance.

The businessmen quickly got Chaplin's attention, however, by offering him $150 a week to make films for Sennett—this was exactly double his Karno salary. Though Chaplin and Reeves had flirted with the idea of filming some Karno skits during their first American tour in 1912, the comedian was still somewhat hesitant to sign. He would be trading the security of Karno for this new, not highly respected medium.

It was untrue that Chaplin still had the first dollar he ever earned, but his impoverished childhood had made him rather tightfisted. Even with his great Karno success, he had continued to bank most of his earnings. The film offer was too tempting, though, and his early hesitancy even enabled him to haggle for a larger contract: $150 a week for the first three months and $175 for the other nine. A popular syndicated newspaper humorist of the day, Frank "Kin" Hubbard, whose aphorisms appeared under the name of Abe Martin, no doubt nicely summarized Chaplin's money concerns when he observed, also in 1913: "Opportunity only knocks once but th' wolf is liable t' drop around any ole time."[28]

CHAPLIN'S FIRST FILMS

Chaplin signed the Sennett contract in May, but his commitment to the Karno tour would occupy him through November. When he arrived in Los Angeles in December, his boyish twenty-four years surprised Sennett, who had been expecting a middle-aged performer; Chaplin had been made up to be much older in the Karno skit Sennett had seen. The Keystone boss, who was then all of thirty-three, was still in the early days of a career that would earn him the title of Father of American Film Comedy. And he was about to give a start to the creator of the most famous icon in cinema history, a tramp named Charlie.

Chaplin's lengthy film career would cover much of the history of the art form. He made his first film for Sennett's comedy company in 1914; it was aptly titled *Making a Living*—Chaplin would do just that in film for the next fifty-two years. His last film, *A Countess from Hong Kong*, would be made in 1966 and star Marlon Brando and Sophia Loren. Between these two dates he would make some eighty-one films.

Many of these works were made during Chaplin's first decade in the industry. In that first year for Sennett he made thirty-five films. This period represented an important apprenticeship for Chaplin. Besides learning everything he could about movies, he very quickly asserted himself both in front of the camera—an early version of his tramp actually appears in his second film—as well as behind it. He was soon writing and directing some of his Sennett films. After 1914 Chaplin wrote and directed *all* his films, making him one of the first film artists in the classical sense, exercising nearly total control in an industry still often defined in collective terms.

Chaplin's career should be approached with five periods in mind: (1) the apprenticeship with Mack Sennett (1914); (2) the film shorts for the Essanay company (1915-1916); (3) the shorts for the Mutual company (1916-1917); (4) the shorts for First National films (1918-1923), which also included the feature *The Kid*; and (5) the ten feature-length films (1923-1966), the majority for United Artists, a company he helped found.

The dominant character in the majority of these films is what has come to be called his "tramp" figure, though the films often show him as employed. He remains in this role from *Kid Auto Races at Venice* (1914) through *Modern Times* (1936), with his toothbrush mustache, baggy pants, floppy shoes, derby hat, and ever-active cane becoming symbols synonymous with comedy the world over. (Figure 1.)

Chaplin retired the tramp, the last holdout from the silent era, after *Modern Times*, because he did not want to threaten either the figure's universality by having him speak or his believability by having him solve problems in a manner that the world had grown too cynical to accept. But it would be misleading to claim that no vestige of the tramp remained after this point in Chaplin's work, because the tramp constantly comes to mind, from the Jewish barber (Chaplin) in *The Great Dictator* (1940), who speedily shaves the customer in strict time to Brahm's Hungarian Dance no. 5, to deposed King Shadov (Chaplin) in *A King in New York* (1957), who finds it necessary to mimic a sturgeon while ordering caviar. Any focus on Chaplin's comedy must begin with The Tramp.

This figure did not emerge immediately with Chaplin's Sennett career. Moreover, despite their later comedy accolades, neither Chaplin nor Sennett was to be overjoyed at the start of their professional relationship. In Chaplin's eyes the Keystone Company was a madhouse of activity, little of it making sense. He was not accustomed to cinema's piecemeal, shot-by-shot construction, often done out of story sequence to save time and money, nor

1. Charlie as a show-off in *Kid Auto Races at Venice,* 1914. (Courtesy Museum of Modern Art/Film Stills Archive.)

was he enamored of Sennett's propensity to close his films with a helter-skelter chase sequence. To Chaplin all this distracted from the key element of comedy, which was based on personality. Sennett, on the other hand, was afraid he was stuck with an overpriced, green kid whose demands for more deliberate comedy pacing would never blend with the Keystone style.

Chaplin's first film for Sennett, shot under the direction of martinet Henry "Pathé" Lehrman, would do little to quiet those fears. *Making a Living* was not the failure many texts describe it as, but Chaplin hardly seemed destined to make the world forget Ford Sterling.

Chaplin's costume in this film debut was a carryover from the pivotal *A Night in an English Music Hall*: top hat, long frock coat, monocle, and walrus mustache. It was more reminiscent of the dandified garb of Max Linder than of the tramp "uniform" that would soon become the Chaplin trademark. Sennett suggested that the comedian put together a new outfit. Legend has it that Chaplin, like a superstitious performer in search of comedy talismans, then pieced together Charlie's costume with clothing from his fellow Keystone clowns. The baggy pants came courtesy of Fatty

Arbuckle, while the giant size 14 shoes belonged to Sterling, with Chaplin having to put the "gunboats" on the wrong feet to keep them on. He then added the undersized coat of Charles Avery to the equally undersized derby of Minta Durfee's father (Minta was the comedienne wife of Arbuckle). Chaplin complemented this clothing menagerie with a dandy's cane, a duck's walk, and a toothbrush mustache, scissored down from one of Mack Swain's. The modest mustache allowed him to soothe Sennett's qualms about youthfulness, without concealing any comic facial expressions.

Chaplin generally followed the preceding account in his autobiography, minus the names, because he was never one for mentioning contemporary comedians. However, the legend is not without a few footnotes. For example, even as a child he had dreamed of putting together a comedy tramp act. Karno music hall comedian Fred Kitchen, whom Chaplin first saw as a child, wore both baggy pants and oversized shoes. And Charles Chaplin, Jr.'s biography of his father has the comedian crediting not that day of inspiration on the Sennett lot but rather a last minute music hall substitution from his youth.[29] He had gone on for a much larger comedian, and by way of wearing his oversized costume, happened onto the tramp outfit. Chaplin, who could often be creative with his life story, does use a similar tale as a subplot in *The Circus* (1928), where Charlie is a spur-of-the-moment fill-in for Rex the tightrope walker, whose costume is much too large.

The peculiar gait, like Harpo Marx's famous "gookie" expression, was drawn from a real-life character. Chaplin was reproducing the splayfooted shuffle of an elderly street person from his youth. And Charlie's delightful cane, which often seemed to have a personality of its own, had been a key weapon in Chaplin's comedy arsenal for Karno. Thus, while things may have come together that momentous day in 1914, the seeds of Charlie the tramp had no doubt been gestating for years.

ANALYZING CHAPLIN'S COMEDY

To understand the life and career of Chaplin, it is necessary to sketch briefly the "why" behind the comedy of the tramp. It is both the foundation of all Chaplin films, even after the tramp has been retired, and a reflection of the comedian's philosophy of life.

In discussing Chaplin's work in terms of comedy theory, no doubt endless definitions could be referred to, beyond Chaplin's smorgasbord approach on those rare occasions when he was moved to examine specific elements of his humor. For example, the early tramp figure was almost a ruffian, who was especially forceful when kicking people with his oversized shoes or jabbing them with the ever-present cane. Roughhouse comedy of this type could easily fall under the comedy theory label of superiority. The premise of this approach is that humor builds upon someone else's humilation or problems.

It would also be possible to reverse this process, focus on frustration, and theorize that we enjoy the Charlie films because we feel superior to him, a premise on which Al Capp once attempted to elaborate.[30] But such a position is much more applicable to the comedy of Laurel and Hardy or of Woody Allen, who focus on frustration.

Other comedy theories, from Eastman's "humor as instinct" to that of the old and venerated comedy of surprise, can be applied on a limited basis to Chaplin's work. Unfortunately, most Chaplin authors avoid comedy theory completely; those who do not, often treat it superficially or prescribe a simple comedy formula as applicable to all the comedian's work. This tendency toward an umbrella approach in any area of comedy theory, which Paul E. McGhee calls "global theories," is problematic, because such theories "discourage attention to important [multilevel] dimensions" in comedy.[31] Thus the method I propose to use, that of incongruity, is not offered as an all-encompassing panacea for Chaplin's humor, but it seems more applicable than any guideline currently in use.

Patricia Keith-Spiegel, in an excellent essay comparing various comedy theories, defines the incongruity approach as "humor arising from disjointed, ill-suited pairings of ideas or situations . . . that are divergent from habitual customs."[32]

Almost everything about the comedy world of Chaplin plays upon incongruity. Its most obvious deployment occurs in the settings that Chaplin selects, especially his propensity to place the tramp in the world of high society, from Mutual films like *The Count* (1916) and *The Adventurer* (1917), where he impersonates the wealthy, to the underrated *City Lights*, where Charlie is befriended by a rich man who knows the tramp only when he (the millionaire) is drunk. *City Lights* produces what is undoubtedly Chaplin's best example of comic incongruity—the scene of the tramp diving out of an expensive limousine, a gift from the drunken rich friend, to beat another tramp to a discarded cigarette butt, after which he returns to his limousine and drives away.

Incongruous settings are not limited to the placing of the tramp in high society. In *Easy Street* (1917) he is a tramp who becomes a cop; in *The Pilgrim* (1923) he is an escaped convict who finds it necessary to play at being a minister; and in *The Gold Rush* (1925) he is seemingly a tramp turned prospector, heading north to the Alaskan gold fields. Incongruous settings such as these—a police station, a church, and the Frozen North— produce much of what is initially funny in his films. This incongruity is especially true of *The Gold Rush*, where the tramp is first seen skidding around the side of what could be a glacier. But Chaplin's use of incongruity goes well beyond setting.

A key to his use of this comic device is in the tramp costume itself. Here is a small figure wearing oversized shoes and pants, an undersized coat, and a well-worn derby and carrying a cane. His gait resembles that of a duck trying to go two ways at once, while his tiny mustache seems more like a chocolate milk smudge than like facial hair. His appearance is not the sort to instill confidence. Obviously this is a tramp, one of society's failures. But very quickly the viewer realizes there is nothing inferior about this character, from the hero who saves Edna from the robbers at the start of *The Tramp* (1915) to the escape artist who whisks the gamin away from the government officials at the close of *Modern Times*.

The viewer is not surprised by these actions because there is something in the original style of the costume, however bedraggled it might look, from the banker's derby to the dandy's cane, that suggests that this character has known better days. There is also an air of independence in his manner, as well as an effortless grace in his movement, the duck walk notwithstanding. It is as if to say, I have had it all once, and if I wanted it again, I could have it. Witness the leisure habits of the tramp in *The Idle Class* (1921), where he travels with a bag of golf clubs, or the ease in which he has cabin owner Hank Curtis (Henry Bergman) taking care of him in *The Gold Rush*. One could liken it to what Walter Kerr has observed as the tendency in Chaplin's work for his character to exist on a level outside of (superior to) the setting in which he is placed, more an additional member of the audience than part of the action being viewed.[33] For that matter, the tramp outfit itself becomes rather natty by the final exit in *Modern Times*.

The narrative of some Chaplin films also accents this comic incongruity by having a dual focus.[34] In certain films, especially the short subjects, this dual focus means that his actions repeat or parallel the actions of another central character. This is best exemplified by Eric Campbell, his comic nemesis in the Mutual films (1916-1917). At Sennett Studios this dual focus was more apt to be on a friendly basis, as in *The Rounders* (1914), where Charlie was teamed with Fatty Arbuckle and they seemed to do everything in tandem. (Figure 2.) However, Sennett also sometimes matched Chaplin opposite the Campbell-like Mack Swain. At Essanay (1915-1916) a friendly dual focus occasionally continued to surface, with Ben Turpin replacing Arbuckle.

This dual focus continues to occur in both the First National productions (1918-1923) and the later features, from the friendly pairing of The Tramp and Big Jim McKay (Swain) in *The Gold Rush* to the comic antagonism between dictators Hynkel (Chaplin) and Napaloni (Jack Oakie) in *The Great Dictator*. This duality is probably best integrated with the story in *The Circus*, where Charlie the clown is paired with Rex the tightrope walker. Because the film first shows Rex performing, Charlie's antics on the tightrope are all the funnier, especially since he manages to succeed. Chaplin also, on occasion, went the dual focus route by playing two parts himself; in *A Night in the Show* he plays the gentleman Mr. Pest and the tramp Mr. Rowdy; in *The Idle Class*, a tramp and a gentleman; and in *The Great Dictator*, a tramp-like Jewish barber and the dictator Hynkel.

2. Charlie and Fatty Arbuckle in *The Rounders,* 1914. (Courtesy Museum of Modern Art/Film Stills Archive.)

The starting point of his dual-focus approach to comic incongruity is often that age-old premise of the comedy team, the contrast of little man/big man. With the physically small tramp often paired with huge men, an initially funny contrast, Charlie's attempts to replicate the actions of some giant are incongruously funny. When he proves himself the victor in these situations, as he usually does, it is all the more comically incongruous. In *Behind the Screen* (1916) Charlie and Campbell are fellow carpenters on a movie set, with director Chaplin actually billing them as "David and Goliath'" in a film title. And it is David (Charlie) who comes out ahead at the film's close.

The greatest example of dual-focus incongruity in Chaplin's work is in his classic film *Easy Street*, generally considered the best film of his Mutual work, already noted as "his most sustained creative period."[35] Film historian Terry Ramsaye also observed, in his own sometimes humorous style, that it was Chaplin's biggest commercial success up until that point, producing "more dimes to the running, linear and cubic foot than any previous Chaplin comedy."[36]

The replication of movement is so firmly balanced that *Easy Street* seems almost choreographed. In fact, Chaplin's second wife, Lita Grey, has written that this was the film a jealous W. C. Fields was referring to when he uttered his famous Chaplin commentary: "He's the world's greatest ballet dancer, and if I ever meet the son of a bitch I'll murder him!"[37]

Easy Street is a story of a skid row derelict, Charlie, who is reformed by a beautiful mission worker (Edna Purviance). The reformed tramp joins the police force, rather an incongruous move in itself for his screen character, and his beat assignment is the ironically named Easy Street. He must contend with street bully Eric Campbell, the other half of the dual focus, who eats cops for breakfast.

Before Charlie joins the police force, director Chaplin crosscuts to shots of Eric and his gang matter-of-factly destroying half the force, with stretchers carrying the wounded into the police station as if it were a war zone. By the film's conclusion, Charlie will have subdued both Eric and the beat in general, turning it into a model street. In the battle between the two characters, each represents the same character at different times—the king of the street. To best understand this dual focus necessitates a close examination of *Easy Street*, as well as of Chaplin's propensity for more conventional uses of comedy through incongruity.

After Eric and the gang finish their tall-tale-style rout of the police, in which they throw the cops around like so much hay, there is the matter of spoils. One of the police has sacrificed his pants in the thick of battle and in so doing produced the spoils (coins). When the coins hit the street, everyone in the group goes for them.

Eric, however, asserts himself against his motley gang and scares them into the buildings on either side of the street. Now possessing sole control of the money and jauntily wearing a policeman's hat, another spoil of battle, he walks up the center of Easy Street alone, in control here, too. This control factor is emphasized by the fact that he occupies the center of the film frame. As he walks, the gang members on the right side of the street venture out of their buildings; when he turns in that direction, they dive back inside. Then the people on the left venture out and the comic process is repeated.

At this point patrolman Charlie innocently walks into this war zone. Eric, initially surprised at the nerve or stupidity of this cop, follows Charlie about in order to size him up. Charlie realizes quickly that he is in a spot, especially after he examines the pile of policemen's clothing still in the street. Although frightened, he manages to appear fairly nonchalant.

Before Eric does anything drastic to this modest-looking cop, he gives him a chance at a heart attack by bending over a gas street lamp to demonstrate his strength. However, Eric, who has already allowed Charlie a few free but ineffective billy club swipes at his head, then makes a mistake. He is so involved in this show of strength that he does not keep an eye on the "victim." Charlie jumps on the bully's back and pulls the gas lamp over Eric's head, and the giant is soon anesthetized. (Figure 3.)

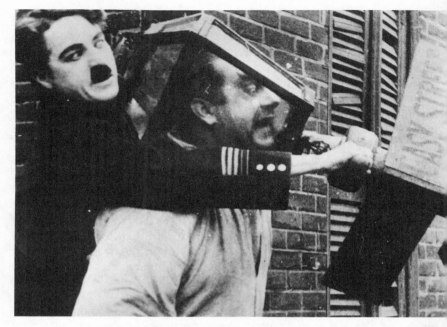

3. "Doctor" Charlie administering gas to Mr. Campbell in *Easy Street,* 1917. (Courtesy Museum of Modern Art/Film Stills Archive.)

After calling the police station for a detachment to come and retrieve the bully, the tramp-turned-cop surveys the terrain of his victory. He begins a stroll down the center of the street, as well as the center of the film frame, that is a repeat of Eric's earlier victory march; now, however, it is Charlie who is in complete control. Once again some people venture out from the buildings on the right-hand side of the street, and Charlie turns, only improving on Eric's movement by making it into a single pirouette, and drives them back inside. And again the process is repeated on the left side of the street. When the flighty detachment of police finally arrives to retrieve Eric's body, director Chaplin even allows himself a topping of these dance-like movements. A child passing by happens to stop in the center of the street and, pointing his finger as a gun, shoots at the police force. The detachment immediately drops back in terror.

Each of these street scenes is funny because of the various levels of incongruity present. Before examining more typical types of incongruity, through understatement and overstatement not dependent on dual-focus narrative, it should be noted that the whole sequence begins and ends with what Edgar E. Willis would define as incongruity stretched to absurdity.[38] That is, the first view of the Easy Street gang shows them massacring the police force tall-tale-style. The extremeness of this is emphasized by the fact that police dummies were introduced at several points in order to make it easier for

Eric to appear to be throwing policemen around. A similar scene will be repeated later at the police station, after he has been momentarily caught. The result is a fight sequence that looks as if it were written for Paul Bunyan; Eric sails the policemen about so easily he might be playing volleyball.

In contrast, the absurd close of the sequence, where the small child frightens the whole police force, is based on the fact that this child is the most diminutive of catalysts. There is just no way that any urchin, regardless of the police force's cowardice, could have produced such fear. In both cases (police massacred by gang, police scared to death by child), the laughter is a result of comic incongruity gone to extremes.

The next movement within the sequence, where Eric asserts his authority over the gang in terms of the money and they fall back from him, is the result of comic incongruity based in overstatement. Though the bully's power has been established on such Herculean levels that there can be no doubt that his gang will be frightened of him, the extreme manner in which they cower before him, from one side of the street to the other, must be labeled an overstatement—comic exaggeration.

The third movement of the sequence, where the gang cowers from side to side before Charlie after he has vanquished the bully, also deals in over-statement. Though the victory over Eric is credible due to the mind-over-matter ingenuity of gassing him, it still seems like the miracle of a David over a Goliath because of the earlier seeming invincibility of the bully. To see the gang shrink from such a modest-sized cop is again comedy of exaggerated incongruity.

It should be added that Charlie's initial encounter with the bully also produces several comic moments of understated incongruity. For example, the bully, who we know is capable of tying Charlie into knots, seems totally incapacitated at the audacity of this little cop invading his territory. Instead of his earlier exaggerated violence, there is almost catatonic puzzlement at just what to do with this Easy Street intruder.

Charlie's reaction to this giant is also one of incongruous understate-ment, so much so that the viewer keeps hoping he will run for safety. But his actions, though tinged with fear, are to stay and deal with the menace. The understated comedy that follows also parallels the thrill comedy of Harold Lloyd, because Eric appears to be every bit as lethal as a fall from a Lloyd skyscraper, maybe more so. Charlie must be careful at every step.

Charlie first tries to call the station, but has difficulty getting at the phone in his police box without arousing the suspicions of the bully, who is standing over him. He disguises the identity of the old-style bell-shaped telephone receiver by using it as a brush, a horn, and a telescope—excellent examples of Chaplin's ability to work a metamorphosis of any object.

Eric buys these transitions, to the point of trying to look through the "telescope." It is here, however, that Charlie momentarily loses his cool and uses his billy club on Eric's head while the bully is distracted by the receiver. Provoked but unscathed, the giant goes into his show of strength by bending the gas street lamp over, giving Charlie the opportunity to gas him.

In another superior example of Chaplin understatement, Charlie the cop takes on the demeanor of a bored suburban doctor. The "doctor" removes the "patient's" gas mask (street lamp) and checks his pulse rate. Finding it still a bit too active, he again returns the "mask" to Eric's head and administers more gas. Needless to say, the bully is eventually reduced to a harmless state.

Though the threat, for the moment, has been eliminated, this scene continues a short while longer in order to project more comedy through understatement. Now that Charlie is free to call the police station, it has become an almost impossible task; his police phone is on the gas lamp street pole that Eric has leveled. Yet, in the most nonchalant manner, Charlie crawls under the pole to make his call flat on his back.

When the task force from the police station arrives, each member scared to death to be in the Easy Street neighborhood, its first sight is that of one small cop, and his giant prisoner laid out on the sidewalk. It is as if a boy fisherman had landed a whale. The understated comic incongruity in the image is increased all the more because Charlie is playing with his billy club, which makes him seem much smaller. When he first sees the other officers he does not even get up, but rather motions to them with a "come on down" air, as relaxed as theirs is tense.

Incongruity, often in terms of dual focus, continues throughout the film. Both characters demonstrate overpowering strength; there is nothing unusual about a man of Eric's size having these capabilities, but Charlie's superman transition is comically incongruous. As is to be expected, Charlie receives overpowering strength completely by chance; he happens to sit on a dope needle and is literally hopped up. This incident also anticipates the "high" Charlie accidently receives from the cocaine-filled salt shaker in *Modern Times*. Thus the *Easy Street* needle, which a member of the neighborhood gang had originally planned for Edna, transforms Charlie into a junior Tarzan.

In the rescue of Edna that follows, Chaplin has the tramp cop take on the street gang and vanquish them just as easily as Eric did the police, to the point of actually throwing people around. Consequently there is a satisfyingly symmetrical nature to the appearance of these epic displays of fighting strength. Eric's battle royal with the police force comes at the film's beginning, while Charlie's conquest of the neighborhood gang closes it.

Comedy through incongruity in Chaplin's work, whether in the abundant examples of conventional understatement and overstatement or in the more rare examples of dual-focus narrative, is actually tied to one of the fundamentals of comedy theory. That is, much of the humor derived from incongruity, and all of it in the case of dual focus, can be defined as repetition. And repetition, as Henri Bergson describes it in *Laughter*, his landmark work on comedy, is "one of the usual processes of classical comedy."[39]

Comedy repetition can be a literal repetition, dual-focus style, where Charlie follows the pattern of someone quite unlike his tramp character within each film, as he does with Eric Campbell. Another example of this is Charlie as the tightrope walker in *The Circus*. There can also be comedy through repetition, where the model for the role exists outside the world of the film. For example, when Charlie becomes a cop in *Easy Street*, part of the reason he is funny is because he is replicating the popular conception of what a tough cop is, another pattern quite unlike his tramp character. Finally, there can be comedy repetition where the dominant model is Charlie himself, from the films where he plays a dual role to those where he has a junior satellite, be it heroine or child, imitating him. This type of repetition is nicely showcased in *The Kid*, where Jackie Coogan's title performance "is clearly another presentation of Charlie, so that we have in this film a dual personality, the adult and the child Charlie."[40]

To state this more succinctly, one has only to repeat another axiom of Bergson's: "Every comic character is a *type*. Inversely, every resemblance to a type has something comic in it."[41] Thus, before his Easy Street encounter with Eric, a bully, director Chaplin has performer Charlie play off the image of the tough cop type. After he defeats Eric, Charlie's actions replicate those of another type—his downed bully of an adversary. And the child that later scares the police force with his "finger pistol" is merely doing a pint-sized imitation of Charlie the cop.

The real thrust of Bergson's *Laughter* is a variation on incongruity; that is, people are comic in terms of their "mechanical inelasticity"—behaving in a rigid and automatic manner incongruous with the concept of being human.[42] In applying this aspect to Chaplin, still one more element of incongruity is revealed.

In film comedy history this "mechanical inelasticity" has seemingly been applied only to the Keystone Kops, and in the most direct manner: they tended to become almost robot-like in their antics, from bouncing out of their Model T squad cars to plowing into very real trees.[43]

A definite strain of this type of comic incongruity can be isolated in Chaplin's work again and again, though on a more sophisticated level, from such quintessential tramp habits as tossing an object to one side and kicking out with the opposite leg to such isolated moments as the nervous breakdown scene on the conveyor belt in *Modern Times*, where he literally becomes a mechanical nut tightener, just like the machines around him.

Probably the best example of this type of incongruity occurs in *Easy Street*, in a scene where Campbell is chasing Charlie around a table in a ghetto flat. Eric starts to weave back and forth on his side of the table, seeing if he can commit Charlie into going one direction or another. But

Charlie finds that by repeating this back-and-forth motion on his own side he can keep the bully confused—at first. Eventually Eric decides to come around one end of the table. Charlie, however, continues to maintain his back and forth motion, as if this weaving in itself is the secret to keeping Eric at bay, and the bully almost catches the undersized cop.

One final element of comic incongruity in Chaplin's tramp even occurs in those rare moments when he does not seem equal to the task. In the beginning of *Pay Day* (1922) he is a construction worker having trouble digging a hole. Each "shovelful" of soil he removes would not fill a teacup. And when he finally manages to improve on this, he has a propensity for hitting his foreman with flying dirt. But whereas anyone else would be fired for such incompetencies, Charlie is given what amounts to a promotion: he becomes a bricklayer, with two assistants. The nature of this switch is accented metaphorically by the fact that he goes from deep in a hole to a bricklaying scaffold several stories up. The wisdom of the switch is then underlined by the magic manner in which he stacks bricks.

The comic incongruity in this example is based on what is often called the wise fool, a character whose every "miscue" eventually proves beneficial, as in Charlie's "accidental" *Pay Day* promotion. At other times these "miscues" can innocently establish a point that otherwise would not be appropriate for the character to make. In a scene in *Easy Street* Charlie visits a ghetto family with about a dozen children in one small room. Instead of expressing his shock at the situation, he "innocently" proceeds to scatter cornflakes on the floor around him, as if the children were so many chickens. By doing the most foolish of actions—throwing food on the floor —he has made a pointed comment: This place is not fit for human habitation.

My reasons for defining much of Chaplin's work in terms of comedy through incongruity have not been presented as an all-encompassing comedy theory for the works of Chaplin. This approach, however, is a very workable model in an area (Chaplin and comedy theory) that suffers from a scarcity of such studies and from a tendency by many theorists to define Chaplin's work in a narrow or self-serving manner.

A fascinating sidelight to Chaplin and comedy through incongruity is suggested by Chaplin's favorite author, Arthur Schopenhauer.[44] This philosopher, writing early in the nineteenth century, was one of the better-known early theorists on comedy through incongruity.

> The cause of laughter in every case is simply the sudden perception of the incongruity between a concept and the real objects which have been through it in some relation, and laughter itself is just the expression of this incongruity.[45]

Comedy for Schopenhauer was a way of meeting the inconsistencies of life, or more precisely, its incongruities. Though Chaplin never articulated his views as such, there is a suggestion of the philosopher's view in one of Chaplin's rare references to comedy theory in his autobiography. "We see in what seems rational, the irrational; in what seems important, the unimportant."[46]

To make this link between Schopenhauer's incongruity theory and Chaplin is mere speculation. I offer it at this point as one more link between Chaplin's work and the theory of comic incongruity. However, having built a case for studying Chaplin's comedy through various levels of incongruity, I believe I have chosen a theory to which he would also have felt somewhat attuned.

Incongruity is also an apt phrase to describe Chaplin's own world view, or lack of one. As he himself noted near the close of his autobiography, "I have no design for living, no philosophy—whether sage or fool, we must all struggle with life. I vacillate with inconsistencies."[47] A close reading of Chaplin's voluminous writing thoroughly illustrates this observation. His only consistent commentary on life's struggles is the intuitive answers he applies to them, what Philip G. Rosen sees as the comedian's conscious opposition to the use of reason in his socio-political thought.[48] The sole exception to Chaplin's adherence to intuition came in his propensity to apply, until late in life, a rational, preconceived framework to his infrequent comments on comedy.

PUBLIC IMPACT

Regardless of how Chaplin or today's student of comedy would analyze the art of Charlie, it is important to underline the huge initial public impact his films had, as well as their staying power. The almost immediate acclaim his tramp figure received in 1914 made him one of the first world media stars. Because of the universality of silent films, he was more of an international star than any comparable figure of today. As a two-part series in *Motion Picture Magazine* put it, "Chaplinitis" had arrived.[49]

What is there about the character of Charlie that made this happen? A popular response is to see the figure as an "everyman," someone to whom the common man could respond at a time when organized bigness had started to dominate every aspect of American life (industry, labor, and agriculture), with the individual lost somewhere in between. The tramp was born in the midst of the Progressive Era (1900-1920), when a great many Americans, largely from the middle class, led a broadly based call for reform, for curbing the corruption of big city machines and trustbusting of large corporations. While bigness was the norm, the Progressive movement was concerned "with improving the plight of the underprivileged individual and the quality of social life throughout the nation."[50]

Bracketing Charlie as an everyman underdog is certainly a viable explanation of his unique rise to prominence. But because Charlie's ongoing battle against society is carried on with such a generally capable intensity, it might seem more logical to see him as a legendary hero of the common people rather than their definitive representative. Film theorist André Bazin suggested this when he observed:

> Charlie is a mythical figure who rises above every adventure in which he becomes involved. . . . For hundreds of millions of people on this planet he is a hero like Ulysses or Roland in other civilizations—but with the difference that we know the heroes of old through literary works.[51]

Any thesis on the sudden wave of "Chaplinitis" following the tramp's motion picture debut must also examine the three-part nature of its timeliness. First, Chaplin was one of the earliest and most truly gifted pantomimists to permanently record his art on film. And without distracting from his unique creative talents, he obviously drew from the long mime tradition that preceded him, such as the previously mentioned material carried over from the Karno years. But as time and memory slip away, all such material becomes indelibly stamped Chaplin.

Second, film was still a new enough medium that "The potentialities of . . . [its mass-market] form of [world] stardom had only begun to dawn on the film industry during the period Charlie entered it."[52] The Chaplin phenomenon seemed all the more distinctive in an era not yet grown accustomed to periodic movie crazes.

Third, the first wave of Chaplin popularity has often been linked with the special comedy needs of humanity while suffering through the darkness of World War I, which also made its debut in 1914. And while the public continued to line up for his films, Allied soldiers often showed their appreciation by using the tramp as a mascot for their military companies. Chaplin's special wartime status is best demonstrated by the huge critical and commercial success of the controversial *Shoulder Arms* (1918), a comedy about the war. It was very daring for the time, because film comedy just did not deal with such serious themes in 1918. But Chaplin's amazing popularity made even this palatable to a large general audience.

Chaplin's image was not to come out of the war completely unscathed, however. Because he was still a British citizen of military age, a number of individuals, especially in the United Kingdom, felt he was shirking his duty by not enlisting. Like many other young men not in uniform, he received white feathers in the mail, though undoubtedly in greater numbers. Later the mail would contain threats, particularly when the United States entered the war (1917). Consequently, while he also received countless letters of thanks for movies that helped keep morale up, that viewpoint more and more came to represent a defensive posture to explain why he was not in uniform instead of one more reason to celebrate Chaplin.

Chaplin's World War I detractors were also undoubtedly given added ammunition by Max Linder's much publicized involvement in the war, where he was severely wounded (initially reported as dead) in action. Two excellent articles the titles of which nicely reflect their patriotic celebration of Linder are Clement F. Chandler's "Max Linder Comes Back!" in *Motion Picture* (February and March, 1917), and Rhea Irene Kimball's "Max Linder, Soldier, Actor, Gentleman," in *Motion Picture Classic* (April 4, 1917).

Harassment by American jingoistic patriots was calmed when Chaplin flunked his 1917 physical. Coupled with this news was a Chaplin statement that reflected the defensive posture already suggested, that he was of more use making films.[53] Kevin Brownlow, in his surprisingly critical look at Chaplin's nonuniformed war involvement in *The War, the West and the Wilderness* (1979), notes that Chaplin sent a similar statement to an English correspondent early in 1918, after the failed physical had not silenced all his British detractors.[54] But William Dodgson Bowman, writing in 1931, seems to have best summarized the pro-Chaplin side of the controversy.

Had he gone to the front the British Army would have gained a recruit of indifferent physique and doubtful value; but it would have lost one of the few cheering influences that relieved the misery and wretchedness of those nightmare days.[55]

A number of historians have also suggested that some of this "patriotic" slander was fanned by competing film companies, which were feeling the pinch of Chaplin's box office power.

Besides the morale-boosting nature of his films, Chaplin lent his talents to the Allied effort more directly through appearances at Red Cross parties, an extended Liberty Bond tour, and the production and donation of a film trailer for the Liberty Loan drive.

Chaplin's two-month tour (spring 1918) for Liberty Bonds, often with close friends Mary Pickford and Douglas Fairbanks, drew huge crowds and raised millions for the war effort. (Figure 4.) The highlight was the White House reception by President Woodrow Wilson, after which Chaplin did an impromptu dance before tens of thousands of capital residents with fellow entertainer-turned bond seller Marie Dressler, who had actually been billed above him in the first feature film comedy, *Tillie's Punctured Romance*. (Chaplin, never one to waste anything, later was able to incorporate his experiences on side trips to Army camps during this tour into the production of *Shoulder Arms*.)

The Liberty Loan trailer was a delightful extended pun on the subject of its plea—the bond. It was comprised of four segments, each of which show-cased a different type of bond: friendship, love, marriage, and liberty. Long-time Chaplin heroine Purviance appeared in the film, as did regulars

4. Chaplin and Marie Dressler in front of the then-Assistant Secretary of the Navy Franklin D. Roosevelt, Douglas Fairbanks, Sr., and Mary Pickford at the April 14, 1918, Liberty Loan Drive in Washington, D.C. (Courtesy Franklin D. Roosevelt Library).

Bergman and Albert Austin; brother Sydney even made a cameo appearance as the Kaiser. The film, which was entitled *Charles Chaplin in a Liberty Loan Appeal* (later retitled *The Bond*), was widely distributed throughout the United States in the autumn of 1918. (Earlier in the year he had made a somewhat similar film, now lost, with Sir Harry Lauder for the British War Loan.)

What Chaplin's drawing power meant financially to the war effort is best related by two now legendary stories of the period. In the first, the Red Cross gatherings with which Chaplin was involved before the United States's entry into the war often allowed the wealthy to rub shoulders with Hollywood royalty for a tax-deductible contribution. At one such dinner a lady donated $20,000 merely to sit next to the comedian. In the second story, during a solo Chaplin bond foray into the South, a former secretary of the Treasury refused to appear with him because Chaplin was merely "a vulgar movie actor." After separate appearances were arranged, Chaplin drew an estimated crowd of forty thousand, while the honorable secretary "packed in" four hundred.

This drawing power had not been lost on Chapln, nor on Sydney, who would manage some of his brother's salary negotiations during the years that paralleled the early part of World War I. Each successive film company change after leaving Sennett would result in a quantum leap in salary. The Sennett contract had started at a respectable $150 a week in December 1913; Chaplin's move to Essanay approximately a year later upped that salary to $1,250 a week. In another year it was on to Mutual for $670,000 annually, or approximately $10,000 a week, plus a bonus. And finally, his 1918 First National signing called for more than a million dollars. After this, except for two late exceptions, his films would be showcased by Chaplin's own company, United Artists, founded by Chaplin, Fairbanks, Mary Pickford, and D. W. Griffith in 1919, though the comedian's First National contract kept him from doing a United Artists title until 1923.

THE FIRST NATIONAL PERIOD

The year 1918 produced both the crowning financial contract with First National and Chaplin's varied wartime contributions. And it was a pivotal year for two additional reasons. In April he would release *A Dog's Life*, which Chaplin's most celebrated biographer, Theodore Huff, has labeled "his first real masterpiece."[56] And in October he would take his first Hetty Kelly-like bride, sixteen-year-old Mildred Harris.

A Dog's Life, his initial First National release, was the story of an extremely down-and-out tramp and his equally down-and-out dog Scraps, who is described in a title as a "thoroughbred mongrel." The film chronicles their hard but successful battle against hunger and humiliation and culminates in an idyllic new life in the country.

There is much that is familiar about the story, from Charlie's ability to best the local toughs to the dual-focus narrative that exists between the tramp and Scraps. The tendency of one's actions to parallel those of the other is even underlined in the film's title, *A Dog's Life*. In fact, the relationship between the two represents a dress rehearsal for the more celebrated dual-focus camaraderie between Charlie and Jackie Coogan in *The Kid*, three years later.

Chaplin's anthropomorphizing of Scraps, attributing human characteristics to the animal, further demonstrates the Victorian roots of his art. Anthropomorphism reached its zenith in Victorian Great Britain, especially in the paintings of Edwin Landseer. His most celebrated work, a stone copy of which now covers his grave, was *Old Shepherd's Chief Mourner*, which movingly details a bereaved collie with its head on his master's coffin. Paintings such as this made Landseer a nineteenth-century culture hero among people not normally familiar with the arts, the same people who would so often be early motion picture patrons.

A more specific comparison between a Landseer canvas and Chaplin's *A Dog's Life* might be made with the painting *Dignity and Impudence*, in which a small terrier comically tries to measure up to a hunting dog. It is amusingly moving, both because it deposits the human frailty of delusions of grandeur on the canine corps and because it undercuts the trait, because the subject is, after all, merely two dogs.

A Dog's Life, though hardly ripe for a title change to *Dignity and Impudence*, does present a small dog seemingly working his way toward being human, a goal as unobtainable as a terrier becoming a hunting dog. And the big "dog" (Charlie), as is his habit, often takes on a superior air—an amusing pose for a tramp, just as a pose of dignity can be amusing for a Landseer dog.

A Dog's Life is a departure for Chaplin in another manner reminiscent of Landseer. The film's humor is more sentimental than slapstick. While sentimentality was hardly new to Chaplin, appearing as early as *The Tramp* (1915), the later film is more self-consciously immersed in the characteristic, be it the tramp's use of Scraps as a pillow in his outdoor "apartment" or Charlie's Rousseau-like grain-planting segment at the close.

The term "departure" also applies to the majority of the seven other First National films Chaplin made between 1918 and 1923. He dared to make a war comedy in *Shoulder Arms*, while *Sunnyside* (1919) mirrors the lyrical praise of the critics a bit too closely—Chaplin even includes a dance of Pan. *A Day's Pleasure* (1919) finds him miscast in a domestic comedy about the frustrations of a short holiday with the wife and children (more reminiscent of what would become W. C. Fields' territory in the 1930s). *The Kid* was the first Chaplin-directed feature, and was much closer to straight drama than anything else he had ever done. In *Pay Day* Charlie is again miscast, this time in a vehicle that anticipates the later standard plots of Laurel and Hardy, right down to the battle-axe wife and the perennial goal of a night on the town with the boys. For the romantic loner who normally places delicate, D. W. Griffith-style women atop pedestals, Charlie's *Pay Day* male camaraderie and domineering linebacker of a wife are especially surprising.

It is only in *The Idle Class* (1921) and *The Pilgrim* (1923) that he returns to comedy themes more closely related to his pre-First National films, particularly those of his Mutual period. Both films revolve around mistaken identities, the former finding Charlie erringly accepted into high society, the latter finding him as a member of the clergy. In each his new social standing then allows director Chaplin the opportunity to return to the familiar ground of social critic, deflating the big wheels on America's main street.

Chaplin's satire of the church in *The Pilgrim* was strong enough to result in its initial banning by state censors in Pennsylvania. But the film's statement seems mild compared to the image of the crooked clergyman he had previously sketched in *Police* (1916). In one *Pilgrim* scene that no doubt bothered censors, "minister" Charlie drop-kicks an unruly child. This also exemplifies Chaplin's return to his earlier, more earthy style, often missing in other First National products. For example, presentation of a child with the famous Charlie boot is radically different from the pleasing yet rather saccharine depiction of little Jackie Coogan in *The Kid*.

There is no doubt that part of the disjointed nature of the First National films is related to his unhappy marriage to Mildred Harris, the second event (after *A Dog's Life*) spotlighted in pivotal 1918. Chaplin himself later observed that the unfortunate union seemed to dry up his comedy ideas.[57] Yet it was rather more complicated than that. Chaplin's fascination with the image of the Victorian child-woman would frequently prove disruptive to his personal and professional career. The Harris marriage was merely the first chapter of a repetitive story that might be labeled "The Search for Hetty Kelly."

The strikingly beautiful teenage film actress Harris completely captivated the comedian—for a time. But Chaplin's nineteenth-century romanticism was equally matched in him with that century's propensity for linear thought, and he was soon too involved in his work to give her even a modicum of the time commitment necessary for the success of any relationship, especially when one partner is so young. Kelly's death in 1921 would forever freeze her in the idealized perfection of a fairy tale sleeping beauty, yet prevent her from making any demands for time upon the workaholic comedian, but the very much alive, continued presence of Harris represented more responsibility than Chaplin was then capable of shouldering.

The marriage was also doomed by its forced nature, and then the suggestion of trickery when Harris later proved not to be pregnant. Moreover, just as Chaplin the artist was ill-prepared for marriage, so was Harris the child. Whereas the comedian entered the union already heavy of heart, Harris was like a little girl about to play house, as misguided by her own sense of romanticism as was Chaplin.

Further cracks in the relationship were provided by the later loss of a three-day-old, malformed baby (whose marker bore Harris's childishly touching nickname for the youngster, "The Little Mouse"), and also by professional friction over her attempt to continue a film career. Chaplin's Victorian belief that a woman's place was in the home was hardly lessened by Louis B. Mayer's attempt to capitalize on the comedian's name when he signed Mildred Harris *Chaplin* to a large film contract.

While the marriage had been professionally disruptive, its dissolution was even more so. After a separation of several months, Harris began to make accusations about mental cruelty and nonsupport, which quickly became newspaper headline material—an ugly proceeding about which Chaplin would learn all too much in the coming years. Yet the observations of journalism's humorists often helped soften the scandal, both then and later. For example, Kin Hubbard's crackerbarrel hero Abe Martin reported, "Mr. an' Mrs. Charley Chaplin have split up. Charley is like a whole lot o' other fellers—he kin make ever' buddy laugh but his wife."[58]

During the divorce proceedings there was the danger that Harris could attach all Chaplin's assets, including the nearly completed *The Kid*, in which he had invested approximately $500,000. An attachment on her part was equally attractive to First National, since the company was in dispute with Chaplin over what the film was worth and expected to obtain its price if the matter were out of his hands.

Because of all this, Chaplin had the film's massive negative, some 400,000 feet, spirited out of Los Angeles under cover of darkness, bound for the haven of Salt Lake City, Utah, safely outside the jurisdiction of California's divorce laws. As with other real events in his life, a legend has grown around the way this getaway was handled. The most common tale, as well as the most colorful, is usually drawn from longtime Chaplin secretary Toraichi Kono.

Kono's explanation has himself and his boss executing something of a Keystone Kops exit from Los Angeles, eventually arriving in Salt Lake City in a physical and economic state commensurate with Chaplin's screen persona: like tramps. With eight cents between them and the most disheveled appearance, at first they even had trouble finding hotel accommodations. When they obtained them, their rooms were immediately turned into a film editing complex. Chaplin essentially corroborates the story in My Autobiography, without going into as much detail.[59]

The flight to Utah precipitated more rapid and reasonable action in the divorce proceedings, though Chaplin would still pay a $100,000 settlement and be subject to a division of property. The cloak-and-dagger exit from California not only officially closed the book on his first marriage, but again demonstrated his lifelong tendency to maximize the drama of his private life.

While the Harris marriage ws the most obviously disruptive force during the artistically uneven First National period, there were other pressures. For example, his United Artists partners (Fairbanks, Pickford, and Griffith) were anxious for him to start production under its banner. But his contractual arrangement with First National would not be fulfilled until 1923, despite attempts to negotiate an earlier exit. Chaplin later observed that his final contract obligations, after The Kid, seemed like an impossible task.[60]

Another stress during this period was many critics' hypothesis that the Chaplin star was fading. This was based upon the critical failure of both 1919 releases, Sunnyside and A Day's Pleasure, as well as the lessening frequency with which his films were appearing. Even before the release of A Day's Pleasure, Harcourt Farmer wrote the provocative article "Is the Charlie Chaplin Vogue Passing?" which appeared in the October issue of Theatre Magazine. Amazingly, Farmer also found fault with a number of Chaplin's pre-Sunnyside film releases, all of which he thought were repetitive. Later in the year James Quirk, writing in the then-influential Photoplay Magazine, opinionated that "Sunnyside was anything but sunny; A Day's Pleasure certainly was not pleasure."[61] The suggestion was again quite clear—Chaplin was slipping.

Such voices were hardly quieted when no Chaplin film was released in 1920, the first time in his career a year had passed without a new Charlie saga. Consequently, the critical and commercial success of *The Kid*, which opened early in 1921, was literally a comeback for Chaplin. Quite possibly those preceding comedy setbacks were instrumental in *The Kid*'s success, encouraging him to construct the film closer to straight drama than any other Chaplin project until this point. But be this as it may, *The Kid* ignited a renewal of Chaplinitis around the world.

Chaplin did nothing to detract from this international chemistry; with customary impulsiveness he decided to make a homecoming visit to England. It was August of 1921, and since the January American premiere of *The Kid* he had finished one film (the as of yet unreleased *Idle Class*) and had completed lengthy preproduction work and a day's shooting on a never-realized film about wealthy plumbers. With all this work, the Harris divorce, and a recent bout with influenza, Chaplin felt himself in need of a holiday.

There was, however, at least one additional factor in his decision to visit England, but this factor varies depending upon which book by the comedian is consulted. In *My Trip Abroad* (1922) he mentions having received a cablegram from London noting the upcoming premiere of the already celebrated *The Kid* and suggesting this to be an opportune time for a return visit, one Chaplin had been promising himself for years.[62] *My Autobiography* (1964) points toward an "insatiable desire" to return to England, a desire which had been growing throughout the summer of 1921.[63] His nostalgia was also heightened during this time by letters he had received from H. G. Wells and Hetty Kelly.

Regardless of just what the keynote reason was, Chaplin closed down his current production and made travel arrangements almost immediately, leaving the film capital the following evening. This quick exit, forever linked with Sydney Chaplin's parting instructions to a member of his brother's party, "For God's sake, don't let him get married," reveals more than an impulsive nature—it shows someone who enjoys surprising people. Chaplin underlined this in *My Trip Abroad* when he observed, "Everyone was shocked [by my quick departure]. I was glad of it. I wanted to shock everyone."[64] Throughout his life he enjoyed saying and doing the controversial. And though this "keep them guessing" trait eventually became most associated with his political comments, the pleasure he derived from shocking people with his sudden 1921 departure for Europe is commentary enough on what a basic Chaplin component this was.

One of the best examples of a shocking Chaplin political comment actually occurred on this trip, before he left the United States. Upon arriving in New York he was asked by a reporter whether he was a Bolshevik. His reply was the provocative "I am an artist. I am interested in life. Bolshevism is a new phase of life. I must be interested in it."[65]

Chaplin's comment came little more than a year after the Red scare in America in late 1919 and 1920, when U.S. Attorney General A. Mitchell

Palmer took it upon himself to conduct his own witch hunting campaign against an almost entirely imagined domestic communist threat. Yet Chaplin, for all the trouble this might have caused him, was most certainly playing for effect. In fact, only the day before, upon his arrival in Chicago, he had answered no to the very same question from the press.[66] As it was, with Chaplin's disembarking, many Americans believed that the comedian was a Bolshevist and was traveling to the Soviet Union.

Chaplin's trip of nostalgia into the past was well served by the ship on which he returned to England. The S.S. *Olympic* was the same vessel that had brought him over for the second Karno tour less than a decade before. But much had changed since 1912, and Chaplin was now returning to a hero's welcome ten thousand times greater than even the fantasy one of his favorite authors had accorded Tom Sawyer, when the boy dreamed of someday returning to St. Petersburg as an imposing pirate.

The crowds that turned out in London and Paris reached frightening proportions, just as one newspaper headline had predicted: "Homecoming of Comedian to Rival Armistice Day."[67] But as was befitting a subject like Chaplin, there was comedy even in his fan statistics. For example, in a three-day period in London he received 73,000 pieces of mail; nearly 700 people claimed to be related; and 9 imaginative women alleged that they were his long-lost mother, all of them asserting Little Charlie was stolen away as a baby. Not surprisingly, most of the "relations" were requesting financial assistance.

Chaplin would meet numerous celebrities during the trip, from H. G. Wells to actress Pola Negri. His *My Trip Abroad* account of the visit might better have been labeled *Famous People I Met*, a title equally applicable to much of his other writing. But as Chaplin biographer Roger Manvell has suggested, "Charlie Chaplin is a Cinderella of the twentieth century."[68] And Charlie's ego was as taken with this fairy tale success as any of his vast public. It is only logical that he would savor such attention.

The Cinderella syndrome provides an additional hypothesis for the key to Chaplin's amazing popularity. His rapid rise to prominence, after the degradation of his youth, no doubt gave promise to the same secret dream most people hold deep inside. And since the underdog tramp of the movies usually finished the films with a victory or a noble account of himself (his stereotype as a victim notwithstanding), the spirit of Chaplin's real-life success was often reflected in his work. Film theorist André Bazin has labeled the ability of an artist to bring personal reality to his art an "example of transposed autobiography."[69] In Chaplin's case the phenomenon seems to have been a major element of his success.

After his return from Europe, Chaplin made *Pay Day* and *The Pilgrim*, which finally fulfilled his First National contract and allowed him to begin production for United Artists, the company he had helped found back in 1919.

UNITED ARTISTS PERIOD

Chaplin's first project for United Artists would create more surprise among his associates than even the quick European exit of 1921. Chaplin had decided to write and direct a serious drama, with no more than a cameo role for himself. The man of comedy was turning to tragedy.

Throughout history comedy has consistently been given a back door to the more "serious" subjects. Quite possibly this neglect started with Aristotle's early definition of comedy as the "imitation of baser men." An even more telling accident of history also involves Aristotle: although mankind has managed to preserve his work on tragedy, his research on comedy has somehow been irrevocably lost.

The attitude toward comedy as something inferior has not been limited to ancient history. In this century, from Henri Bergson's *Laughter* (1900) to Walter Kerr's *Tragedy and Comedy* (1967), major theorists who have made otherwise great contributions to comedy theory continue to hedge in giving comedy parity with tragedy.

Ironically, this second-class identity has often been subscribed to by comedy artists themselves, including Chaplin. As early as 1915 he had attempted to do a serious film entitled *Life*, but his comedy obligations had kept it from being completed. Articles on Chaplin that appeared after that date often reported his interest in or preference for tragedy, such as the February 1922 *Current Opinion* piece, "Charlie Chaplin, as a Comedian, Contemplates Suicide." Thus his decision to make a serious film was hardly without earlier precedents.

The story for what would become *A Woman of Paris* (1923) was a love triangle involving a wealthy Parisian sophisticate (played by Adolphe Menjou), his mistress (Edna Purviance), and the young artist she knew before, in an earlier and simpler time (Jean Millet). Inspired by the colorful gold digging career of Peggy Hopkins Joyce, one of several beauties to whom Chaplin had been linked romantically after his return from Europe, the film was also a special gift to long-time leading lady Purviance.

She had been starring in Chaplin films since 1915, was nearing her matronly thirties, and was no longer the Victorian child-woman he needed as heroine. But both Chaplin and Purviance were hopeful that *A Woman of Paris* would launch her dramatic film career. Unfortunately, what was to have been the birth of a new career was stillborn. Despite excellent reviews and such praiseworthy feature articles about her as Adela Rogers St. Johns's "Hollywood Mystery Woman," which appeared in *Photoplay* (February 1924), the public could not accept her outside the realm of nineteenth-century innocence in which thirty-four earlier Chaplin films had typecast her.

The Purviance failure was especially ironic since, with what we now know of her relationship with Chaplin, the love triangle in *A Woman of Paris* might be seen as the dual role she played for a time in the comedian's life. For nine years she had played the idealized heroine to Charlie the tramp, occupying a pedestal not unlike that the young artist of *Paris* placed her upon. Yet in the first of those years she also had been the real-life lover of Charles Chaplin, the increasingly sophisticated and world-famous film director. Again, this was hardly different from her role as Menjou's mistress in *Paris*.

Throughout the film Purviance manages to maintain a certain rural innocence, which complements the country setting in which the character begins and ends the story. And though rural wholesomeness seems rather incompatible with the life of Peggy Hopkins Joyce, it was perfect casting for Purviance. One has only to read some of the interviews-articles that appeared while she was with the Chaplin company, such as "Little Miss Happiness," "My Heroes," "A Star Who Longs for Pretty Clothes," "In Placid Mold," and "The Serene Goddess," to see how much of her real country upbringing seemed to stay with her in Hollywood.[70]

The ending of the film, where Purviance's character breaks with Menjou's and slips into anonymity, foreshadows the actress's future, for the conclusion of *Paris* also terminated the Purviance-Chaplin professional relationship, though he would keep her on salary until her death in 1958. Very soon after *Paris*, she too would slip into comparative anonymity.

Like Purviance's reception, *A Woman of Paris* received critical raves but was not commercially successful, especially outside large metropolitan areas. But its subtle understatement and biting irony quickly had it labeled a classic, and it is said to have inspired the sophisticated comedies of Ernst Lubitsch. Chaplin had more than achieved "his ambition to do at least one big dramatic feature to show the world that he could be something else besides a clown."[71]

In March 1924 Lillita McMurray, using the professional name Lita Grey, signed a film contract that made her Chaplin's new leading lady. Little did anyone suspect that in seven months she would also own that title in private life.

Grey was not quite sixteen and a relative unknown, though she had had small parts in two previous Chaplin productions. She and her mother had played maids in *The Idle Class*, and Lita had also excelled as the delightfully tempting angel of the dream sequence in *The Kid*. In 1924 life would imitate art, as Lita Grey became Chaplin's own special tempting angel.

According to her *My Life With Chaplin* (with Morton Cooper, 1966), there would be innumerable meetings after the signings, at first nothing more than innocent public appearances for the media, complete with chaperone. Other meetings would not be so innocent, and by autumn there would be an unenviable Chaplin encore—his second marriage would also be a shotgun affair.

As their premarital relationship involved subterfuge, so did the marriage ceremony, which took place in Mexico on November 24, 1924. Chaplin used his then current production, *The Gold Rush*, as the cover for the wedding, claiming the number of location sites was being expanded. But since everyone knew the film was a comedy about the frozen North—Will Rogers had even referred to it as a "snow picture," with Chaplin being "as busy as an Eskimo trying to keep warm with a Palm Beach suit on"[72]—the new locations ruse did not exactly fool all the press. Newspaper reporters anticipated a story, but since Grey was still the heroine of *The Gold Rush* (to be replaced soon afterwards by Georgia Hale because of Grey's pregnancy) and was therefore not out of place on a "location" trip, the exact nature of the news was not immediately obvious. A final Chaplin diversion, sending the technical crew out to shoot ocean footage, allowed a press-free ceremony, though reporters were never far off.

Eventually there would be headlines of shock that the bride was only sixteen years of age (Chaplin was thirty-five), which the Los Angeles school district accented by ruling that she must still comply with required school attendance. Yet it was not a scandal of film-career-ending proportions, which would often be the case in the 1920s. America's favorite cracker-barrel hero, Will Rogers, put it all in perspective when he observed, "This girl don't need to go to school. Any girl smart enough to marry Charlie Chaplin should be lecturing at Vassar College on 'Taking advantage of your opportunities.' "[73]

Chaplin, once again in an unhappy domestic situation, poured himself even more into the production of *The Gold Rush*. The result is a film that is still often judged the greatest cinema comedy of all time. Chaplin himself called it the film he wanted to be remembered by. And at the time of its initial release, 1925, it was his greatest critical and commercial success, rather lofty plaudits in and of themselves, in a career that had known little else.

In *The Gold Rush* he had directed Charlie's nomadic shuffle northward to the turn-of-the-century Klondike, where fortunes were made and lost daily. And as is befitting such an acclaimed comedy work, Charlie metaphorically strikes gold with the heroine, after literally hitting pay dirt with his mining partner (Mack Swain).

As Woody Allen suggests at the close of *Annie Hall*, however, getting things right is what art is all about, since life is so seldom the way one plans. *The Gold Rush* fade-out presented a millionaire tramp finding love at last, while a newspaper photographer recorded the event. But the happy ending of Chaplin's greatest professional triumph would be followed by a comparably infamous personal debacle, recorded by a legion of newspapers—the long, scandalous divorce from Lita Grey. Because the proceedings followed the famous film, and Lita's lawyer (her uncle, Edwin McMurray) was able to obtain such a large settlement, the divorce even became known as the second "Gold Rush."

Several items increased the sensationalism of the case. First and foremost was a forty-two-page divorce complaint which "extended sensationally from 'cruel and inhuman treatment' and infidelity to every sin she, or her legal advisers, cared to devise."[74] There was no denying Chaplin was an often difficult, often contradictory person with whom to live. But at the same time there was little denying that her divorce "brief" was, in the language of the streets through which she dragged it, a hatchet job. Even Lita was later moved to describe the document, which had been constructed by her uncle, as going beyond "just asking for support. I was smearing Charlie's name, maybe beyond repair."[75] The atypical nature of the divorce complaint was further accented when within two days of its January 10, 1927, submission to the court some enterprising duplicating "expert" turned it into a Los Angeles street corner best seller.

Chaplin was the target of countless newspaper attacks, though even then there were many who felt the battle rather one-sided. (See the Rollin Kirby drawing, Figure 5.) The result was probably the most celebrated observa-

WHAT REMAINS UNTOUCHED

5. "What Remains Untouched"—Chaplin the Artist. A Rollin Kirby drawing of Charlie done during the scandalous 1927 divorce proceedings with Lita Grey Chaplin. (Courtesy Nostalgia Press.)

tion to come out of the whole case, that of acid humorist H. L. Mencken. "The very morons who worshipped Charlie Chaplin six weeks ago now prepare to dance around the stake while he is burned; he is learning something of the psychology of the mob."[76] This defense of Chaplin the man (a cynic like Mencken could hardly be expected to celebrate Chaplin's romantically sentimental art) allowed Mencken another shot at the people, of whom he had a low view and whom he once delightfully labeled "homo boobiens."

The two children that had been born to the short union, Charles Jr. and Sydney, also fueled the controversy when the question of their adequate child support became an issue during the lengthy proceedings. (Chaplin later noted in his autobiography that it was because of his fondness for the boys that nothing of his relationship with their mother would be mentioned.)[77]

The final element of sensationalism, which according to Lita forced Chaplin into a settlement (the case had become nearly stalemated after countercharges by the comedian), was her threat to name five prominent actresses with whom he had been involved during their marriage. Whether true or not, in a period when Hollywood had already subjected itself to self-censorship (the Hays Office) after several scandals had made it fear federal intervention, Lita's threat shook the film capital. The forthcoming large settlement considerably eased Hollywood's mind, though as Will Rogers suggested, a number of other Americans remained curious about those names.

> Good joke on me. I left Hollywood to keep from being named in the Chaplin trial and now they go and don't name anybody. Not a name was mentioned but Charlie's bank. Charlie is not what I would call a devoted husband, but he certainly is worth marrying.[78]

On August 22, 1927, Lita was awarded a settlement of $625,000 and given custody of the boys, each of whom was also awarded a trust fund of $100,000. After court costs and legal fees Chaplin would be out nearly a million dollars, which produced a collective low whistle of amazement across the country, no doubt dissipating a great deal of any remaining Chaplin hostility. Most importantly for the comedian, he could now return to work on the nearly completed The Circus, whose production the Grey divorce proceedings had interrupted, just as the Harris case had blocked distribution of The Kid. And once again, Will Rogers nicely capsulized the curiosity of a nation about its controversial but still favorite screen comedian.

> Just been over visiting Charlie Chaplin at his studio, and watching him work. I wanted to see how a man acted that had just been separated from a million. That would be the supreme test

of a comedian. He is funnier than ever. He showed me the new
[almost completed] picture. If the next wife settles for a cent less
than two and a half million, she is a chump.[79]

The divorce proceedings had not been the only thing that made the completion of *The Circus* difficult. Monetarily, the demands of the production, which necessitated setting up and maintaining a complete circus for over a year, would nearly match the cost of the Grey settlement. And at the same time, the U.S. government informed Chaplin he owed back taxes of $1,133,000. This would take the next several years to settle.

Beyond these financial pressures were a number of professional ones. First, Chaplin had to try to top his last and greatest, possibly *the* greatest, comedy of all time, *The Gold Rush*. Second, his primary feature-length comedy competitors were much more prolific. While Chaplin was now letting years slide by between his productions, Harold Lloyd was producing a quality comedy each year and the amazing Buster Keaton was doing it twice annually. And in the period between the release of *The Gold Rush* (1925) and *The Circus* (1928), a popular new Chaplin-like performer had arisen named Harry Langdon.

Langdon had nowhere near Chaplin's range, but still there was a sense of the master in his pathos. James Agee said it best when he likened Langdon to a musician with merely "one queerly toned, unique little reed. But out of it he could get incredible melodies."[80] Langdon, under the guidance of Frank Capra, became the sensation of 1926 and early 1927 with three very popular features: *Tramp, Tramp, Tramp* (1926), *The Strong Man* (1926), and *Long Pants* (1927). Langdon would fade quickly after his 1927 split with Capra, which is often ascribed to the comedian's attempt to emulate the sole auteur status of Chaplin. But for a short time, during Chaplin's 1926-1927 hiatus from the screen, it appeared that he had a serious rival in the mixing of comedy and pathos, something Lloyd did awkwardly and Keaton generally avoided.

A third professional concern was how the sensationalism of the Grey divorce would affect the future box office of his films. At one point during the messy proceedings there was even a question of whether there would *be* a future, since women's clubs had secured the banning of Chaplin films in several U.S. cities, an action which precipitated the comedian's 1927 nervous breakdown. Though the case clearly was not as damaging as the Fatty Arbuckle sexual scandal, where a death was involved, Hollywood had already demonstrated a willingness to offer up sacrificial lambs when its collective neck was in trouble.

That the protracted production of *The Circus* was a traumatic experience for Chaplin might best be demonstrated by the way he links it, in a mere passing reference in *My Autobiography*, to the death of his mother.[81] Though he movingly describes Hannah Chaplin's death (he had brought her to the United States in 1921) as occurring while the film was in production, other Chaplin references consistently give *The Circus* a January 1928 release date, while August 28, 1928, has long been established as the day his mother died. But regardless of who is correct, it seems significant that he links this most difficult time period with the loss of the individual who had the greatest single impact on both his professional and personal life.

Earlier in this chapter I noted Will Rogers' observation that finishing *The Circus* would be "the supreme test of a comedian." It is a tribute to Chaplin's talent that this is probably his funniest feature. Though without the poignancy of the boot-eating scene in *The Gold Rush*, where starving Charlie must prepare a Thanksgiving meal from one of his oversized shoes, *The Circus* is a proverbial laugh riot that seldom deviates from continuous comedy. It is as if his deteriorating personal life demanded an all-out comedy production to keep his world in balance.

The Circus is not, however, merely an early Mack Sennett-like collection of gags the only common denominator of which is comedy. Chaplin's material is more tightly integrated by two factors. First, the circus setting ties each of Charlie's individual adventures together, from getting trapped in the mirror maze to getting locked in a cage with a lion. Moreover, Charlie's jack-of-all-trades nomadic nature seems well suited for a circus life-style, while in most of his other films there is a basic comic incongruity between Charlie and his setting.

The second key integrator is a theme that asks what it takes to be funny. Charlie is a successful circus clown only when he is not aware of what he is doing. For example, his initial "performance" takes place when a cop chases him into an ongoing big top show, causing his comic interaction with various acts. Later there is an even more inspired "performance" when a circus donkey pursues him into the midst of the evening's entertainment. With each successive deflating of an act, the crowd is further enthralled, a response decidedly different from its ho-hum attitude toward the old routines of the regular circus clowns. Because of Charlie's propensity for accidental comedy (director Chaplin has him fail a clown audition, using set routines), the villainous ringmaster retains the tramp as a property man even after he has unknowingly become the star of the circus. And while Charlie eventually triumphs over the ringmaster, his comedy escapades continue to be based on accidents.

Chaplin's special focus on the nature of comedy in *The Circus* seems appropriate for a director coming away from his most acclaimed work while suffering through a most trying personal time. And his cinematic answer to the question, that comedy is the result of forces outside one's control, is consistent with the rest of his world view, which was always heavily influenced by nineteenth-century romanticism. Ironically, the divine inspiration-like answer of *The Circus* is an observation he usually omitted from his voluminous writing and interviews until near the end of his life.

The film was well received, and the Academy of Motion Picture Arts and Sciences presented Chaplin with a special Oscar for 1927/1928 (the first year awards were given), citing his "versatility and genius in writing, acting, directing and producing *The Circus*."[82] This award has often suffered from the same anonymity that has attached itself to the film. When Chaplin was given his special lifetime achievement Oscar in 1972, it was, and often still continues to be, reported as his first statuette.

Why has *The Circus* not claimed the visibility of other Chaplin works? There are two key reasons. First, it falls between his two most celebrated works, *The Gold Rush* and *City Lights*. Second, except for Charlie's decision to go it alone at the end, *The Circus* does not mix pathos with its comedy—a mixture that has become *the* Chaplin trademark. *The Circus* never attempts to be more than simply a very funny movie.

The coming of sound motion pictures also distracted from the original 1928 release of *The Circus*. After the huge success of the partial talkie *The Jazz Singer* (1927), the public demanded more and more sound films. And while silent movies continued to be made for a few more years, their number and significance declined radically with each passing year. By 1931, which was the release date of Chaplin's next film, the still silent *City Lights*, anything but sound was considered anachronistic. Hollywood expected *City Lights* to fail, yet it would be hailed as a masterpiece.

Why did Chaplin continue the silent tradition when the rest of the film industry was jumping to sound? First, it allowed him to maintain the universality of his tramp character. Charlie spoke in a language understood around the world—pantomime. Anything less, such as adopting English dialogue, would have undercut the everyman nature of his character severely. Chaplin's writing from this period would also apply that same universality to all of silent cinema, celebrating the specialized art form it represented.[83] Chaplin's friend and contemporary Mary Pickford articulated this sentiment in the most provocatively succinct manner when she observed: "It would have been more logical if silent pictures had grown out of the talkie instead of the other way around."[84]

Second, a universal character also could be equated with a universal box office. Being confined to one language would limit his large market abroad. Good business for others dictated a transition to sound, while just the opposite was true for Chaplin, though he did add a synchronized score and sound effects to *City Lights*.

Like filmmaker and theorist Sergei Eisenstein, Chaplin believed that sound could be used as an additional tool in what would still be essentially silent cinema. He was appalled that early sound films so surrendered themselves to this new development, especially when the sound quality was often very primitive. Chaplin even satirized this technical limitation at the opening of *City Lights*, where two pompous public speakers "broadcast" distorted sounds instead of words.

A third reason to continue the silent tradition, suggested by his oldest son, Charles Chaplin, Jr., was purely to save the tramp figure, which had become his father's alter ego. Because if Charlie's universality was not to be compromised with a voice, the character itself would need to be retired. "But knowing my father, . . . he simply could not make the move that might destroy the Little Tramp. *City Lights* was my father's signed reprieve."[85]

City Lights was a long two-year production, fraught with many anxieties besides the gamble of going on with a silent film. For director Chaplin, the not always benevolent dictator of the set, his two key players besides the tramp created production exasperations. Henry Clive, who was playing Charlie's sometime millionaire friend, refused to do a comic drowning scene until the water was warmed. Chaplin saw several shades of red and Clive was fired, despite the fact that scenes involving his character were all but completed. He was replaced by Harry Meyers, who was superb in the role, but it took months to reshoot the now discarded scenes involving Clive.

The same fate nearly befell Virginia Cherrill, who played the blind flower girl with whom the tramp falls in love. In real life she was a recently divorced free spirit who often showed signs of the previous night's partying—hardly the desired look for the virginal maiden she played. Chaplin seriously considered replacing her with the heroine of *The Gold Rush*, Georgia Hale, with whom he was then romantically involved. But Hale did not meet the requirements of the role, and Cherrill was retained after being given a stern pep talk.

A final challenge of the *City Lights* production was Chaplin's composition of the film's synchronized score. He had supervised the sheet music for theater musicians since *The Kid*.[86] But this was his first original composition for a feature, something which would be a regular part of Chaplin's duties on each subsequent film.

Because Chaplin could not read music (though he played several instruments by ear), his composition sessions often proved to be a comic nightmare for the professional musicians hired to transcribe or translate his recorded humming of the desired melody. When this tedious process was coupled with Chaplin's never-ending demand for perfection, it is easy to see how numerous music assistants were driven to distraction. Yet, as Theodore Huff wrote in his excellent September 1950 article in *Films in Review*, "Chaplin As Composer: His Unique Gift for Scoring His Films" (which later became the foundation for Chapter 25 of his celebrated biography of the comedian), "Chaplin's music is an integral part of his conception of the film."

City Lights proved to be a huge critical and commercial success, combining the elements of comedy and pathos on a level comparable to that of *The Gold Rush*, though not quite of the epic "man against nature" scope of the

Klondike story. The conclusion of *City Lights*, where the haunting close-up of Charlie's face reflects both joy that the blind girl can now see and sadness that he is not the benefactor she dreamed of, has often been called cinema's greatest moment. Certainly it is the most memorable moment in a career of memorable moments created by Chaplin.

The film's close also brings the story full circle, from the pity Charlie felt for the blind girl in the beginning, to that which she feels for the tramp and/or herself now, pity he is not the knight in shining armor she imagined. Yet, as is so often true of a Chaplin work, the film's close is open-ended. One might still hope there is a chance for Charlie. After all, he won Georgia after a less than encouraging beginning in *The Gold Rush*. And while the former blind girl is not pleased at the modest physical specimen before her, she has yet to see the magic Charlie can coax from the everyday world around him, from the ongoing personality of his anarchistic cane to the delightful one-time dance of the rolls in *The Gold Rush*.

To adequately showcase the release of *City Lights*, he completely organized its New York premiere, personally handling everything from prices to publicity. He then combined another pilgrimage to England with the London opening of the film, much as he had done ten years earlier with *The Kid*. And just as he had proved the industry wrong with the giant success of *City Lights* in America, his 1931 English reception surprised many by being just as tumultuous a celebration as the earlier one.

English homage turned into a global affair as the London visit became an around-the-world trip. He chronicled his adventures in *A Comedian Sees the World* (1933, often said to have been ghostwritten), which first appeared in a five-part series in the magazine *Woman's Home Companion*. Like the 1922 *My Trip Abroad*, the work is essentially a travelogue, though not so fresh as the comedian's first account of international fame. And unlike the comedy travelogues of a favorite author, Mark Twain, who had often deflated the importance of celebrated foreign places and personages, Chaplin was most respectful.

However, the 1930s meetings with world leaders and dignitaries went beyond the heady experience they must have provided an individual of Chaplin's originally meager background. The contacts allowed him to bounce a wide assortment of personal views on world issues off the very people most directly involved. Like many people of limited formal education, Chaplin overcompensated in his personal study. Consequently, he was fairly bursting with theories on global problems, especially ones related to the infamous 1930s Depression, which would be the setting for his next film, *Modern Times* (1936).

THE TRAMP'S LAST FILM

Modern Times represents a watershed point in Chaplin's career, for it is both the final appearance of his timeless tramp and his last silent film. At the time, however, not even Chaplin, who was letting more and more time pass between productions, had decided on the future fate of Charlie. But a close, often metaphorical, reading of the film suggests that there were few or no other options available. This view rests upon three key factors to which Chaplin subjected (however subliminally) the character of Charlie.

First, the concept of "modern times" had never before intruded so strongly into the tramp's world—for the first time his ongoing existence seemed threatened by change. As Robert Warshow has suggested, prior to *Modern Times* Charlie and society often were at odds but there seemed to be no real threat to the continued independence of a professional free spirit like the tramp. But after the early 1930s, changes in society had created a condition that represented an ongoing threat to the individual.[87] Not surprisingly, the machine society of *Modern Times*, as well as the fascist one of *The Great Dictator* (1940), quite literally threaten the life of Chaplin's underdog alter ego.

Modern Times is structured upon the institutionalism of this change in society. As if comically anticipating contemporary documentary filmmaker Frederick Wiseman's obsession with institutional life, Chaplin's film divides its time between a factory, a prison, and a huge department store. In each case, and particularly that of *the factory* (which was an early title for the film), these institutions have a markedly debilitating effect on Charlie.

In the factory Charlie's job is to tighten nuts on an assembly line—a line whose speed is constantly being increased, as if in reference to the ever-changing clock face over which the opening title (*Modern Times*) is superimposed. Eventually Charlie's enslavement to the assembly line (he misses tightening a nut, and proceeds to go after it) causes him quite literally to be swallowed up by the machine. As Theodore Huff has put it, "the endless nut-tightening finally drives Charlie 'nuts.'"[88] Yet this comic breakdown (equipped with two wrenches, he tries to tighten everything in sight, including some provocatively placed buttons on a woman's blouse) represents a defeat over Charlie to which no other living antagonism has ever come close.

The road to the sanitarium is also assisted by other modern elements in the factory. For example, Charlie is the victim of a factory boss who anticipates by well over a decade the "Big Brother is watching you" situation of George Orwell's *1984*. With factory monitors placed in strategic places, Charlie cannot even steal a quick smoke in the washroom without the boss watching.

The tramp's mental and physical health is further endangered by the boss's desire to increase productivity by slipping workers into an automatic feeding device that will allow them to work through lunch. Charlie gets to be the guinea pig for this machine, which begins to malfunction early in the demonstration, attacking the defenseless Charlie with everything from a renegade ear of corn to a blotter-like mechanical napkin that keeps smacking him in the mouth. And most appropriately, for a machine, it attempts to force-feed him some steel nuts mistakenly placed on his dessert dish.

In the prison setting (thought to be a communist leader, he has mistakenly been jailed), Charlie's life-style is completely institutionalized, from the matching cells to the mass dinner scene where, row after row, the prisoners sit down at long gray tables. And though nothing occurs here that is quite so metaphorically dramatic as being swallowed by a machine, Charlie reveals the extent of his institutionalization merely by not wanting to leave the prison, even after he is pardoned.

Times must really have changed when a "tramp" cannot get along in the outside world, especially one who has formerly been so fiercely independent. Yet as the congested city montage that opens the section suggests, Charlie is no longer up to this type of stress after his release from the sanitarium. As if to underline this, not long after his release from prison he dines on a huge restaurant feast for which he has no money—in order to return to prison. (Red Skelton would later base his annual Freddie the Freeloader Christmas television show on this premise.)

This is not the spirit of the Charlie of old, but rather an old Charlie. The hallmark of his earlier work was the innovative manner in which he *avoided* the law, from the lively escapes of the short subject years, such as his ability in *The Rink* (1916) to literally "roll" circles around the police, to the quiet dignity his escapes had achieved by the time of *City Lights*, where the tramp aristocratically avoids a cop by simply walking through an expensive automobile parked nearby. On those earlier occasions when the authorities did catch him, director Chaplin rarely allowed the viewer the sight of Charlie in a lock-up. If anything, prison in a Chaplin film had formerly represented an occasion for a brilliant escape, such as the lively chase of *The Adventurer* (Figure 6) or the lovely irony of clerical disguise in *The Pilgrim*. Significantly, both of these films start *not* with an incarcerated victim but rather with an already escaping Charlie.

For these reasons it is a shock to find the *Modern Times* tramp so enamored of the safety of the penal cell, even one sporting the added bourgeois touch of a picture of Lincoln. Granted, he does have near free rein here, but that is only because he has single-handedly *stopped* an earlier escape attempt by others. But unhappily for Charlie, he is pardoned. When he later escapes arrest after the "free" lunch he originally took to return to prison, it is only because of the childlike intensity of the lovely, coaxing gamin (Paulette Goddard). But when had Charlie ever needed coaxing to escape before?

The apparent age of the comedy character is another factor at this point. As early as *City Lights*, the tramp is starting to show signs of age. In *Modern Times*, much of this is minimized by the general lack of close-ups—something film theorist Béla Balázs has claimed was necessary in order that Chaplin avoid any apparent mechanical problems the absence of

6. Charlie had already escaped at the start of *The Adventurer,* 1917.
(Courtesy Museum of Modern Art/Film Stills Archive).

sound would have implied in dramatic close-up.[89] Still, *Modern Times* presents the viewer with a noticeably older tramp, and age does not set well with his comedy character.

The ability of any comedy character to age relates directly to the premise on which the character is based. For example, with clowns of childlike innocence, such as Chaplin contemporaries Stan Laurel and Harry Langdon, the aging process is devastating—they literally lose their premise for comedy. Conversely, with characters like Groucho Marx or W. C. Fields, where comedy is based upon cynical worldly experience (and more than a touch of the dirty old man), age actually enhances their appeal.

The comedy persona of the tramp, though hardly based in innocence, still does not age well. Because of Charlie's ability to master almost any task and his ease at taking on other shapes and forms (he successfully assumes the pose of a floor lamp in *The Adventurer*), authors have often seen the magic of Charlie in godlike terms—particularly as Pan. Robert Payne actually entitled his biography of the comedian *The Great God Pan: A Biography of the Tramp Played by Charlie Chaplin.*[90] Such comparisons were being made so early in Chaplin's career that they probably caused the rather self-conscious, though delightful, dream sequence of *Sunnyside* (1919), where Charlie dances with four lovely wood nymphs in a meadow.

Needless to say, gods do not age. And though nothing in *Modern Times* is quite so shocking as the Lillian Ross photograph of Chaplin in retirement assuming the pose of Pan (from her 1980 book, *Moments with Chaplin*),[91] Charlie shows enough age in the 1936 film to suggest that the saga of the tramp had best close.

The final institutional setting is that of a multistoried department store, where Charlie briefly finds work as a night watchman. The store's many showroom settings seem to represent a microcosm of "modern times," and as if to accent the ever-accelerating pace of life, Charlie finds it necessary to don roller skates to maintain the speed required for his rounds.

But just as the Marx Brothers would find that there is nothing simple about even a microcosm (in their own *Big Store*, 1940), so Charlie would also encounter a problem. His heart would go out to fellow victims of "modern times"—unemployed workers who were robbing the store, workers who were also friends from the factory assembly line days. When authorities discover the robbery at the store's opening the next morning, a "closing" of sorts takes place for Charlie—he is returned to prison. His "meeting" with his former factory mates and the resulting trip back to the hoosegow bring his three-part encounter with institutionalism full circle.

The second key factor that serves as a harbinger of the tramp's swan song focuses on his relationship with the lovely gamin. Goddard, as Huff has noted, is "different from both the old, passive Chaplin heroine, and the tempestuous Georgia" of *The Gold Rush.*[92] But whereas Huff drops his Goddard focus after noting her "vitality and spontaneity," it is necessary to take this perception of her distinctiveness one step further.

This "vitality and spontaneity" very much reflect that this is the first and only time we have a heroine created in the image of Charlie. Inspired by his close relationship with Goddard (who he is said to have secretly married in 1935 or 1936, though there appears to be no evidence to prove it), Chaplin saw the gamin as the catalysis of the whole film.[93]

Traditionally, Charlie acted as a father figure for his heroines, from his masterly scrubbing of Edna Purviance's face in *The Vagabond* (1916) to his care for the blind girl in *City Lights*. But in *Modern Times* this parental role is most definitely shared, almost as if director Chaplin is acknowledging the new role of women in "modern times." There is no doubting this gamin is often the one who takes care of Charlie—a unique reversal. She does everything from finding them a rickety but serviceable home to getting him a job as a singing waiter. But most importantly, just as Goddard represents an inspiration for Chaplin as director, the gamin works the same magic on the character of the tramp. For example, she is the catalyst for Charlie's escape from the "free lunch" arrest he had originally orchestrated as a ticket back to the safety of prison. From this point on, it is the spirit of the Charlie of old that has returned, a true "Artful Dodger," in the semantic sense (to borrow from Dickens, a Chaplin favorite). He again has no need of prisons and regains his old elusiveness during run-ins with the law.

The gamin makes this possible because she is a younger, "streetwise" version of Charlie. Whereas earlier heroines were often several notches above him in social class (especially Purviance), the gamin has been orphaned into the streets. Moreover, she takes to this tramp-like situation with all the physical intensity of a young Charlie (previous heroines were rather restrained in their actions). She shows tenacity in caring for her young siblings, reminiscent of the tramp's care of Jackie Coogan in *The Kid*, and she brings grace to her improvisational street dancing that is much like Charlie's salute to Pan in *Sunnyside*.

Chaplin continues to allow the tramp some parental action, such as getting the gamin food in the department store cafeteria and tucking her in for the night in the bedding supply section. But she still comes across as more of an equal than any other Chaplin heroine. The comedian seems to accent this by the film's close—the gamin accompanies Charlie down one final road, the first and only time the exit shuffle, his classic film signature, has been shared.

The third and final element that seems to signal that *Modern Times* will be the close of Charlie's career comes in the often derivative nature of the comedy material itself. That is, many of the routines, though delightfully funny, are merely close variations of things Chaplin has done before, from his skill in the skating scene, so reminiscent of *The Rink*, to his problems as a waiter, a comedy situation he had essayed on several earlier occasions, starting with *Caught in a Cabaret* (1914).

A certain degree of such derivation is to be expected when dealing with what theorist Balázs calls "true personalities of the screen," among whom he lists Chaplin—those stars who do not so much act as play the "same personality" in each film, where the heavy viewer identification is a product of the fact that this "old acquaintance" turns up in each new film.[94] But the often derivative nature of *Modern Times*, despite the time update, seems to go beyond the needs of viewer identification. Balázs's hypothesis asks not for recycled routines but rather recycled spirit—a consistency of attitude in the character as he responds to *new* situations.

There is nothing new about the problem of derivative material, if indeed it is a problem. For example, as numerous writers have noted, the Marx Brothers essentially remade the same movie again and again. Yet, it does not distract from the greatness of a specific comedy pattern, though as Woody Allen has noted, it does suggest a failure to grow.[95]

When *Modern Times* came out, however, the derivative nature of the film often met celebration rather than criticism, because of the great popularity of Charlie and the rarity with which he was appearing. It was as if to say an old Charlie was better than no Charlie. For example, *New York Times* reviewer Frank S. Nugent closed his glowing review of the film, after chronicling several derivative strands, with: "This morning, there is good news: Chaplin is back again."[96] But "to some people, Chaplin now seemed like a creature from another world. His comedy . . . [was] remote from the new types."[97] More than anything else, this is a reference to his refusal to abandon the silent form.

Whereas Chaplin's loyalty to silence in *City Lights* had seemed quite justified because of the early crudeness of Hollywood's transition to sound, which he satirized at the start of the film, many saw the continued silence of *Modern Times* as an anachronism. Chaplin himself noted that he approached his next project, what would become *The Great Dictator*, with the "feeling that the art of pantomime was gradually becoming obsolete, . . . a discouraging thought."[98]

Modern Times, therefore, begins to take on the quality today's recording industry might label "Chaplin's Greatest Hits" (Huff calls it a "Chaplin anthology"),[99] a phenomenon that does not traditionally appear until the close of an artist's career. Chaplin seems to accent this final quality by the one *new* element he brought to the film—allowing Charlie to speak briefly for the first and only time. The speech is actually a delightful gibberish song, "a sort of Katzenjammer French,"[100] whose nonsense lyrics he improvises after losing the originals. Thus director Chaplin creates a lovely device with which to preserve the formerly silent universality of Charlie's character: the tramp is given his own language. Chaplin had, however, put himself in a corner.

What kind of sound encore could he do? Gibberish would hardly work on an expanded scale; yet limiting himself to merely one language would immediately destroy the air of universality. There was also the problem that this *tramp* would be speaking with an English accent, hardly the stuff of an everyman universality. Therefore, to preserve the uniqueness of Charlie, retirement was the only real option.

The preceding observations *now* seem to "document" *Modern Times* as the logical close to the celebrated career of the cinema tramp. Chaplin would go on to create a number of other film characters, often with tramp-like qualities, but Charlie belonged to the ages.

After the opening of *Modern Times*, Chaplin took Goddard on a five-month holiday to the Orient, where they may have been married. But for reasons that have never been revealed, both Chaplin and Goddard refused to disclose the exact nature of their relationship upon their return. And the illicit suggestion this secrecy produced in the censorship-conscious 1930s is often said to have cost Goddard the coveted role of Scarlett in *Gone With the Wind* (1939). Chaplin would not refer to her publicly as his wife until 1940, shortly before they separated. Once again he seemed to be exposing his love of the contradictory.

FILMS OF CONTROVERSY

Modern Times was followed by *The Great Dictator* (1940), the most controversial film in Chaplin's career to that point. The film was a devastating parody of Adolf Hitler, with Chaplin playing both the dictator, Adenoid Hynkel, and a tramp-like Jewish barber who closely resembles Hynkel. The inspiration for the project, originally suggested by Alexander Korda in 1937, was based on the toothbrush mustache similarity between Hitler and Charlie and the opportunity it provided for a comedy of mistaken identity.

At the same time, however, the role of Hynkel allowed Chaplin to explore new comedy areas, especially in sound, that had been forever closed to Charlie. For example, his delicious travesty of Hitler as an orator, with its "Demokratien shtoonk!" and "Frei Sprecken shtoonk!" allowed Chaplin to showcase his exceptional talents for both verbal mimicry (well honed from performances at Hollywood parties) and pointed political satire.

This celebrated performance of German gibberish was, of course, complimented by Chaplin's ongoing ability to give his work numerous levels of comedy richness. Thus the viewer's easy comic understanding of such Hynkel comments as "Libertad shtoonk!" is effectively milked for further humor by the comic overstatement of an unseen narrator who translates the obvious, while also becoming a victim of parody with his "diplomatic" decoding, such as "Demokratien shtoonk!" becoming "Democracy is fragrant." (Woody Allen would include a similar translation scene in *Bananas*, 1971, with a parody of another dictator, Castro.) Moreover, the distorted speech of Chaplin's dictator (echoed in his name, *Adenoid Hynkel*) is punctuated by more traditional moments of Chaplin visual comedy, from the microphone that is physically repelled by Hynkel's verbal attack, to the overheated speaker stopping to pour a glass of drinking water in the front of his pants—a slapstick commentary on the almost sexual nature of Hitler's impassioned speech.

As in so much of Chaplin's work, there is also an underlying suggestion of a comic literary tradition in this film. But while Dickens and Cervantes are often used to explain Chaplin's films, the oratorical spoof in question seems more reminiscent of the tongue-in-cheek essays of a Chaplin favorite named Mark Twain, particularly that author's biting comments on "The Awful German Language," which is actually part of a longer Twain work with a title to which one might expect Chaplin to be drawn—*A Tramp Abroad* (1880).

Chaplin took numerous chances with the production of *The Great Dictator*. There was the threat of censorship from the Hays Office, as well as personal threats from right-wing extremists through the mail (shades of his World War I white feather letters). And as with the controversial *Shoulder Arms* wartime release twenty-two years earlier, some questioned the appropriateness of *Dictator* appearing with Europe already engaged in World War II. He was also stepping away from Charlie, probably cinema's most popular character, though the presence in *Dictator* of the sometimes tramp-like barber was meant to soften this. In addition, Chaplin was playing a world leader despised even then. Finally, by its very nature black comedy, which best describes *Dictator*, searches out controversy, whether it be Jonathan Swift's eighteenth-century "Modest Proposal" of baby eating or Stanley Kubrick's cinema poem to the Apocalypse, *Dr. Strangelove: or How I Learned to Stop Worrying and Love the Bomb* (1964).

Chaplin took these chances because he was determined that both Hitler and Nazi racism be ridiculed.[101] And the film's political focus continued the trend, begun with *Modern Times*, of dealing more pointedly with social issues, a characteristic that had received little attention in his work since the Mutual Film days (1916-1917). But because *The Great Dictator* addressed political issues so much more baldly than any preceding Chaplin work, the film also marks the first step of the final stage of his career—where the personal social views of the man take precedence over everything, including comedy, with no Charlie to make the often resultant controversy more palatable.

The Great Dictator mixed controversy with curiosity (besides being Chaplin's first film after Charlie's retirement, it was his first sound film), making it the biggest box office success in his career to that point. The reviews, however, were mixed; rather than praising the film as a whole, the critics were more likely to praise individual scenes, such as Hynkel's gibberish speech or his ballet-like dance to world power. But one scene received much criticism—the closing speech by the little barber, where he seems to step out of character in order to address the viewer directly, instead of the audience within the film. And while the merits of this final speech continue to be debated by film historians and critics, it nicely symbolized the more personalized direction his future work would take.

Chaplin's controversial close to *The Great Dictator* was hardly unusual, given the volatile time in which it was set. Several other major then-contemporary productions with political themes also included self-conscious conclusions. For example, William Dieterle's controversial film about the Spanish Civil War, *Blockade* (1938), concludes with Henry Fonda dropping any pretense of story and making an impassioned plea to the film audience. Moreover, John Ford's 1940 adaptation of *The Grapes of Wrath*, with Ma Joad's (Jane Darwell) uplifting final speech, tacked on by producer Darryl Zanuck to avoid a pessimistic conclusion, remains a controversial contradiction of John Steinbeck's original novel. And finally, Alfred Hitchcock's stylish Nazi warning, *Foreign Correspondent* (1940), concludes with an emotional radio broadcast by reporter Joel McCrea that quickly becomes a self-conscious message to America.

It now seems somehow appropriate that Chaplin should have opened the 1940s with a controversial film, because for much of the decade he would be involved in continuous controversies. For example, while the United States's entry into World War II helped dissipate right-wing criticism of Chaplin generated by *The Great Dictator*, his Second Front support for our new ally, the Soviet Union, again left him vulnerable to conservative extremists. Ironically, Chaplin's pro-Soviet activity was merely an extension of the anti-Nazi nature of *Dictator*. In fact, as Roger Manvell observes, the comedian's July 22, 1942, Second Front speech by telephone to sixty thousand trade unionists in Madison Square Garden closely followed the closing speech of *The Great Dictator*.[102]

The early 1940s also found the comedian involved in two sex scandals. One would produce lurid headlines for years, while the other was soon recognized by outsiders as the perfect love both he and his former screen alter ego, Charlie, had for so long been seeking. The first case involved a beautiful but unstable girl named Joan Barry, with whom he became professionally and romantically involved during the early 1940s. (Chaplin and Goddard had separated in 1941 and were said to have been divorced in 1942, but their Mexican divorce was just as vague as their earlier marriage claims. In fact, the *New York Times* reported that "so secretive was the action that an entry of the decree had been ordered removed from the record by the jurist who issued it.")[103] When Chaplin ended the Barry relationship in early 1942, she began to harass him, doing everything from breaking windows in his house to actually breaking in and holding him at gunpoint. In 1943 Barry named Chaplin in a paternity suit, which was followed in 1944 by a federal grand jury indictment of the comedian for violation of the Mann Act (the transfer of a woman across a state line for sexual intentions). The latter accusation, also allegedly involving Barry, was soon shown to be ludicrous, and the charge was dropped. But the paternity suit was upheld in court through the slanderous melodramatics of Barry's lawyer, despite a blood test that proved conclusively that Chaplin could not have been the father.

The second "scandal" would normally not have been pigeonholed as such, but it became inevitable because of its timing and Chaplin's proven proclivity toward young women. Thus, at approximately the same time as the paternity suit was filed, the comedian secretly married eighteen-year-old

Oona O'Neill, daughter of playwright Eugene O'Neill. Chaplin was fifty-four. And though this fourth marriage would become *the* success of his private life, lasting as it did until his 1977 death and producing a family of Victorian size (eight children), the union only intensified the ballyhoo against him in 1943.

The preceding examples were merely the most prominent of Chaplin's 1940s controversies. Additional problems included more tax differences with the government and a continued tendency in post-World War II America to antagonize the political right and some moderates with such actions as his support of Henry Wallace. Wallace, the former third-term vice-president under Franklin Roosevelt, had been President Truman's Secretary of Commerce until a falling out over Truman's "get tough" policy with the Soviets. Wallace felt world peace could be maintained only by better relations with the Soviet Union; thus he opposed such presidential actions as the Truman Doctrine and the Marshall Plan. In 1948 Wallace ran for president on the Progressive Party ticket, which supported closer ties with the Soviets. He finished last in a four-way race ultimately won by Truman. Candidate Wallace and supporter Chaplin might best be described today as idealistically naive liberals who underestimated the patently disruptive nature of the Soviets in Europe after World War II. However, they were most certainly not communist sympathizers, a charge frequently leveled against them at the time.

Chaplin did not always even have to do something to be controversial. For example, he was widely criticized during the 1940s and early 1950s for not relinquishing his British passport and becoming an American citizen, because he had lived in this country since 1913. Chaplin's defense, that he felt himself a citizen of the world, did not fall on many sympathetic ears, though there were countless other unhounded artists in Chaplin's position. One such individual was his celebrated understudy from Karno days, Stan Laurel. John McCabe notes that Laurel, who kept his British citizenship throughout his fifty-four-year residency in the States, was forever irked that Chaplin should be so singled out.[104]

With these frustrations as a backdrop, Chaplin's decision to make another black comedy statement film seems most logical. The result was *Monsieur Verdoux* (1947), with Chaplin playing a dapper former bank clerk, Henri Verdoux, who marries and murders little old ladies for a profit. The film was inspired by the "career" of Frenchman Henri Landru, better known as the "modern Bluebeard," who was guillotined in 1922 for liquidating ten of his girlfriends.

Orson Welles had originally approached Chaplin about the role of Landru in one of a series of simulated documentaries the young director was contemplating. But Chaplin's often macabre sense of humor was more drawn to the comic potential of the material, just as the cannibalism of the snowbound Donner Party had inspired some of the most poignantly funny scenes in *The Gold Rush* or Hitler's Nazism had led to *The Great Dictator*.

While *Monsieur Verdoux* was closest to the black comedy political focus of *The Great Dictator*, in terms of the comedian's previous work *Verdoux* did not have the broad-based popular appeal of an Adolf Hitler parody. And although both films had didactic tendencies, a message on the negativism of dictatorship is much more palatable in this country than a warning about the murderous inclinations of big business.

Monsieur Verdoux was also operating under some other restraints. For example, despite the tongue-in-cheek richness of the often woman-plagued Chaplin becoming a "Lady Killer" (the working title of the script, much of which was written during the Joan Barry scandal), the film's cynicism was ahead of its time. In addition, like Preston Sturges' black comedy from the following year, *Unfaithfully Yours* (1948), which features Rex Harrison murdering his wife in three different daydream sequences, the public just did not expect this type of comedy from Chaplin. Thus, while both *Monsieur Verdoux* and *Unfaithfully Yours* are now critically acclaimed, neither film had a good box office on its initial U.S. release. And finally, *Monsieur Verdoux* was hurt financially by the previous Chaplin controversies. In a number of areas it was banned and/or picketed by organizations like the American Legion.

The degree to which the right wing used *Monsieur Verdoux* to get at its creator is best demonstrated by the shocking treatment Chaplin received at the United Artists press conference in New York on April 12, 1947, one day after the opening of the film. The transcript of the proceedings reads like a scenario on how to conduct a witch hunt. Chaplin was rudely questioned on a number of "patriotic" topics, from his foreign citizenship to his controversial friendships. The only bright spot in the inquisition was the tribute paid to him by author and critic James Agee, who posed an ironically rhetorical question on just what having a free country meant.

Agee continued his defense of Chaplin through a three-part celebration of *Monsieur Verdoux* in *The Nation*.[105] First the critic itemized and answered a number of complaints about the film; then he addressed the key thrust of the work: murder as a "metaphor for business," with Verdoux as a "metaphor for the modern personality."[106] And though Agee probes several other aspects of the film, such as Verdoux's ties with Charlie, the writer is at his best delineating the metaphorical substructure upon which the film is built. His three-part review often is credited with keeping the critical reputation of the film alive until a time when the public was better able to judge the work as separate from the life of the artist.

The year 1947 provided other Chaplin controversies besides those often focused on through *Monsieur Verdoux*. These included an old friend's lawsuit for plagiarism of *The Great Dictator* and demands for his deportation by a U.S. congressman. Also, Chaplin was led to believe he would be called before the House Un-American Activities Committee, a request which was later withdrawn.

By the late 1940s the controversies that clung to Chaplin had somewhat died down. The years from then until the release of his next production, *Limelight* (1952), were personally rather quiet ones for the comedian. The home that had once served as a Hollywood tennis party center (Chaplin was a keen student of the game) was no longer a drawing card. Because people did not want to risk controversy by association, he was often avoided. Chaplin, however, finally had a happy home, a good marriage, and a growing family.

Limelight is set in 1914 London, far from the controversies of the 1940s. The central character, an aging, no longer popular clown named Calvero the Tramp Comedian, bears more than coincidental ties with Chaplin himself. The film's May-December relationship between Calvero and Terry, the young ballerina (Claire Bloom) who makes him happy once more is reflective of Oona's effect on Chaplin's real life. And the London music hall scene of Chaplin's youth is frequently showcased. Even the 1914 date has special significance for Chaplin, since it marked the appearance of his first film and the official close of his music hall days. Though far from being a Chaplin biography, *Limelight* is, as Denis Gifford suggests, often "true in spirit" to the comedian's life.[107]

The film opens with Calvero thwarting an attempted suicide by the ballerina. Terry has tried to take her own life because she cannot find work as a dancer. Still depressed after Calvero's rescue, she claims paralysis in both her legs despite a doctor's prognosis that there is nothing physically wrong. The old clown is eventually able to coax Terry from her depression and physical disorder, using a combination of intense platonic devotion and a nonstop enthusiasm for life. Calvero's drive, though sometimes didactic, prepares the ballerina for a seemingly unlimited professional future, and she eventually returns the favor (bringing the story full circle) by helping him to realize one last great performance before he dies.

Limelight has also come to be seen as Chaplin's one last great performance, towering over his final two films; *A King in New York* (1957) and *A Countess from Hong Kong* (1966). Yet at the time much of the glory was negated by a single action of U.S. Attorney General James McGranery. Chaplin and family were en route to Europe by ship after the New York premiere of *Limelight* when he was informed by cable that McGranery was barring his reentry into this country (Chaplin was still a British subject) pending an appearance before an immigration board of inquiry. The comedian would have to answer rather vague moral and political charges hearkening back to the overblown Chaplin scandals already delineated in this text. The nature of this smear can be equated with the man in which it was implemented: Chaplin had been granted a reentry permit before he disembarked, but it was cancelled as soon as he left.

The witch hunting had gone on long enough for Chaplin, and he decided to stay abroad permanently. Oona briefly returned to the United States to oversee the removal of Chaplin's sizable fortune, which the comedian had good reason to fear might be blocked by the government. However, no problems developed and the family eventually settled on an estate in Switzerland, the Manoir de Ban in the village of Corsair. This was to be Chaplin's last home.

A King in New York, shot in England, is rather an indirect response to Chaplin's shabby treatment in 1952. The film satirizes a gamut of American subjects, from McCarthyism to rock 'n roll. Unfortunately the movie is not on a par with his earlier work. The main plot, in which a deposed king learns the big business value of a royal title in the United States, is an excellent premise for a satire on American values. But the story is bogged down by didactic comments too often to realize its satirical potential. And Chaplin's character is the least sympathetic or arresting of all his post-Charlie roles, though there are redeeming moments, such as his surprise at the taste of a liquor for which he is doing a commercial or his adolescent-like interest in the lovely television advertiser (Dawn Addams).

Ten years later Chaplin would try one final film—writing and directing *A Countess from Hong Kong,* a romantic comedy with Marlon Brando and Sophia Loren. It was a critical and commercial failure. And whereas *A King in New York* at least had had the sometimes saving grace of Chaplin's on-screen presence, he allowed himself only a brief cameo in *A Countess.*

Roger Manvell has described the Switzerland chapter of Chaplin's life as the "halcyon years."[108] And while there is much to this, since he had his ever-growing family around him (Oona would have four more children in Europe, doubling the size of their family) and a home far from witch-hunting America, the failure of his two final films was most disappointing.

On April 10, 1972, much of the hurt from these and other disappointments was undoubtedly lessened when the Academy of Motion Picture Arts and Sciences awarded Chaplin a special Oscar for his contributions to cinema. His was a most triumphant return, coming precisely twenty years after McGranary had negated Chaplin's U.S. reentry permit. America had finally tendered an apology of sorts for its past treatment of the clown. This Oscar was but one of the many hosannas he would receive in his final years; others included the Venice Film Festival's Golden Lion statuette (1972) and being knighted by Queen Elizabeth II of England (1975).

Chaplin died on Christmas Day 1977. His gift of Charlie will forever brighten the human experience; in the chaotic modern world, people relate much more closely to the ironies of comedy than to the flaws of tragedy. Chaplin himself had inadvertently stumbled onto this when he noted:

> I am not a bit funny, really. I am just a little nickel comedian trying to make people laugh. They act as though I were the king of England.[109]

For most people, he represented much more.

56   Charlie Chaplin

NOTES

1. Terry Ramsaye, *A Million and One Nights: A History of the Motion Pictures through 1925*, 2 vols. (1926; rpt., in 2 vols. in 1; New York: Simon and Schuster, 1964), pp. 648-649.
2. Denis Gifford, *Chaplin* (Garden City, New York: Doubleday, 1974), p. 11.
3. Robert F. Moss, *Charlie Chaplin* (1975; rpt. New York: Harcourt, Brace, Jovanovich, 1977), p. 12.
4. R. J. Minney, *Chaplin: The Immortal Tramp* (London: George Newnes, 1954), p. 6.
5. John McCabe, *Charlie Chaplin* (Garden City, New York: Doubleday, 1978), p. 9.
6. Charles Chaplin, *My Autobiography* (1964; rpt. New York: Pocket Books, 1966), p. 22.
7. Chaplin, *My Autobiography*, p. 24.
8. Chaplin, *My Autobiography*, p. 366.
9. McCabe, *Charlie Chaplin*, pp. 16-17.
10. Roger Manvell, *Chaplin* (Boston: Little, Brown, 1974), p. 51.
11. Charlie Chaplin, *Charlie Chaplin's Own Story* (Indianapolis: Bobbs-Merrill, 1916), p. 172.
12. Chaplin, *Charlie Chaplin's Own Story*, p. 175.
13. Buster Keaton with Charles Samuels, *My Wonderful World of Slapstick* (Garden City, New York: Doubleday, 1960), p. 13.
14. Chaplin, *My Autobiography*, pp. 24, 239.
15. McCabe, *Charlie Chaplin*, p. 27.
16. Raoul Sobel and David Francis, *Chaplin: Genesis of a Clown* (London: Quartet Books, 1977), p. 179.
17. George De Coulteray, *Sadism in the Movies*, translated by Steve Hult (New York: Medical Press, 1965), pp. 163-177.
18. Sobel and Francis, *Chaplin: Genesis of a Clown*, p. 181.
19. Manvell, *Chaplin*, p. 60.
20. Charles Chaplin, Jr., with N. and M. Rau, *My Father, Charlie Chaplin* (New York: Random House, 1960), p. 29.
21. See especially Gerith von Ulm, *Charlie Chaplin: King of Tragedy* (Caldwell, Idaho: Caxton, 1940), p. 57; Charles Chaplin, Jr., *My Father, Charlie Chaplin*, p. 29.
22. Theodore Huff, *Charlie Chaplin* (1951; rpt. New York: Arno Press and the New York Times, 1972), p. 18.
23. Chaplin, *My Autobiography*, pp. 119, 136-137.
24. McCabe, *Charlie Chaplin*, p. 39.
25. Huff, *Charlie Chaplin*, p. 19.
26. Huff, *Charlie Chaplin*, p. 19.
27. Chaplin, *My Autobiography*, p. 46.
28. Frank "Kin" Hubbard, *Back Country Folks* (Indianapolis: Abe Martin, 1913), p. 45.
29. Charles Chaplin, Jr., *My Father, Charlie Chaplin*, p. 23.
30. Al Capp, "The Comedy of Charlie Chaplin," *The Atlantic*, February 1950, pp. 25-29.
31. Paul E. McGhee, "On the Cognitive Origins of Incongruity Humor: Fantasy

Assimilation versus Reality Assimilation," in *The Psychology of Humor: Theoretical Perspectives and Empirical Issues*, ed. Jeffrey H. Goldstein and Paul E. McGhee (New York: Academic Press, 1972), p. 62.

32. Patricia Keith-Spiegel, "Early Conceptions of Humor: Varieties and Issues," in *The Psychology of Humor: Theoretical Perspectives and Empirical Issues*, p. 7.

33. Walter Kerr, *The Silent Clowns* (New York: Alfred A. Knopf, 1975), p. 77.

34. I owe a debt to my friend and teacher Rick Altman of the University of Iowa (French and Comparative Literature Departments) for his work in dual focus narrative. See his "The American Film Musical: Paradigmatic Structure and Mediatory Function," *Wide Angle: A Film Quarterly of Theory, Criticism and Practice*, vol. 2, no. 2, 1978, pp. 10-17.

35. Huff, *Charlie Chaplin*, p. 65.

36. Terry Ramsaye, "Chaplin—And How He Does It," *Photoplay*, September 1917, p. 138.

37. Lita Grey Chaplin with Morton Cooper, *My Life with Chaplin* (New York: Bernard Geis Associates, 1966), p. 143.

38. Edgar E. Willis, *Writing Television and Radio Programs* (Chicago: Holt, Rinehart and Winston, 1967), p. 288.

39. Henri Bergson, *Laughter* (1900), rpt. in the anthology *Comedy*, ed. Wylie Sypher (Garden City, New York: Doubleday, Anchor Books, 1956), p. 107.

40. Peter Cotes and Thelma Niklaus, *The Little Fellow: The Life and Works of Charles Spencer Chaplin* (1951; rpt. New York: Citadel, 1965), p. 109.

41. Bergson, *Laughter*, p. 156.

42. Bergson, *Laughter*, pp. 66-67.

43. Gerald Mast, *The Comic Mind: Comedy and the Movies* (Indianapolis: Bobbs-Merrill, 1973), p. 50.

44. Cotes and Niklaus, *The Little Fellow*, p. 46.

45. Arthur Schopenhauer, *The World as Will and Idea* (1818; English translation, R. B. Haldane and J. Kemp, 1883) in *Theories of Comedy*, ed. Paul Lauter (Garden City, New York: Doubleday, 1964), p. 355.

46. Chaplin, *My Autobiography*, p. 226.

47. Chaplin, *My Autobiography*, p. 535.

48. Philip G. Rosen, "The Chaplin World View," *Cinema Journal*, Fall 1969, pp. 2-12.

49. Charles J. McGuirk, "Chaplinitis," *Motion Picture Magazine*, July and August 1915.

50. George Mowry, *The Progressive Era, 1900-20: The Reform Persuasion* (1958; rpt. Washington, D.C.: American Historical Association, 1972), p. 12.

51. André Bazin, "Charlie Chaplin," in *What Is Cinema?*, vol. 1, selected and trans. Hugh Gray (1958; rpt. Los Angeles: University of California Press, 1967), p. 144.

52. Manvell, *Chaplin*, p. 16.

53. Sobel and Francis, *Chaplin: Genesis of a Clown*, p. 155.

54. Kevin Brownlow, *the War, the West and the Wilderness* (New York: Alfred A. Knopf, 1979), p. 40.

55. William Dodgson Bowman, *Charlie Chaplin: His Life and Art* (1931; rpt. New York: Haskell House, 1974), p. 74.

56. Huff, *Charlie Chaplin*, p. 95.

57. Chaplin, *My Autobiography*, p. 249.

58. Frank "Kin" Hubbard, *Abe Martin the Joker on Facts* (Indianapolis: Abe Martin, 1920), p. 64.

59. Chaplin, *My Autobiography*, p. 259. The best version of Kono's tale is found in Gerith von Ulm's *Charlie Chaplin: King of Tragedy* (Caldwell, Idaho: Caxton Printers, Ltd., 1940), pp. 117-125.

60. Chaplin, *My Autobiography*, p. 318.

61. Huff, *Charlie Chaplin*, p. 109.

62. Charlie Chaplin, *My Trip Abroad* (New York: Harper and Brothers, 1922), p. 2.

63. Chaplin, *My Autobiography*, p. 284.

64. Chaplin, *My Trip Abroad*, p. 3.

65. Chaplin, *My Trip Abroad*, p. 8.

66. Chaplin, *My Trip Abroad*, p. 5.

67. Manvell, *Chaplin*, p. 162.

68. Manvell, *Chaplin*, p. 3.

69. André Bazin, "The Grandeur of Limelight," in *What Is Cinema?*, vol. 2, selected and trans. Hugh Gray (1971; rpt. Los Angeles: University of California Press, 1972), p. 136.

70. Hazel Simpson Naylor, "Little Miss Happiness," *Motion Picture*, April 15, 1918, pp. 75-77; Adela Rogers St. Johns, "My Heroes," *Photoplay*, June 1919, pp. 34+; Maude S. Cheatham, "A Star Who Longs for Pretty Clothes," *Motion Picture Classic*, November 1919, pp. 54+; Clyde Stuart, "In Placid Mold," *Motion Picture Magazine*, February 1922, pp. 28+; Maude S. Cheatham, "The Serene Goddess," *Motion Picture Classic*, August 14, 1922, pp. 20+.

71. Huff, *Charlie Chaplin*, p. 169.

72. Will Rogers, "Out for the Jack," (May 18, 1924, syndicated weekly newspaper article), in *Will Rogers' Weekly Articles*, vol. 1, *The Harding/Coolidge Years: 1922-1925*, ed. James M. Smallwood (Stillwater: Oklahoma State University Press, 1980), p. 235.

73. Will Rogers, "We Save Money, Egypt Loses It" (December 14, 1924, syndicated weekly newspaper article), in *Will Rogers' Weekly Articles*, pp. 333-334.

74. Manvell, *Chaplin*, p. 176.

75. Lita Grey Chaplin with Morton Cooper, *My Life with Chaplin* (New York: Bernard Geis, 1966), p. 225.

76. Huff, *Charlie Chaplin*, p. 205.

77. Chaplin, *My Autobiography*, p. 328.

78. Will Rogers, "Will Rogers Explains One Joke Is on Him" (August 25, 1927, syndicated daily telegram), in *Will Rogers' Daily Telegrams*, vol. 1, *The Coolidge Years: 1926-1929*, ed. James M. Smallwood (Stillwater: Oklahoma State University Press, 1978), p. 121.

79. Will Rogers, "Will Rogers Studies Effect of a Man Losing a Million" (September 16, 1927, syndicated daily telegram), in *Will Rogers' Daily Telegrams*, p. 128.

80. James Agee, "Comedy's Greatest Era," (September 3, 1949, *Life* essay), in *Agee on Film*, vol. 1, *Review and Comments* (New York: Grosset and Dunlap, 1969), p. 12.

81. Chaplin, *My Autobiography*, pp. 310-311.

82. Nathalie Frederik, *Hollywood and the Academy Awards* (Beverly Hills: Hollywood Awards Publications, 1971), p. 46.

83. See Gladys Hall, interviewer, "Charlie Chaplin Attacks the Talkies," *Motion Pictures*, May 1929, pp. 28+; Charlie Chaplin, "Pantomime and Comedy," *New York Times*, January 25, 1931, p. 6.

84. Kevin Brownlow, *The Parades Gone By . . .* (1968; rpt. New York: Ballantine Books, 1970), p. 667.

85. Charles Chaplin, Jr., with N. and M. Rau, *My Father, Charlie Chaplin*, p. 42.

86. Huff, *Charlie Chaplin*, p. 237.

87. Robert Warshow, "Monsieur Verdoux," in *The Immediate Experience* (1962; rpt. New York: Atheneum, 1972), p. 208.

88. Huff, *Charlie Chaplin*, p. 258.

89. Béla Balázs, *Theory of the Film*, trans. Edith Bone (1952; rpt. New York: Dover, 1970), p. 237.

90. Robert Payne, *The Great God Pan: A Biography of the Tramp Played by Charles Chaplin* (New York: Hermitage House, 1952).

91. Lillian Ross, *Moments with Chaplin* (New York: Dodd, Mead, 1980), p. 59.

92. Huff, *Charlie Chaplin*, p. 257.

93. Chaplin, *My Autobiography*, p. 415.

94. Balázs, *Theory of the Film* trans. Edith Bone, pp. 284-285.

95. Gene Siskel (interviewer), "Woody Allen, A Joker More Mild Than Wild," *Chicago Tribune* Arts and Fun, September 24, 1978, sec. 6, p. 3.

96. Frank S. Nugent, review of *Modern Times*, February 6, 1936, in *New York Times Film Reviews, 1932-1938* (New York: New York Times and Arno Press, 1970), p. 1252; see also Mark Van Doren, review of *Modern Times*, *Nation*, February 19, 1936, p. 232.

97. Huff, *Charlie Chaplin*, p. 254.

98. Chaplin, *My Autobiography*, p. 420.

99. Huff, *Charlie Chaplin*, p. 253.

100. "Charlie Chaplin," in *Current Biography 1940*, ed. Maxine Block (New York: H. H. Wilson, 1940), p. 158.

101. Chaplin, *My Autobiography*, p. 426.

102. Manvell, *Chaplin*, p. 198.

103. Huff, *Charlie Chaplin*,. p. 281.

104. McCabe, *Charlie Chaplin*, p. 203.

105. James Agee, "Monsieur Verdoux," in *Agee on Film*, vol. 1 (New York: Grosset and Dunlap, 1969), pp. 252-262. (Originally appeared in *Nation*, May 31, June 14, and June 21, 1947).

106. Agee, "Monsieur Verdoux," p. 257.

107. Gifford, *Chaplin*, p. 114.

108. Manvell, *Chaplin*, p. 214.

109. Lewis Jacobs, *The Rise of the American Film: A Critical History* (1939; rpt. New York: Teachers College Press, 1971), pp. 231-232.

2

CHAPLINITIS

"I am here to-day." Chaplin's popularity was so great in the teens and twenties that theater owners had only to display a cardboard image of the tramp with this short statement to draw a large audience. Before examining the long-range impact Chaplin's art has had on film comedy and study, as well as on popular culture in general, it is important to underline the huge initial effect his comedy had on the public. One of the first world media stars, Chaplin enjoyed a popularity that was not limited to any one age group, as is often the case with performers today. While adults celebrated the tramp in song and dance, the world's children had numerous jingles about their favorite figure; one jingle in Puerto Rico was about "Chali Chaplin" and kitties, and an English version was set to the music of "Gentle Jesus."[1]

His popularity touched off marketing schemes that are still with us. There were Charlie Chaplin lapel pins, hats, socks, ties, complete costumes, spoons, Christmas decorations, statuettes, buttons, paper dolls, games, playing cards, squirt rings, comics, dolls, and anything else on which his likeness could be reproduced. In his autobiography Chaplin also notes having been approached about diverse products such as Charlie toothpaste and Charlie cigarettes.[2]

"Chaplinitis" was fed all the more by countless other entertainers from assorted media who cashed in on Chaplin's popularity. Song writers cranked out such numbers as the "Chaplin Waddle," "Funny Charlie Chaplin," the "Charlie Strut," "Charlie Chaplin: The Funniest of Them All," and the "Chaplin Wiggle." In total there would be at least twenty Chaplin songs, with the most successful efforts being Leslie and Gottler's "Those Charlie Chaplin Feet" and Downs and Barton's "That Charlie Chaplin Walk."[3]

Both vaudeville and film suddenly had an overflow of tramp imitators. Stage versions included no less a figure than Chaplin's one-time Karno understudy Stan Laurel, long before his teaming with Oliver Hardy. Chaplin's most capable screen copier was Billy West; other prominent film imitators included Billie Ritchie (another former Karno member) and Mexican actor Charles Amador, who even changed his name to Charles Aplin. Chaplin sued and eventually won a judgment again Aplin in 1925 that decreed Chaplin's tramp suit and shuffle to be his own property.[4]

The world started to take on a certain "trampish" look. The Charlie mustache became the fad. Adults grew them, and children pasted them on or smudged charcoal on their upper lips. "His clothes, his boots, his postures and gait were all imitated by would-be humorists."[5] Chaplin, always the connoisseur of beautiful women, would later express bemused regret that even Ziegfield Follies girls marred their loveliness with Charlie mustaches and baggy pants.[6] Moreover, theaters everywhere were capitalizing on the craze by having Charlie Chaplin look-alike contests; the winner of one such Cleveland competition was a youngster named Leslie T. Hope; he is better known today as Bob Hope.[7] As a lark, Chaplin himself is said to have entered one of these contests—and finished third. The saturation level of 1915-1916 Chaplinitis is nicely articulated in one of several Charlie jokes then makng the rounds.

> "You appear worried."
> "Well, you see I have two invitations to dinner. At one home the young daughter is learning to play the piano and at the other the son gives imitations of Charlie Chaplin."[8]

While it was not possible to clone Chaplin himself, his early films, which he did not control, underwent a similar fate—they were constantly reissued with new titles to fool the public. This was especially true of his Keystone films, which came first both in chronology and quantity. For example, *The Rounders* (1914) later appeared under six different titles: *Revelry, Two of a Kind, Oh What a Night, Going Down, The Love Thief,* and *Tip Tap Toe. The Property Man* (1914) knew five additional titles: *Getting His Goat, The Roustabout, Props, Charlie on the Boards,* and *The Vamping Venus.*[9] Additional "Charlie films" were created "by using a few clips and close-ups from old Chaplin prints and adding scenes done by imitators."[10]

Chaplinitis enthralled intellectuals as well as the masses, bringing fresh interest to a fairly new art form struggling for recognition. Film critic and historian David Denby even suggests, "In a sense, it was Chaplin who created film criticism, perhaps because his combination of slapstick and pathos was a recognizable art form—mime."[11] Historically, the beginning of serious Chaplin analysis is generally attributed to Broadway actress Minnie Maddern Fiske's 1916 article, "The Art of Charles Chaplin."[12]

The Fiske essay is important on two counts. First, she was a prominent member of the legitimate arts (theater; at a time when being in the movies was still often considered theatrical slumming), and her celebration of the comedian's skills helped establish a Chaplin-as-artist precedent. Second, she justified historically the only real complaint (from a group later defined as "middle-class elders"[13]) then still occasionally lodged against his work—that it had vulgar tendencies. Her defense observed quite correctly that broad comedy has always had a certain degree of vulgarity, whether it be a play by Aristophanes or a novel by Fielding.

Through the years a great number of important artists and film scholars have endorsed the Fiske stance. George Bernard Shaw observed that Chaplin was the only genius that had developed in motion pictures; noted historian Gerald Mast likened the comedian to a cinematic Shakespeare. Film critic Richard Schickel was once even moved to begin an essay on the comedian with a list of Chaplin accolades from the highest level of film comedians and scholars, adding, "One could fill an essay with such quotations and still have plenty left over, . . . [including] nearly every critic and every artist one respects."[14]

Chaplin's greatest and most enduring impact has been on screen comedy. Even today he is the standard by which all film comedians are measured. His balancing of a successful comedy persona with moments of equally successful pathos has been difficult for other comedians to master. Film biographer Bob Thomas goes so far as to call the urge to accomplish this the "Chaplin disease," because so many have failed.[15] A list of these would include Harry Langdon, Lou Costello (of Abbott and Costello), Bob Hope, Jerry Lewis, and Richard Pryor.

The secret to Chaplin's ongoing film comedy influence is better understood by examining his work in relation to basic traditions in American humor, an area where little analysis has been done. A key factor in this neglect is the question, Is the tramp essentially a capable or an incompetent comedy hero?

Incompetent would seem the most obvious answer. In thinking of film comedy, one first sees a "little fellow" in baggy pants, derby hat, and floppy shoes shuffling down a dirt road. This image is also probably cinema's most famous icon: Chaplin's defeated tramp going down still one more road as the film comes to a close. Certainly every student of film has a favorite variation on this theme, whether the dusty road of *The Tramp* (1915) or the abandoned grounds of *The Circus* (1928). Through film compilations and picture book anthologies of memorable screen moments, this image is well known to the most casual of filmgoers. It is fully chronicled by film scholarship, starting with the very dean of American film historians, Lewis Jacobs, for whom the tramp was "a humble and pathetic figure in search of beauty, the butt of jests, harassed by poverty, the law, and social forces that he can neither understand nor resist."[16] All this is not to say that film scholarship has completely neglected the tramp's capable side; however, thirty years after Jacobs wrote *The Rise of the American Film*, Raymond Durgnat still felt called upon to note that "so heavily has the stress been laid on Chaplin as waif, as a sentimental clown . . . and so on, that criticism has all but lost sight of the complementary pole of his inspiration."[17]

The bittersweet closing icon of the defeated tramp has, therefore, become overextended. Defeat does not represent a fair commentary on all of Chaplin's tramp films and film endings or even a sizable number of them. A close examination of the majority of his films, from the shorts at Keystone, Essanay, Mutual, and First National to the features at United Artists, Attica-Archway, and Universal, indicates quite a different situation.[18]

Chaplin's tramp milieu is much more likely to be upbeat, and despite his English background, his screen tramp is heavily immersed in American humor. Chaplin adjusted quite readily to a country he found to be very much like himself, young and ambitious. Chaplin's close friend, writer Max Eastman, remembers the comedian saying quite early, "Of course, I am essentially American. I feel American, and I don't feel British—that's the chief thing."[19] Similar feelings would be repeated over forty years later in Chaplin's autobiography (1964), even after his experiences with McCarthyism. Because of the tramp's immersion in American humor, if one were to divide American screen comedians into a simple dichotomy of "winners" and "losers," the tramp would most definitely be in the former category. A film dichotomy of this nature would follow the traditional breakdown already established in American fictional humor, which gravitates toward two types. There is the nineteenth-century capable "winner," often associated with "the Yankee," the beginning point of American humor, and the twentieth-century incompetent loser, the comic antihero. The latter category first fully blossomed in the late 1920s in the *New Yorker* magazine, especially in the writings of Robert Benchley, Clarence Day, James Thurber, and S. J. Perelman and in the films of Leo McCarey's Laurel and Hardy.[20]

The antihero who tries to create order in a world where order is impossible is actually not new to American comedy; few comedy types are. This kind of antihero existed in earlier forms of American humor but usually not at center stage, which was reserved for the seemingly rational world of the capable hero.

Chaplin first appears on screen in 1914, when the capable comedy hero is still dominant in American humor. Though some elements of the antiheroic are no doubt in his work, the guiding comedy force throughout is that of the capable figure. The key exception would be the frustrations of *Modern Times*. Chaplin himself underlined the uniqueness of that film situation by the fact that he retired his tramp character after that film.

A thorough study of these two figures, the capable versus the antiheroic, indicates that they differ in five essential ways. The capable type is usually employed, whereas the antihero has a great deal of leisure time. The former is involved in political issues; the latter ignores the subject of politics. The first is successful; the other is constantly frustrated. The hero is a father type; the antihero is a child figure. And finally, the capable figure is from the country and the incompetent from the city.

In order to dislodge some of the tramp's one-sided discoloring—the image of a defeated figure—it would seem fruitful to examine him in relation to these five characteristics that differentiate the capable hero from the comic antihero in American comedy. First, with regard to the tramp's use of time, the logical choice would be to put him in the leisure class. The stereotype of the Chaplin character would suggest that he is nothing but a tramp; actually, he is more often gainfully employed. Robert Sklar has stated, "No comedian before or after him has spent more energy depicting people in their working lives: his first motion picture was the prophetically titled *Making a Living*."[21] One might also add the title of one of Chaplin's Essanay films, *Work* (1915).

In Chaplin's Mutual films (1916-1917), which rate special attention because they were made during "Chaplin's most fertile years, his most sustained creative period, . . . where he made twelve almost perfect comedies," he manages to play a fireman (Figure 7), a floorwalker, a car-

7. Charlie performing firehouse duties in *The Fireman*, 1916. (From the author's collection.)

penter, a pawnshop clerk, a waiter, and a cop.[22] Moreover, *The Immigrant* (1917), another Mutual film, ends just as he and the heroine have acquired jobs. Much of the same occurs in his feature films, from his role as prospector in *The Gold Rush* (1925) to his collection of positions in *Modern Times* (1936): factory worker, maintenance apprentice, night watchman, and waiter-singer.

Even in *City Lights* (1931), where plot demands make more of an issue of his tramp state in order to juxtapose him with his wealthy friends and with the blind girl's belief that she has a rich benefactor, employment still manages to be a major focus. The tramp needs money so that the blind girl can have an eye operation. This need results in Charlie becoming first a streetcleaner and then a boxer.

The second manner in which Chaplin follows the characteristics of the capable figure is that his films often center on politics. One might call them a primer of social issues. This is particularly true of the Mutual films, which appeared at the culmination of the Progressive Era in America, a time of great reform for individual rights, 1897-1920.[23]

In eleven of the twelve Mutual films, Chaplin places the tramp in situations that focus on, and possibly in the case of alcohol capitalize on, Progressive issues. These films are best divided into five social areas: (1) urban corruption, *The Floorwalker* (1916) and *The Fireman* (1916); (2) the plight of the urban poor, *The Pawnshop* (1916), *Easy Street* (1917), and *The Immigrant*; (3) the idle rich (not a specific concern of Progressives but a tangential area to both urban poverty and corruption, especially when contrasted with Chaplin's image of the poor), *the Count* (1916), *The Rink* (1916), and *The Adventurer* (1917); (4) elitism, *Behind the Screen* (1916), which endorses the antistrike stance of the Progressives; and (5) alcoholism, *One A.M.* (1916) and *The Cure* (1917).

Questions might be raised about the inclusion of alcoholism, since comedy and drinking go back to the Greek god of wine Dionysus and to the very origins of comedy. Chaplin also combined drinking with comedy in later films. Yet alcohol was a topical issue at the time the Mutual Films were made: Progressives favored prohibition, and in 1917 Congress passed the whiskey-limiting Lever Act and then the Eighteenth "Prohibition" Amendment, submitting it to the states for ratification. Given Chaplin's "understandable aversion to alcohol, which had brought such tragedy to his family,"[24] the subject of alcohol seems a legitimate final category of the Mutual Films.

Not everything Chaplin did at Mutual fit smoothly into the Progressive mold. In *The Immigrant* he plays upon irony in the promise of America and the Statue of Liberty, juxtaposed with the cattle-like treatment the newcomers receive on their arrival (Figure 8). In this film Chaplin would seem to take a big city problem, the plight of the underprivileged immigrant, too far for many Progressives. The typical Progressive was nativist in

8. Charlie and Edna Purviance approach America in *The Immigrant,* 1917. (Courtesy Museum of Modern Art/Film Stills Archive.)

viewpoint and felt immigration restriction was the answer; legislation along these lines was eventually passed in the early 1920s. It is only fitting that Chaplin, the most famous immigrant of the day, should have expressed the plight of less fortunate immigrants.

Even here, however, Chaplin appeals to the Progressives' nonimmigration stance, because other than the innocent heroine (Edna Purviance) and her mother, the immigrant passengers are portrayed in a comically negative light, as humor antagonists for Chaplin. Their behavior includes gambling, fighting, the drawing of a pistol, and the robbing of an elderly woman. Moreover, once Chaplin's immigrant character is in New York, he has no job and no money. It is only through the kindness of an artist that he receives employment as a model, a position one assumes can only be temporary. To many Progressives this sympathetic portrayal was an example of why they felt the immigrant was a drag on American society.

Chaplin's Mutual films represent a neglected comic survey of several Progressive issues at the very close of the era. Occurring too late to be called Progressive muckraking in the tradition of Upton Sinclair's *The Jungle* or Ida Tarbell's *History of the Standard Oil Company*, the Mutual films were instead a final summing up of what the Progressive Movement had tried to be.

Chaplin continues to touch on political stances in his later features. This is probably exemplified best by the close of *The Great Dictator*, where his Jewish barber, mistaken for the "great dictator" Hynkel, gives a speech against totalitarianism directly to the viewer. Yet it is only through the "Progressive" Mutual films that some semblance of a political form is brought to the broad-based humanism of Chaplin's films.

The third reason the tramp is more logically placed in the realm of capable comedy is that he is generally successful at what he does; this also flies in the face of the image of the pathetic little tramp. To examine his tramp films closely is to discover a character generally so adept at the task at hand that the "loser" label seems to represent more of a taunt to his larger antagonists than a genuine description of a true state of affairs. In *The Rink* Charlie quite literally skates rings around his perpetual Mutual Films antagonist, Eric Campbell. In *The Adventurer* (Figure 9) even the police find him impossible to catch, in part due to his metamorphic abilities; at one point he loses them by imitating a hall lamp. Even in the most basic task, from carrying chairs in *Behind the Screen* to stacking bricks in *Pay Day* (1922), his skills are amazing.

The capable figure's comedy counterpart, the antihero, is most often frustrated by a wife and/or machines. Such frustration is generally not the case with Charlie. Indeed, to break one more misconception, the stereotype of the tramp as a loser at love is largely false. He consistently wins the

9. An on-the-lam Charlie makes like a society chap to Edna Purviance in *The Adventurer,* 1917. (From the author's collection.)

heroine's hand, from the Mutual films with Edna Purviance to the later feature work with Paulette Goddard. These films also literally avoid what has become a traditional comedy premise, the battle of the "married" sexes, by seldom going beyond the courtship period.

Chaplin seems to underline this luck at love in the close of the Mutual film *Behind the Screen*, when, after Charlie has defeated the anarchist strikers and won Edna's heart, he steps out of character by facing the camera and winking at the audience, just after kissing Edna. It is as if to ask, Was there ever any doubt? Much the same effect is also achieved at the close of the last "tramp" picture, *Modern Times*, when Charlie goes down one final road, this time accompanied by a lovely gamin (Paulette Goddard). By now no wink is necessary to explain what the student of Chaplin has seen occur repeatedly—the girl usually belongs to the tramp by the final fade-out. Exceptions, as in the solo close of *The Circus* (1928), are often a result of a deliberate decision by the tramp to remain alone.

The tramp's interaction with mechanical objects, the other usual frustration of his antihero counterpart, is more problematic, though his dexterity almost always wins out. Frustrating moments can occur, such as the alarm clock that suffers a fatal operation at the hands of Charlie in *The Pawnshop* or the debilitating conveyor belt of *Modern Times*. But for every such stumbling block there are numerous mechanical victories: the Chaplin cop of *Easy Street*, who so adeptly manages to etherize the giant bully (Eric Campbell) with a gas street lamp, or the Chaplin soldier of *Shoulder Arms* (1918), who converts a Victrola horn to a breathing device so he can sleep underwater in his partly submerged bunker. Often when Charlie does not resolve a mechanical mess, such as the dismantled clock in *The Pawnshop*, it is because of a personal whim rather than incompetency; he has fun taking apart a customer's clock but has no particular need or desire to put it back together. In contrast, antiheroes like Laurel and Hardy would not have been able to put a clock together even if they wanted to.

With the exception of *Modern Times*, the film world of Chaplin's tramp has actually not yet reached the mechanized state of the world of Laurel and Hardy, and Charlie is just not as surrounded by gadgets. However, as has been implied, if and when the tramp desires it, he is quite capable. He flaunts this ability in *Police* (1916), when he breaks into an icebox as if it were a safe.

If the situation demands, Charlie is even capable of inventing mechanical gadgets, which is in the best tradition of Yankee ingenuity. This ability is exemplified by the day care center for one that he constructs in *The Kid* (1921). Anticipating the eccentric inventions Buster Keaton will later feature in some of his 1920s films, the tramp's "baby machine" replaces the conventional rocker with a baby-sized hammock within easy access to a rope-suspended baby bottle, which is actually a converted coffee pot and rubber glove. Underneath all these contraptions, and specifically under the baby's posterior, is a potty-chair fashioned from an old seat and a spittoon.

Appropriately, Mary Pickford's nickname for Charlie was the "Little Philosopher."[25] And though it might sound overly ponderous, Charlie has a pronounced tendency to philosophize, from the lecture on life he gives the suicidal millionaire in *City Lights* (1931) to the pep talk for the gamin at the close of *Modern Times*. Film titles make short work of both these and other examples (coming, as they do, from silent film), but seen in this manner, Chaplin's later, often controversially verbal, post-tramp films do not seem so atypical.

Chaplin himself seems to underline his belief in the capable nature of the tramp by the minor changes he made in the 1942 re-release of *The Gold Rush*. For example, where as the original 1925 version had the tramp mistakenly receiving an encouraging note from the heroine (her old boy-friend was playing a joke), in 1942 the editing at no time suggested an error had been made. Thus, the heroine's love for Charlie is established long before the concluding scenes, while in the original version it was uncertain until then.

Charlie as the master of most situations remains a much more defensible position. Celebrated Chaplin biographer Theodore Huff nicely capsulizes this finesse, as well as the comedian's tendency to place the character in professional settings: "Super-waiter, super-boxer, super-policeman, super-tightrope walker: . . . Chaplin's best efforts have been gained through super expert professional dexterity."[26]

The fourth characteristic, as the baby-oriented mechanics of *The Kid* suggest, is that the "capable" tramp is also something of a father figure. Certainly there is a large dose of the child in all comics and in all comedies, and Chaplin's tramp films represent no exception. Yet in his filmic interactions with society, the tramp generally cares for others instead of being cared for himself, as the antihero must be. His relationships with women are constantly as father to daughter, protecting and caring for the waif figure of the woman, again in direct contrast with the often amazon "boss" females of the antiheroic world, probably exemplified best in the film world of Laurel and Hardy.

This fatherly role is reiterated throughout Chaplin's tramp career, with the most memorable example (after *The Kid*) probably being his care of the blind girl in *City Lights*. And it is in the celebrated *The Vagabond* (1916), which has been called "a prototype of *The Kid*,"[27] that the parental duties are most thoroughly marked out. The tramp's fatherly treatment of the girl (Edna Purviance) in *The Vagabond* also nicely contradicts one more Chaplin-directed cliché, that the girl in his films was always an idealized object on a pedestal. After all, taking care of a child is quite different from seeing someone on an idealized perch. In a wonderfully thorough scene on personal hygiene, Charlie vigorously washes her face, taking special time to roll a corner of his washcloth into a dipstick of sorts to get at the always

elusive ears and nostrils. He then proceeds to give her scalp a careful examination for fleas, not calling a halt to this extensive project until after he has
set her hair with homemade curlers. The film also manages to present
Charlie at such parental tasks as fixing supper and setting the table. The
Vagabond model anticipates his care of the girl in the often neglected
feature *The Circus*, especially the scene in which he "lectures" her on the
dangers of eating too fast. The Chaplin father figure misses few tricks.

The fifth and final characteristic that places Charlie more comfortably in
the capable comedian category is that he seemingly is rural in origin. The
world of Chaplin's tramp, which itself is an outgrowth of pastoral America,
depicts the nineteenth- and early twentieth-century view of the city, which
as seen by rural America is a dirty, corrupt, and dangerous place. And as
the earlier comments on politics and the Progressive Era suggest, Charlie
constantly seems to be in the midst of this urban decadence. This focus is
kept plausible because the tramp often seems to be new to either setting, as
an apparent stranger in a small rural town or as an immigrant to the city.

Much of the humor in these situations evolves from the quick-witted
country tramp's rapid adjustment to each new urban challenge, from curbing the street fighting of the *Easy Street* slums to passing as upper crust at
the society masquerade in *The Idle Class* (1921). In probably his most
pointed expression as a stranger in difficult circumstances, Charlie manages
in *The Immigrant* to get a free meal in the toughest restaurant in New York
(where giant Eric Campbell is the combination waiter-bouncer), to acquire a
job, and to marry a beautiful girl, all on his first day in America.

As with the work of Charles Dickens, which always fascinated Chaplin
for the parallels he saw between it and his own rags-to-riches story, his
scenes in the country are equally significant; yet they are fleeting.[28] In
contrast with the lengthy exposés of city problems and ugliness, the country
scenes are times of restoration and safety and female beauty. In *The Tramp*
(1915) both the setting and the country girl who cares for Charlie's wound
from the foiled robbery very much resemble the setting of *Oliver Twist* and
Dickens' young Rose, who cares for Oliver's wound during his sojourn in
the country after another bungled robbery.[29] As is to be expected, such
juxtaposition gives high praise to the country, the place of the capable
hero's origins and/or aspirations. And though no setting is without
problems, such as the tough farmer in *Sunnyside*, with whom Charlie the
hired man must contend, director Chaplin's image of the country is generally
one in which the tramp's "church [is] the sky and his altar the landscape."[30]

In considering Chaplin's use of the country in his films, an interesting
"coincidence" between his real life and his art should be pointed up. In his
autobiography he notes that just prior to his entry into film his goal was to
save enough money to buy himself a farm. Over twenty-five years later, in
The Great Dictator (1940), Chaplin makes this the goal of Hannah, the
girlfriend of the Jewish barber (Chaplin). The farm is to be their sanctuary

from the Nazis. And though the film will go on to show that by 1940 not even the country is safe from such dangers (another reason for the permanent exit of the tramp earlier in *Modern Times*), director Chaplin continued to play upon the metaphor of the country as a haven.

It is appropriate that late in Chaplin's career he underlined the significance of the country by the title song he composed for the 1959 re-release of *The Pilgrim* (1923). It appeared, along with *A Dog's Life* (1918) and *Shoulder Arms*, in a special film compilation called *The Chaplin Review*. The song, "Bound for Texas" (which is repeated frequently in *The Pilgrim*), referred to being weary of the city and the factory and ready for the wide open spaces.

As a final postscript on the uniqueness of the country to the world of Chaplin's tramp, it should be remembered that numerous authors have seen the magic of Charlie in terms of a modern Pan. Nature often plays a key role in his films, whether it is the tree he hides in in *The Vagabond* (1916), or the tree he literally becomes in *Shoulder Arms*, where it is his disguise for reconnaissance.

Charlie as Pan is constantly suggested by the recurring image of a flower, which is almost as much a part of his costume as the derby and cane. Flowers often symbolize love to the tramp, whether it is for dear Edna in *The Tramp* (1915) or the blind flower girl of *City Lights* (1931). And they also represent freedom, from the "wild flower" he plucks during his dance of Pan in *Sunnyside* (1919) to the equally "wild flowers" of the Mexican border close of *The Pilgrim*, when the sheriff releases him by having Charlie pick a bouquet across the border. But in general, like the single flower of Jean Renoir's classic *Grand Illusion* (made in 1937 by the renowned director who was greatly influenced by the comedian), the flower of a Chaplin film symbolizes beauty in an otherwise gray world.

Because of the five characteristics enumerated here, the propensity of Chaplin's tramp to be in a profession and to be political, successful, fatherly, and rural—all characteristics closely associated with America's capable comedy figures—the tendency to see the tramp as only a defeated figure is very misleading. Why, then, has this defeated tramp image persisted? Herein lies the key to Chaplin's ongoing popularity and influence.

While the central impetus for the eventual ascension of the comic antihero in American humor took place in the 1920s, there were numerous antiheroic foreshadowings, in a host of mediums, that paralleled Chaplin's 1914 film beginnings. These included the comic strips of George Herriman ("Krazy Kat," 1913) and George McMannus ("Bringing Up Father," 1913) and the movie comedies of John Bunny (1910-1915).

Chaplin's prefilm medium, vaudeville, offered its own antiheroic foreshadowing. In fact, in *American Vaudeville as Ritual* Albert F. McLean, Jr., notes that again and again after 1900 critics implied that a "new humor" had developed in this country. And though he mentions other media, he gives the biggest nod to vaudeville, because it "was both the major market and the leading innovator in this revolution in popular taste."[31]

The primary manner in which this new vaudeville comedy seemed to anticipate the antiheroic comedy was in its focus on the urban area. Big industry had come to the cities, and behind it tens of thousands of immigrants, anxious for success (this group also comprised a large part of the early film audience). Yet as in Upton Sinclair's *Jungle*, few of these immigrants succeeded. Thus McLean suggests that urban-based frustrations created a demand for a "new humor."

> The task of relieving social tensions had been taken from the
> . . . deadpan. . . . A whole new generation of comics, for the
> most part city-bred, . . . had sensed the utility of humor in
> oiling the psychic wheels of an industrial democracy.[32]

While Chaplin's comedy was of the capable school, it also embraced the problems of urban living, as demonstrated by its often markedly Progressive stance: the rural and/or immigrant Charlie up against varying elements of the big-city system. Chaplin, of course, was more pointed in his look at urban frustration, and also allowed Charlie more room for success, or at least escape (down one more road). In contrast, antiheroic comedy depoliticalized urban frustration, making it appear humorously inevitable, or at least more palatable, by packaging the problem in a world of comic absurdity. Examples would include Krazy Kat's love for Ignatz Mouse, who is forever creasing Krazy's head with a brick, only to be arrested by Offissa B. Pupp, the dog in love with Kat, to Laurel and Hardy's never-ending tit-for-tat battle with every aspect of the city, from mechanization to madness. Consequently Chaplin could capitalize on this key comedy element of urban frustration (with Charlie offered more of a chance for success) while still maintaining a screen persona based on the then more familiar and traditional capable comedian. With such a broad base of appeal, Chaplin's legacy has had a phenomenal impact on film, both in its production and in the critical analysis applied to those productions, as well as on popular culture in general.

William Cahn's biography of Harold Lloyd, done in close collaboration with Chaplin's chief box office rival of the 1920s, observes:

> Chaplin's humor had an amazing effect on almost all the
> comedians of his era, and after. For many years, there was
> scarcely a comedian in the United States, and in many other
> parts of the world, who could operate without showing some of
> the [Chaplin] influences.[33]

Lloyd himself became established playing a figure named "Lonesom Luke" (1915-1917), whom comedy historian Kalton C. Lahue has labele "a sort of hayseed copy of Chaplin's character."[34] Lloyd did not actuall perform a literal imitation of Chaplin, à la Billy West and so many others but his costume (which attempted to reverse the tramp's baggy attire wit tightness) and story situations were often reminiscent of Chaplin's rough and-tumble comedies at Keystone. And even some of his post-Luke, earl Lloyd-horn-rimmed-glasses films have strong parallels with previou Chaplin shorts. For example, Lloyd's *Fireman Save My Child* (1918) ha much in common with Chaplin's *The Fireman* (1916), while *Pipe th Whiskers* (1918) draws from *The Cure* (1917). Lloyd, of course, eventuall evolved his own distinctive comedy identity, closely tied to the America success story, though today he is best remembered for the "thrill comedy' of such films as *Safety Last* (1923). But it is an excellent gauge of Chaplin' influence that one of silent comedy's pantheon members (Chaplin, Keaton Langdon, and Lloyd) should have toiled so long in Chaplin's shadow.

Of these celebrated Chaplin contemporaries, however, Harry Langdo owed the most to Chaplin. Though without the physical comedy capabilitie of the tramp, Langdon's mixing of pathos and humor was second only t Chaplin's (Figure 10). Moreover, as Mordaunt Hall observed in his *Nev York Times* review of *Long Pants* (1927): "Mr. Langdon is still Charle Spencer Chaplin's sincerest flatterer. His short coat reminds one o Chaplin, and now and again his footwork is like that of the great screer comedian."[35] Appropriately enough, Langdon's greatest period of success both critically and commercially, was to occur during one of Chaplin's firs sustained absences from the screen. Mack Sennett, who gave Langdon hi film start in 1924, just as he had Chaplin ten years earlier, has noted, "Th two were the same in their universal appeal. They were the little guys copin with a mean universe."[36] The on-screen successes of their comedy persona are dependent, however, upon a completely different set of circumstances Whereas Charlie's capableness eventually pulls him through, Langdo knows success only through the grace of God.

On occasion even the mature work of Lloyd and Keaton was not immun to Chaplin's influence. The success of *The Gold Rush* (1925) was so grea that the next films by both Lloyd (*The Freshman*, 1925) and Keaton (*G West*, 1925) seem to be consciously striving for Chaplin pathos. Thei highly regarded contemporary reviewer, Edmund Wilson of *The Nev Republic*, was so struck by this development that he reevaluated his view on 1920s film comedy.

And I prophesied [in a September 2, 1925 review of *The Gold Rush*] that Chaplin, with his finer comedy [of pathos] and less spectacular farce, would not be able to hold his popularity against [the comedy of Lloyd and Keaton, but] . . . *The Gold Rush* has

10. Charlie momentarily down on his luck in *The Gold Rush*, 1925. (Courtesy Museum of Modern Art/Film Stills Archive.)

had a great success; and, so far from playing Chaplin off the screen, Buster Keaton and Harold Lloyd have taken to imitating him. What is striking in their new films is the reduction of the number of gags and the attempt to fill their place with straight drama. . . . [They] have tried to follow Chaplin's example by allowing their comic characters to become genuine human beings.[37]

If Wilson had saved his overview on the influence of Chaplin's film until May 1926 he could have included the whole silent comedy pantheon, for that was when Langdon's *Gold Rush* derivative feature, *Tramp, Tramp, Tramp*, appeared. Not only was its pathos influenced but the plot itself borrows from or plays upon a number of scenes from *The Gold Rush*. Hall's review of *Tramp, Tramp, Tramp* focuses on three of the most obvious parallels: Langdon hanging by a mere nail from a dizzying height is reminiscent of the cabin over the cliff scene in *The Gold Rush*, where Charlie opens the door and nearly strolls into nothingness; Langdon's frequent battles against a high wind occur just as frequently in the Chaplin film; and each film has a comic scene dependent upon the flying feathers of a formerly stuffed pillow.[38] Hall might have added several other Chaplin similarities, from the on-the-road central theme (a cross-country foot race), to a heroine very much upon a pedestal. Even the title *Tramp, Tramp, Tramp* reminds the viewer of Chaplin's most popular nickname (as well as occasionally fooling today's revivalist audiences into expecting Charlie).

Chaplin's impact on silent film comedy assumes an almost surrealistic quality when it is realized that he was a major influence on the era's most celebrated cartoon figure—Felix the Cat. Anyone who has ever seen a Felix cartoon immediately recognizes the Chaplinesque qualities of the cat, from his ability to metamorphose himself and other items when necessary (his tail would even become a cane) to the wickedly pleasing direct address grin and wink he periodically gave the viewer. Felix was actually called "the Charlie Chaplin of cartoon characters."[39]

The chief animator for the original Felix film cartoons was Otto Messmer, who had previously worked on a cartoon film series of Chaplin. The former project had given Messmer "the opportunity to study Chaplin's pantomime and body movements, which profoundly affected his future work."[40] There is even a delightful "in" joke reference to Chaplin in *Felix in Hollywood* (1922), where the cat does an imitation of Charlie only to run into him and be accused of stealing.[41]

Chaplin's effect on film comedy did not end with sound. His routines have continued to footnote the films of other great comedians, from the Marx Brothers' use of the mirror sequence in *Duck Soup* (1933, employed by Chaplin in *The Floorwalker*, 1916) to recycled variations upon the *Modern Times* (1936) automatic feeder in Bob Hope and Bing Crosby's

Road to Hong Kong (1962) and Woody Allen's *Bananas* (1971). More importantly, Chaplin's ability to mix comedy and pathos continues to be *the* film standard, especially in the later work of Jerry Lewis and Woody Allen.

Chaplin's influence on foreign cinema is equally immense. And nowhere is it more effectively shown than in French film, the second most significant of all national cinemas, where it is best exemplified by the work of two great French satirists, René Clair and Jean Vigo, the latter of whom died tragically after completing only four films. Because Chaplin was the pivotal hero to both directors, their films are often not only infused with a Chaplinesque quality, but sometimes populated with figures made to look or act like Charlie. For example, in Clair's *The Imaginary Voyage* (1925), a lovesick young bank clerk dreams about a seemingly unattainable heroine (shades of Chaplin's *The Bank*, 1915). But after the fantasy assumes a macabre twist in a wax museum, the endangered hero is rescued when the figures of Charlie Chaplin and Jackie Coogan come to life. Celia McGerr, author of an excellent Clair reference, calls the film's dream sequence "almost an *hommage* to Clair's hero Charlie Chaplin."[42]

Chaplin's greatest compliment from Clair came, however, at a time when the French director might have embarrassed him. After *Modern Times* (1936) was released, the producers of Clair's *Liberty for Us* (1931) sued Chaplin for plagiarism. The 1937 suit claimed that Chaplin had borrowed material from the earlier film, especially the conveyor belt sequence. But Clair refused to join his producers, Filmes Sonores Tobis, claiming if there had been any borrowing he was flattered, since he had borrowed so much from Chaplin. Moreover, he stated, "My romance [*Liberty for Us*] is a typical Chaplin romance, only lacking his genius."[43] Filmes Sonores Tobis later dropped its suit.

How much, if at all, Chaplin was influenced by the sequence will never be known, but there is a most definite Chaplin stamp on numerous other elements of *Liberty for Us*. For example, there was a Chaplinesque central character (Emile) who is comically proficient at kicking tails Charlie-style, yet who knows the pathos of thinking a girl's smile for another was meant for him (shades of *The Gold Rush*). Several other Chaplin touches occur before being topped off by the stereotyped Charlie down-the-road exit, this time by two characters (Emile and Louis) assuming the "occupation" of tramp.

While the Chaplinesque elements of various Clair films might be discussed ad infinitum (for example, *The Two Timid Souls*, 1928, and *Under the Roofs of Paris*, 1930), the shortness of Vigo's career necessitates focusing on his *Zero for Conduct* (1933). Vigo's film occurs in a tyrannically run boy's school, where young exuberance is stifled by a martinet system. The boys revolt against regimentation like so many young Charlies against the establishment. Appropriately, their joyful destruction of the dormitory, in a feather "snowfall" of broken pillows, seems drawn directly from Chaplin's own joyful feather "snowfall" scene in *The Gold Rush*. Moreover, the film's narrative makes the iconoclastic tramp a natural hero for the boys, since the school's only sympathetic teacher manages a delightful imitation of Charlie.

The boys, who are secretly watching their teacher perform his tramp impersonation, complement this Chaplin footnote by adding their own Chaplinesque response. Each time the teacher turns in their direction (he is shuffling back and forth à la Charlie), the boys duck out of sight, just as the street people responded to both Charlie and Eric in *Easy Street* (1917).

Vigo adds several other Chaplin footnotes, including the rooftop final exit of the boys, reminiscent of Charlie's chimneytop dexterity at the close of *The Kid* (1921). But the most amusing reference to the world of Charlie is Vigo's casting of a three-foot midget as the school's principal, a symbolic undercutting of authority just like the three-foot German commander in *Shoulder Arms* (1918).

Clair and Vigo are but two prominent examples of Chaplin's influence on foreign directors. A number of other filmmakers might be mentioned, however, without even leaving France, from comedian-director Jacques Tati, (the very name of whose delightful film persona Mr. Hulot suggests the French label for Charlie—Charlot), to the country's greatest director, Jean Renoir. In fact, Renoir pays constant tribute to Chaplin, whether it is the story of an iconoclastic tramp in *Boudu Saved from Drowning* (1932, which opens with a tribute to Pan) or the *Modern Times*-ish conclusion of *The Lower Depths* (1936). Renoir's greatest film, *The Rules of the Game* (1939), makes direct reference to Chaplin's *The Count* (1916) by the manner in which it replicates that short subject's high society chase and confusion of identities. The French director even credits Chaplin with inspiring the theme of nonviolence in a Renoir film seemingly far removed from the world of the tramp, *The River* (1950), which focuses on a crippled war veteran of India.[44] Therefore it is not surprising that Renoir states, after a momentous film career originally inspired by the tramp, that "the master of masters, the film-maker of film-makers, for me is still Charlie Chaplin."[45]

Chaplin's influence on Italian film, the next most significant national cinema after those of the United States and France, has been equally impressive. This is best demonstrated by briefly examining two of Italy's greatest directors, Vittorio De Sica and Frederico Fellini, both of whom were profoundly influenced by Chaplin. In fact, De Sica was doubly stirred by the comedian, since he considered his two teachers to be Chaplin and the Chaplin-influenced Clair.

> Do you know that I am obsessed by two "monsters"? They make life completely impossible. They are Charlie Chaplin and René Clair. . . . After them the cinema has become almost impossible! Those two discovered everything.[46]

And Clair has even gone so far as to return the ultimate compliment to De Sica by calling him "Chaplin's most authentic successor."[47]

While Chaplin often seems to pervade the De Sica world, whether in the folk fantasy of a *Miracle in Milan* (1951) or in the combination slapstick-pathos of an old man and his dog in *Umberto D* (1952—*A Dog's Life* thirty-four years later), the creator of the tramp is even more strongly felt in Fellini films.

One has only to view *The Road* (*La Strada*, 1954) and the bewitching performance of Giulietta Masina (Fellini's wife) as Gelsomina, the clown-like servant to Anthony Quinn's strongman, to appreciate the depth of Chaplin's influence on Fellini. The film's mixing of comedy and pathos, Masina's delightful mimicry, even the title—*The Road*—all suggest the world of Charlie. More specifically, one could define the character of Gelsomina, the lightheartedly loyal but ill-used servant, as a somber variation on the lightheartedly loyal Charlie of *City Lights*. Though Charlie is never so mentally simple as Gelsomina, nor so defeated (Gelsomina's eventual hurt destroys her will to live), both beautifully portray first the humor of complete devotion, and then the pain of rejection when that love is not returned. Appropriately, Fellini "singles out *City Lights* (1931) as a masterpiece among the silents."[48] The fact that Fellini has made the fate of Gelsomina even darker than that of Charlie in *City Lights* might be explained by Fellini's favorite film—Chaplin's black comedy *Monsieur Verdoux* (1947). Coming just a few years before *The Road*, Fellini considers this comedy of murders to be "the most beautiful film he has ever seen."[49]

The Chaplinesque nature of *The Road* is most significant, especially since Fellini considers the work his "most representative film," as well as the one in which he feels closest to the characters.[50] Yet there is no shortage of other Chaplin-flavored Fellini films, from the *Nights of Cabiria* (1956), with Masina's touchingly comic streetwalker who longs for love, to *The Clowns* (1970), which often evokes individual scenes from Chaplin films, as well as including Victoria Chaplin in the cast, as an "homage to her father."[51]

De Sica and Fellini are the most pivotal examples of Chaplin's followers among Italian directors, yet several other outstanding filmmakers could have been examined. They include Pier Paolo Pasolini, especially in *The Hawks and the Sparrows* (1966), which was inspired by the early Charlie films and features the Chaplin contemporary Toto; Lina Wertmuller, who often focuses on a Chaplinesque underdog fighting the system, such as in *The Seduction of Mimi* (1972); and Franco Brusati, whose *Bread and Chocolate* (1974) is constantly footnoted with Chaplin touches, while still maintaining an identity of its own.

Similar stories of Chaplin's influence are to be found in the histories of nearly all other national cinemas. Japanese film history, once obscure in the West because of cultural and political differences, is now one of the most celebrated of Asian film traditions here and often displays characteristics of the tramp films. This is best shown in the works of Kiyohiko Ushihara, who studied with Chaplin in the mid-1920s, and Heinosuke Goshu, who was greatly moved by *A Woman of Paris* (1923) and the Chaplin-influenced *Marriage Circle*.[52]

Charlie's popularity also generated a number of Japanese imitations. But whereas this phenomenon had generally occurred elsewhere in the 1910s and early 1920s, *Chaplin! Why Do You Cry?*, a Japanese variation on *City Lights*, would have a major impact in Japan as late as 1932. (Director Enjiro Saito generally maintained the Chaplin story line, though the Charlie figure became a Japanese sandwich man.) Chaplin's Japanese popularity is assisted by the fact that he represents

> the personification of . . . [their] comic ideal. The kind of humor which allows one both to laugh and weep is particularly admired by the Japanese, and when Chaplin visited the country in 1932 the nation overwhelmed him with attention. . . . Even today Chaplin remains something of a national hero. His way of walking is still imitated, usually by sandwich men, appearing complete with cane, derby, and oversize shoes. Packed houses always greet a revival of *The Kid*, one of the early Chaplin films still playing in Japan.[53]

These, then, have been some of the major filmmakers influenced by the comedy of Chaplin—filmmakers so moved as to footnote or recreate the mood of the Charlie films frequently in their own works of art. Yet besides the unbelievably high standard he established for film comedy, Chaplin bequeathed to them an even greater heritage. He gave the genre a legitimacy it had not had before, and he established a comedy production precedent of personal control that later film generations would label auteurism. Phrased more succinctly, Chaplin made it easier for the comedy filmmakers who followed him to do what they had to do—make people laugh. The fact that many ambitious later comedy projects by bona fide auteurs failed (for example, Stanley Kramer's *It's A Mad Mad Mad Mad World*, 1963, and Steven Spielberg's *1941*, 1979) merely underscores the intuitive comedy genius of Chaplin, who never lost sight, amidst all that production power, of the need for a central hero to whom an audience could relate.

Moreover, the Chaplin model has not been without other snags for prospective disciples. For example, some emulators of his pathos, such as Harry Langdon in *Three's a Crowd* (1927, after his split with Frank Capra) or Jerry Lewis in *Cinderfella* (1960), have mistakenly overplayed the sentimental, while providing no counterbalancing elements of character capableness. Thus the viewer was apt merely to feel pity for these clowns, rather than smile the bittersweet smile normally reserved for the pathos of Charlie.

Interestingly enough, Woody Allen, whose film comedy persona is diametrically opposed to that of Chaplin's (the frustrated antihero versus capable Charlie), has probably followed Chaplin's behind-the-camera career model more closely than any other major comedy filmmaker. Each realized early the need for both a consistent, easily identifiable character capable of generating sympathy and the necessity for production control via writing and directing as well as starring. Allen has long admired Chaplin for having the artistic daring to move beyond the security of the Charlie films.

> What happens with a more serious artist, like Chaplin, is you try to do other things. You don't go to your strength all the time. And you strike out so people think you're an ass or pretentious, but that's the only thing you can do.[54]

Thus, in films like *Manhattan* (1979) and *Stardust Memories* (1980), Allen has attempted to move beyond the antihero, just as Chaplin attempted to move beyond Charlie with films like *The Great Dictator* (1940) and *Monsieur Verdoux* (1947). Also, as with Chaplin's production of *A Woman of Paris* (1923), Allen felt a need to prove himself artistically by writing and directing a serious film in which he would not appear. *Interiors* (1978) was the result, a critical success unattended by the American masses, just as *A Woman of Paris* had been. Allen is still a comparatively young filmmaker with, it is hoped, many more productions to come. Yet regardless of the direction these productions take, it seems safe to assume that he will continue to look for the artistic challenge, just as his model always did.

Chaplin's influence on cinema has not been limited to filmmakers. He has had an equally significant impact on the history of film theory and criticism. In the infancy of the medium his work helped give film the artistic legitimacy to be written about, as well as a standard with which to gauge other performers. In the years since then, authors from seemingly every possible film methodology have attempted to include Chaplin's art in their camps, as well as frequently illustrating their systems via the comedian's films. And though this has resulted in many valid insights, the seeming need to utilize Chaplin has also created many provocative twists of their methodologies in order to accommodate the Charlie persona, or the persona has been bent to better match the given "ism."

This theoretical fascination with Chaplin is best demonstrated in film study by probing the work of four pivotal film theorists: Rudolf Arnheim, Sergei Eisenstein, Béla Balázs, and Siegfried Kracauer. In each case Chaplin's unique effect on film has inspired both insights and theoretical gerrymandering.

Arnheim, the traditional standard-bearer for formalist film theory, which accents the media over the subject, was fascinated with Chaplin's comedy, referring to it at length over a dozen times in his *Film As Art* (1933). He justified this fascination from four different perspectives, which I have labeled (1) traditional formalism, (2) forgiven primitivism, (3) forgotten rules, and (4) denial of sound.

First, Arnheim's greatest praise for Chaplin's comedy occurs when the comedian displays formalistic tendencies, for example, whenever Chaplin displays a self-conscious use of the film medium. Arnheim's two primary examples focus on comic surprise through camera placement: the apparently seasick Charlie leaning over the side of the boat (his back to camera) in *The Immigrant* and the backside of what appears to be a sobbing husband, whose wife has left him, in *The Idle Class*.[55]

In both cases Charlie soon turns around and completely negates what the complacent viewer has been tricked into assuming by the camera placement. In the first example Charlie has been fishing, and a rather healthy bite has necessitated that he lean over the side to pull it in. When he turns around, you meet a proud fisherman instead of a seasick tramp. In the second case of the apparently sobbing male who has lost his wife, Charlie's turn reveals that he is preparing some drinks in a cocktail shaker, without a thought to sadness.

Arnheim is impressed with this formalistic filmmaking technique, which he emphasizes by making it the first rule of his "Summary of the Formative Means of Camera and Film Strip," stating that "Every Object Must Be Photographed from One Particular Viewpoint!"[56] Yet in relation to Charlie's style, Arnheim is misleading. He would seem to suggest that such formalistic techniques as camera placement dominate the comedy situations in Chaplin, when just the opposite is true.

The Chaplin style is essentially that of a realist. His mime ability was so great, his interaction with props so versatile, that he generally found it necessary to shoot the majority of his scenes in long take and long shot and direct camera placement to underline the fact that he alone, the performer, was the cause of this veritable comedy magic. To have overindulged in editing and tricky camera placements would have shed doubt on what were indeed real Chaplin skills.

Arnheim indirectly acknowledges this fact by his second justification for embracing the Chaplin milieu. This justification I have labeled "forgiven primitivism." Chaplin's dominant realistic tendencies are explained away as part of a very early period of cinema history, as

> a film style before the "discovery" of the camera and montage. In these early films, camera and montage serve mainly as technical recording devices for what is acted out on the scene, and are therefore unessential.[57]

Arnheim's phrase for this early film state is "pre-technology." Thus he is in the awkward position of pooh-poohing Chaplin's comedy production know-how as somehow primitive, just after praising the comedian for comedy technique that is formalistic, and therefore superior according to Arnheim.

This qualifying strengthens the misconception that Chaplin, as well as "early American film comedies" in general, was limited in his technical production abilities, that he was a comedy artist despite this primitivism. Arnheim neglects to explain why Chaplin continued this "pre-technology" approach throughout his lengthy career, long after he should have seen the formalistic light.

Arnheim's third justification goes beyond even the rather tenuous nature of the first two, as I have suggested with the phrase "forgotten rules." Arnheim praises Charlie's ability to create "unexpected associations . . . between very divergent objects," the prime example being drawn from *The Pawnshop* (Figure 11).

11. Charlie about to perform a fatal operation on Albert Austin's alarm clock in *The Pawnshop,* 1916. (Courtesy Museum of Modern Art/Film Stills Archive.)

Charlie as assistant to a pawnbroker examines the alarm clock brought in by a customer as if he were a doctor examining a patient. He puts a stethoscope to his ears and listens to the clock ticking (heartbeat—clockwork), then . . . [he] takes off the back with a can opener (food can—alarm clock).[58]

These "unexpected associations" are one cornerstone of Chaplin's comedy art, his ability to transform any object into something else. In recognizing this phenomenon Arnheim has departed completely from his formalistic shaping process and embraced a realistic subject, complete with minimal editing, long takes, and long shots. Whereas before he seemed to bend his rules for Chaplin, at this point he literally breaks those rules. His apparent defense of this inconsistent stance is that a Chaplin comedy transformation of an object is comparable to the editing process itself.

It is with Arnheim's fourth Chaplin justification, his position on sound, that he is on his most solid ground, though the theorist does not expand this greatly. Arnheim opposes the addition of sound to motion pictures, with which Chaplin had concurred by keeping the comedy world of the tramp silent, although both acquiesce on the use of sound effects. Chaplin had even written more than one defense on the aesthetics of silent cinema (the most well known being "Pantomime and Comedy," 1931.)[59] This Chaplin work no doubt influenced Arnheim's film theory book (it predates *Film As Art* by two years) and might explain Arnheim's reluctance to expand on the point, since Chaplin had already dedicated a well-known essay to it.

To defend film as art, as opposed to simple recording, Arnheim underlines the nonrealistic tendencies of film and denies the use of technical innovations of a realistic nature, such as the addition of sound or color, as well as the deployment of realistic techniques such as long takes and long shots. "For Arnheim, every medium, when used for artistic purposes, draws attention away from the object which the medium conveys and focuses it on the characteristics of the medium itself."[60] The film artist must concentrate on the visual and translate any message into this form. If it cannot be translated into the visual, it is not meant to be a film. When it can be translated, the limitations placed upon the medium—in this case the absence of sound—act almost as a strainer; they create a purified statement. The same formalistic argument could be used to explain why sculpture is not painted.

For Arnheim the silent cinema was just such a purified medium, and with regard to Chaplin, speech is translated into purified pantomime.

> He does not *say* that he is pleased that some pretty girls are coming to see him, but performs the silent dance, in which two bread rolls stuck on forks act as dancing feet on the table (*The Gold Rush*).[61]

It is only with this last theoretical stance (on sound) that Arnheim uses Chaplin's comedy art as an example in a truly legitimate manner, legitimate in the sense that it was typical of the comedian's work. Otherwise, Arnheim is rather "creative" in his use of a favored artist to showcase his theory.

The second major theorist to consider is Sergei Eisenstein, whose initial writings and film work first appeared in the 1920s, actually predating Arnheim. I have placed him second, however, because Eisenstein, also a formalist, did not really come to grips with Chaplin theoretically until late in the 1930s, specifically in the essay "Word and Image" (1939).[62] Prior to this, Eisenstein's work is most often associated with a montage of collision, his unique approach to film editing.

For Eisenstein the editing process is what made film an art form. But instead of what was then, in the 1920s, the traditional approach to editing, the linking of content-related shots of film to advance a narrative, Eisenstein placed conflicting shots together—hence collision—to produce a new meaning. For example, in his film *October* (1927) he shows President Kerensky of Russia to be pompous by juxtaposing his image with busts of Napoleon and later that of a peacock.

Such an approach to film as art has little to do with the minimal editing of Chaplin's long-take work. J. Dudley Andrew has noted: "Early in his career [1920s] he [Eisenstein] chided filmmakers who used extensive takes. What could be gained by continuing to gaze at an event once its significance has made its imprint?"[63] Thus there is little of Chaplin in Eisenstein's early theoretical writings. Only later, with Eisenstein's revision of his montage approach in "Word and Image" (also known under the more self-explanatory title of "Montage 1938"),[64] is Chaplin legitimized in Eisenstein's world of theory.

Eisenstein's revised look at montage, no doubt due in part to the Soviet government's disapproval of his 1920s formalism, negates traditional editing and concentrates on the movements of the film actor. These individual actions of the performer constitute, for Esienstein, a metaphorical sense of montage. Appropriately enough at a time when he was turning his traditional approach to montage upside down, his definition of this new montage of acting was based on Chaplin. Eisenstein quoted George Arliss on "restraint" versus "exaggeration" in screen writing, with Arliss using Chaplin as the ideal example of screen acting.

> I had always believed that for the movies, acting must be exaggerated, but I saw in this one flash that *restraint* was the chief thing that the actor had to learn in transferring his art from the stage to the screen. . . . The art of restraint and suggestion on the screen may any time be studied by watching of the inimitable Charlie Chaplin.[65]

Arnheim seems to have anticipated Eisenstein's "Montage 1938" by several years when he cited the fun house mirror scene in Chaplin's *The Circus* as an example of the comedian's surprising and amusing multiplication of man without montage or lense distortion.[66] The scene refers to a house of mirrors chase, with Charlie being pursued by a pickpocket who has planted stolen goods on the tramp and now wants the goods back—and a cop who thinks Charlie did the stealing. Although there are several hilarious interactions, Arnheim's reference is to the relationship between Charlie and the pickpocket. When each makes his move, Charlie to escape and the pickpocket to reclaim the stolen goods, there are suddenly, due to the mirrors, innumerable Charlies and pickpockets in the frame.

A montage of acting, though not without interest, severely stretches the formalistic positions of both Arnheim and Eisenstein by its propensity for the long take. Indeed, when one compares Eisenstein's collision montage with his acting montage, there is a temptation to rechristen the latter as self-indulgent montage. Both Arnheim and Eisenstein kept Chaplin at the center of their proofs.

The third major theorist Béla Balázs, whom Andrew has shown to be the transitional figure between formalism and realism, is the most sympathetic of the theorists toward the comedy art of Chaplin, with the possible exception of André Bazin (who will be dealt with in Chapter 4).[67] Balázs' writing has less of a tendency to be bound by ironclad rules, other than his weakness for the close-up. There are, however, several Chaplin justifications that can be fallen back on if friction occurs between his theory and the art of the comedian.

First, as with Arnheim's pretechnology statements, which I labeled forgiven primitivism, Balázs is not as critical in his demands of early slapstick, in which he includes early Chaplin.

> Thus a definite variety of film art [slapstick] with a distinctive
> style of its own was born *before* the specific new method of film
> art and the new form-language of the film was developed.[68]

In speaking of the primitive comedy chase, he approaches the winsome, though questionable, implication that said chases cannot be critically examined, due to inherent properties not unlike the universal appeal of children and animals in film.

Second, Balázs praises the unique art form that was silent cinema, paralleling the sentiments of Arnheim and Chaplin. "A glance from . . . Chaplin spoke volumes—more than the words of many a good writer."[69] Yet Balázs verged from Arnheim's strict path in that he did not deny technological progress in motion pictures, such as sound, as long as it was used in a formalistic manner.[70] Balázs states:

> If Chaplin's last [tramp] films were nevertheless great artistic
> achievements, they were so not because of their silence but in
> spite of it. There was nothing in these films which would have
> justified their silence as an artistic necessity.[71]

But Balázs does not hold Chaplin to this. He fleshes out in detail the reasons for this exception.

> Charlie, the little man, would have had to invent some specific manner of speech which would have been as different from the speech of other men as his appearance was different from the appearance of other men.[72]

This exception, with regard to Charlie's need for silence, surfaces again in what one might expect to be another factor in Balázs' praise of Chaplin, the close-up.

For Balázs the close-up is a guide to the human soul, to a special humanistic truth—it is the equally special gift of the art of film.

> The language of the face cannot be suppressed or controlled. However disciplined and practisedly hypocritical a face may be, in the enlarging close-up we see even that it is concealing something, that it is looking a lie. . . . It is much easier to lie in words than with the face and the film has proved it beyond doubt.[73]

Balázs, who refers most movingly to the human close-up as a "silent soliloquy," has even come to be called "the poet of the close-up."[74] However, even here Balázs is willing to make exceptions in the name of Chaplin. Balázs forgives the technical limitations and general lack of close-ups in *Modern Times*; as noted earlier, he felt Chaplin needed to avoid any apparent mechanical problems that the lack of sound would have suggested in dramatic close-ups.

Balázs' final and yet most consistent line of suport between his theory and his inclination to praise Chaplin focuses on the comedian as one of the first true personalities of the screen, someone who played himself. The art of film, for Balázs, is closely tied to viewer identification with the performer, and no one better symbolized this for the theorist than Chaplin.

> If Charlie Chaplin came to be the best-loved darling of half the human race, then millions of men and women must have seen in his personality something . . . that lived in all of them as a secret feeling, urge or desire, some unconscious thought, something that far transcends the limits of personal charm or artistic performance.[75]

Siegfried Kracauer, the fourth major theorist to consider, is a realist, as the title of his work so elegantly phrases it: *Theory of Film: The*

Redemption of Physical Reality (1960). Formalistic theory had largely dominated film study until that time, with the result that film realism was often neglected or discredited. Since the comedy art of Chaplin more generally falls in the realist camp, due to such techniques as the long take and the long shot, one would expect many predictable points of agreement to be expostulated on by Kracauer. Yet what comes forth from the theorist, though in praise of Chaplin, is often hardly predictable.

This ability to surprise the reader is best exemplified when Kracauer deals with fantasy and Chaplin; for example, the theorist is especially taken with the tramp's dream of heaven in *The Kid*, which he describes in a quote from Theodore Huff's *Charlie Chaplin*.

> The grimy slum court is transformed into a place of celestial bliss, with its inhabitants posing as white-clad angels; even the little dog grows wings, and the bully plays a harp as he flies about with the others between the flower-decorated facades.[76]

Because this dream is a parody of heaven and Chaplin underlines its staginess, Kracauer sees fit to praise this in realistic terms: "Their very staginess denotes that they spring from a primary concern for physical reality."[77]

Kracauer, who has little time for editing and is rather enamored of the long shot (Chaplin realistic specialities he does not deal with), truly seems to seek the controversial in the Chaplin scenes he chooses to justify. Thus, in addition to "realistic" fantasy, Kracauer is also capable of interpreting Arnheim's formalistic camera placement as realistic debunking, right down to using the same Chaplin example. That is, Kracauer also uses, as Arnheim did, the scene from *The Immigrant* in which Charlie appears to be seasick but is actually fishing. But whereas Arnheim focuses formalistically on the initial ability of the camera placement to fool the viewer, Kracauer keys on the eventual truth (reality) the camera placement shows. For Kracauer it is a realistic task to "make you see."[78]

Kracauer is also a realist hesitant about the use of sound; in a section entitled "Speech undetermined from within," he praises the opening of Chaplin's *City Lights*, in which the comedian substitutes distorted sound for the speech of a pompous city official.[79] Kracauer is afraid of a "theatrical" situation, in which dialogue would displace the visual. Sound for Kracauer should reinforce the visual, which is just what the Chaplin example does. Yet Kracauer is quite capable of a flip-flop to include another favorite comedian, the highly verbal Groucho Marx, in his film theory. He justifies Groucho's dialogue along the same sound distortion lines as he does Chaplin's speech in the opening of *City Lights*. Kracauer's theory also rings very close to those of the formalists already examined; thus "Kracauer's realism was as cautious and conservative as Balázs' formalism was."[80] Indeed, Kracauer is also quick, despite this cautious realism, to support Chaplin's decision to keep Charlie silent. "Realist" Kracauer seems most adept at praising the nonrealistic aspects of the comedian.

As was the case with the Chaplin-influenced filmmakers, there are just too many similarly moved cinema theorists and critics to attempt to name all of them, or even a sizable percentage. But the four examples cited, Arnheim, Eisenstein, Balázs, and Kracauer, have historically had both the most sustained impact on film theory, as well as being the most creative in their ability to utilize Chaplin as an example or a proof of a given axiom. Many of the Chaplin authors scrutinized in the bibliographical essay in this book (Chapter 4) also labor under a degree of Chaplinitis. But they tend to employ the comedian in personal pantheons that seem more consistent with what Chaplin represented. For example, Bazin's theory of realism meshes quite nicely with Chaplin's production values.

Chaplin's amazing impact on film comedy and film study is easily matched, if not surpassed, by his influence on popular culture. The tramp icon that graced so many marketing schemes in the teens and twenties remains very much alive today. One can still buy everything from Charlie playing cards to Charlie music box figurines, which twirl to the tune of "Smile," from *Modern Times*. Moreover, his image, or its interchangeable coat of arms (various arrangements of Charlie's oversized shoes, cane, and derby) continue to be appropriated for a wide variety of subjects, from a recent video and print ad campaign for computers to a logo for a chain of comedy nightclubs.

The symbol of Charlie has become what the record industry has long labeled a "hook," a subject which is both immediately recognizable and which exerts an equally direct emotional response. And Charlie represents the most effectively complex of symbols. Thus he can be used in the most logical manner, as *the* emblem of what a comedy night club is striving for (laughter), or on a more abstract level, he can bring warmth and humanity to an ad campaign for the most cold and mechanical of products, the computer. And all this takes place decades after the last Charlie film was made and even several years since the death of his creator. "Chaplinesque" has become a well-known, and possibly overused, term the world around.

Charlie also continues to be a highly visible figure in the popular arts outside of cinema. Television's two most memorable and durable clowns, Red Skelton and Lucille Ball, owed much to Chaplin's comedy tradition. For Skelton, Chaplin has been a lifelong idol, and there is more than a little of Charlie the tramp in Skelton's most celebrated character, Freddie the Freeloader, who often did skits entirely in pantomime. (The show, which ran from 1951 to 1971, also featured a silent spot.) As noted earlier, Skelton's popular annual Christmas story, with broke Freddie ordering and consuming a huge meal so that he might know the warmth of a jail cell, is largely taken from Chaplin's *Modern Times*. And there were other Chaplin-influenced Skelton routines, such as the sketch in which he played a starving tramp who is mistaken for an actor in costume. Forced to play out a scene with an actress, hunger eventually causes Skelton's tramp to mistake the heroine's hand for a scrap of chicken, from which he then takes imaginary morsels in the most delicate mime. The routine beautifully salutes *The Gold Rush* Thanksgiving scene, bringing to mind both the tramp's methodical eating of his stewed boot (Figure 12) and Mack Swain's hunger-induced hallucination of Charlie as a chicken.

12. Charlie eating his boot in *The Gold Rush,* 1925. (Courtesy Museum of Modern Art/Film Stills Archive.)

Chaplin's importance to Skelton might best be capsulized by his key reason for buying Chaplin's former studio (which was by then quite antiquated).

> It had once belonged to the Master pantomimist of all time.
> . . . The aura of Chaplin still hung over every . . . sound stage
> and dressing room. And once Red became its owner, he would

be able to sit in the very same office He used, and at the same desk He ruled from, and control his own destiny much in the way He did.[81]

Lucille Ball's slapstick comedy in the famous "Lucy" shows, which ran between 1951 and 1974, also seems to have been greatly influenced by Chaplin, from an occasional television story line that allowed her to do a costumed impersonation of the tramp to the physical sight gags with which she became so frequently involved. Like Skelton, she tended to utilize the less capable components of the tramp for her humor. And again like Skelton, possibly her greatest skit seems to have been drawn directly from *Modern Times*. The sketch in question finds Lucy and close friend Ethel Mertz (Vivian Vance) working on a candy shop conveyor belt wrapping chocolates. Like Charlie's *Modern Times* factory job, where he finally cannot keep up with his own conveyor belt, Lucy and Ethel soon suffer the same comic fate. Besides being a delightful Chaplin footnote, it remains one of Ball's favorite *I Love Lucy* episodes.[82]

The most celebrated of the more traditionally oriented contemporary mimes, from Marcel Marceau to Shields and Yarnell (Robert Shields and Lorene Yarnell), all owe a huge debt to the artistry of Chaplin. In fact, the award-winning Marceau largely credits his idol Chaplin for his decision to study pantomime. Interestingly enough, Chaplin's daughter Victoria is currently a circus clown and tightrope walker, as if she were specifically stirred by her father's film, *The Circus*.

Chaplin's influence on theater has been equally impressive. For example, the comedian had a profound effect on German playwright Bertolt Brecht, "whose dramas are said to have done more to shape the modern theatre than any playwright since Ibsen"[83] The Chaplin touch can be seen in such Brecht productions as *Herr Puntilla and His Knight Matti*, which features a *City Lights*-like millionaire who is humane to a poor man only when he (the moneyed individual) is drunk; Brecht's *Caucasian Chalk Circle* has thematic parallels with *The Kid*; and the physical comedy of the playwright's *In the Jungle of Cities* is often seen as a general tribute to Chaplin. An even more impressive yet frequently overlooked Chaplin influence can be seen in the sequel-like nature to *The Gold Rush* of Brecht's *The Rise and Fall of the City of Mahogany*.[84]

During Brecht's "American exile" (1941-1947, after his fleeing of Nazi Europe), biographer Frederic Ewer notes:

He met and became friendly with Charlie Chaplin, whom he had admired since his boyhood, and who inspired so many of his own ways of thinking [both as a playwright and in his writing on stage theory and epic theater method]. Now a closer association only served to strengthen that admiration.[85]

Brecht's plays, however, often come to rest upon a helpless irony that is neither derivative nor equally applicable to Chaplin's work, despite film historian Gerald Mast's comparison of *Easy Street*'s conclusion with that of Brecht's *Threepenny Opera* and *The Good Woman of Setzuan*.[86] This is not to deny Chaplin any sense of irony in his productions but rather to draw attention to both the indestructible underdog persistence of the tramp, as well as the genre expectations of the comedy. While I will be discussing this at length in Chapter 4, suffice it to say that the Chaplin-Brecht relationship, in terms of influence, was not a two-way street, at least during the Charlie years.

Chaplin's impact on theater can also be demonstrated in any number of non-Brechtian ways, from a forthcoming Broadway show on his life and times to his effect on Nobel Prize-winning author Samuel Beckett. Beckett's writing, particularly his most celebrated work, *Waiting for Godot*, often shows signs of Charlie. For example, *Observer* theater critic Kenneth Tynan noted that the tramps of *Godot* "converse in the double-talk of vaudeville: one of them has the ragged aplomb of Buster Keaton, while the other is Chaplin at his airiest and fairiest."[87] Beckett would later attempt to cast Chaplin in his avant-garde movie *Film* (1965), in a part which eventually went to Keaton. Not surprisingly, Beckett biographer Deirdre Bair observed that as a child the playwright "never missed a film starring Charlie Chaplin."[88]

Chaplin's continued influence on writers outside of film cannot be limited to theater but also includes fiction and poetry. Fiction showcases an especially diverse Chaplin panorama, from James Agee's use of Charlie as one of the special ties between a 1915 father and son in his Pulitzer Prize-winning *A Death in the Family*, to the sometimes Chaplinesque nature of James Joyce's celebrated Leopold Bloom (see especially Mary Parr's *James Joyce: The Poetry of Conscience*, Inland Press, 1961). And Chaplin's life has sometimes even become a source for popular "fiction," such as John Baxter's rather bald use of Chaplin's biography as the basis for his "novel" *The Kid* (Viking Press, 1981). Baxter, who has also written several film texts, tells the story of one Tommy Timpson, a former Dickensian waif in turn-of-the-century London who becomes *the* film comedian of all time. The "coincidences" with Chaplin's life are endless and include everything from Tommy Timpson having a Japanese "man Friday" named Koto (Chaplin's long-time Japanese assistant was named Kono) to Timpson being knighted by the Queen of England. This left-handed salute to Chaplin is topped off with a dust jacket caricature of Charlie (Tommy's comedy costume matches the tramp's exactly, right down to the toothbrush mustache) and a book title that does not exactly distract from the comparison.

Countless poets have been inspired by Chaplin's artistry (including myself), and the comedian himself acknowledges the phenomenon by the inclusion in his autobiography of Hart Crane's "Chaplinesque," which the poet personally dedicated to Chaplin in appreciation of *The Kid*. Poet and painter e. e. cummings was even moved to create a delightful pencil drawing abstract of Charlie as Pan, which Parker Tyler used as the frontispiece in his book *Chaplin: Last of the Clowns*.

As with all great artists, Chaplin's work has had the poignancy to be seen and enjoyed at many levels, from intellectual stimulation to the sheer joy of laughter. But unlike many great artists whose uniqueness is dulled by the passage of time and popular culture's absorption of their innovations, Chaplin's gift of comedy remains as bright today as it was back in 1914 at the birth of Charlie.

The preceding examples that helped document this ongoing Chaplin heritage merely represent a surface scratching of the comedian's impact on film and popular culture. As important though this influence has been, it says little about the given factor behind all of it—Chaplin's awesome ability to "just" make millions upon millions of people laugh, generation after generation. As René Clair observed as early as 1929, "the masses do not know that Chaplin is the greatest author, the greatest creator of fiction, living today."[89] The masses merely know that he is funny, and from this all else continues to evolve.

NOTES

1. Gerald D. McDonald, Michael Conway, and Mark Ricci, eds., *The Films of Charlie Chaplin* (New York: Bonanza Books, 1965), p. 13.

2. Charles Chaplin, *My Autobiography* (1964; rpt. New York: Pocket Books, 1966), p. 183.

3. Gerald D. McDonald, *The Picture History of Charlie Chaplin* (New York: Nostalgia Press, 1965) [p. 25].

4. Theodore Huff, *Charlie Chaplin* (1951; rpt. New York: Arno Press and the New York Times, 1972), p. 65.

5. William Dodgson Bowman, *Charlie Chaplin: His Life and Art* (1931; rpt. New York: Haskell House, 1974), p. 70.

6. Chaplin, *My Autobiography*, p. 183.

7. Charles Thompson, *Bob Hope* (New York: St. Martin's Press, 1981), p. 8.

8. McDonald, *The Picture History of Charlie Chaplin* [p. 16].

9. Raoul Sobel and David Francis, *Chaplin: Genesis of a Clown* (London: Quartet Books, 1977), pp. 233, 234.

10. Huff, *Charlie Chaplin*, p. 64.

11. David Denby, "Introduction," in *Awake in the Dark: An Anthology of American Film Criticism, 1915 to the Present*, ed. David Denby (New York: Vintage Books, 1977), p. xxi.

12. Minnie Maddern Fiske, "The Art of Charles Chaplin," *Harper's Weekly*, February 6, 1916, p. 494.

13. Huff, *Charlie Chaplin*, p. 6.

14. Richard Schickel, "Hail Chaplin: The Early Chaplin," *New York Times Magazine*, April 2, 1972, p. 13. (Ironically, after Schickel opens with these quotations of praise, he assumes a rather critical position on Chaplin.)

15. Bob Thomas, *Bud & Lou* (Philadelphia: J. B. Lippincott, 1977), p. 130.

16. Lewis Jacobs, *The Rise of the American Film* (1939; rpt. New York: Teachers College Press, 1971), p. 247.

17. Raymond Durgnat, *The Crazy Mirror: Hollywood Comedy and the American Image* (1969; rpt. New York: Dell, 1972), p. 80.

18. There were also single Chaplin features at Keystone (*Tillie's Punctured Romance*, 1914), First National (*The Kid*, 1921), Attica-Archway (*A King in New York*, 1957), and Universal (*A Countess from Hong Kong*, 1966).

19. Max Eastman, *Heroes I Have Known: Twelve Who Lived Great Lives* (New York: Simon and Schuster, 1942), p. 200.

20. For more information on this area see especially Walter Blair, *Native American Humor* (1937; rpt. San Francisco: Chandler, 1960); Wes D. Gehring, *Leo McCarey and the Comic Anti-Hero* (New York: Arno Press, 1980); Jennette Tandy, *Crackerbarrel Philosophers in American Humor and Satire* (New York: Columbia University Press, 1925); and Constance Rourke, *American Humor: A Study of the National Character* (1931; rpt. New York: Harcourt, Brace, Jovanovich, 1959).

21. Robert Sklar, *Movie-Made America* (New York: Vintage Books, 1976), p. 110.

22. Huff, *Charlie Chaplin*, p. 65.

23. A paper on this subject, entitled "Charlie Chaplin and the Progressive Era: The Neglected Politics of a Clown," was presented by the author at the Second International Conference on Humor, Los Angeles, August 25, 1979. It was published in the Autumn 1981 issue of *Indiana Social Studies Quarterly*, pp. 10-18.

24. Huff, *Charlie Chaplin*, p. 18.

25. Charlie Chaplin, Jr., *My Father, Charlie Chaplin* (New York: Random House, 1960), p. 242.

26. Huff, *Charlie Chaplin*, p. 296.

27. Huff, *Charlie Chaplin*, p. 70.

28. For this fascination with Dickens, see especially Charles Chaplin, *Charlie Chaplin's Own Story* (Indianapolis: Bobbs-Merrill, 1916), and to a lesser extent his *My Autobiography*. The first text reads very much as if Chaplin were transcribing from a copy of *Oliver Twist*. In fact, it has been noted that "critics in 1916 found this autobiography a mixture of fact and fiction. Because of embarrassment, the comedian eventually had the book withdrawn from the market." See Donald W. McCaffrey, ed., *Focus on Chaplin* (Englewood Cliffs, New Jersey: Prentice-Hall, 1971), p. 27 (footnote). More recent criticism suggests that *Charlie Chaplin's Own Story* was ghostwritten. See John McCabe, *Charlie Chaplin* (Garden City, New York: Doubleday, 1978), p. 90.

29. Charles Dickens, *Oliver Twist* (1841; rpt. New York: Times Mirror, 1961), pp. 281-289.

30. A film title in Chaplin's *Sunnyside* (1919).

31. Albert F. McLean, Jr., *American Vaudeville as Ritual* (Lexington: University of Kentucky Press, 1965), p. 106.

32. McLean, *American Vaudeville as Ritual*, p. 110.

33. William Cahn, *Harold Lloyd's World Comedy* (London: George Allen and Unwin, 1966), p. 61.

34. Kalton C. Lahue, *World of Laughter: The Motion Picture Comedy Short, 1910-1930* (1966; rpt. Norman: University of Oklahoma Press, 1972), p. 90.

35. Mordaunt Hall, March 29, 1927, Review of *Long Pants* [the influence of Chaplin on Langdon], in *New York Times Film Reviews, 1913-1931*, project manager Abraham Abramson (New York: New York Times and Arno Press, 1970), pp. 356-357. See also Donald W. McCaffrey, *4 Great Comedians: Chaplin, Lloyd, Keaton, Langdon* (New York: A. S. Barnes, 1968), p. 105.

36. Mack Sennett with Cameron Shipp, *King of Comedy* (1954; rpt. New York: Pinnacle Books, 1975), p. 141.

37. Edmund Wilson, "Some Recent Films" [the impact of *The Gold Rush* on Lloyd and Keaton], *New Republic* (December 16, 1925), p. 109. See also Edmund Wilson, "The New Chaplin Comedy," *New Republic*, September 2, 1925, pp. 45-46.

38. Mordaunt Hall, May 24, 1926, review of *Tramp, Tramp, Tramp* [the influence of *The Gold Rush*], in *New York Times Film Reviews, 1913-1931*, p. 313.

39. Leonard Maltin, *Of Mice and Magic: A History of American Animated Cartoons* (New York: New American Library, 1980), p. 24.

40. Ibid., p. 22.

41. I frequently use Felix cartoons in my film history class, and *Felix in Hollywood* always receives the best response, no doubt assisted by the caricatures of other Hollywood personalities besides Chaplin. See also Maltin, *Of Mice and Magic*, p. 24.

42. Celia McGerr, *René Clair* (Boston: Twayne, 1980), p. 44.

43. Ibid., p. 104.

44. Jean Renoir, *My Life and My Films*, trans. Norman Denny (New York: Atheneum, 1974), p. 205.

45. Ibid.

46. Roy Armes, *Patterns of Realism: A Study of Italian Neo-Realist Cinema* (New York: A. S. Barnes, 1971), p. 144.

47. Ibid.

48. Edward Murray, *Fellini the Artist* (New York: Frederick Ungar, 1976), p. 32.

49. Ibid., p. 32.

50. Ibid., p. 83.

51. Ibid., p. 197.

52. Joseph L. Anderson and Donald Richie, *The Japanese Film: Art and Industry* (1959; rpt. New York: Grove Press, 1960), pp. 51, 357.

53. Ibid., p. 99.

54. Eric Lax, *On Being Funny: Woody Allen and Comedy* (1975; rpt. New York: Manor Books, 1977), p. 172.

55. Rudolf Arnheim, *Film As Art* (1933; rpt. Los Angeles: University of California Press, 1971), pp. 36, 51.

56. Ibid., p. 127.

57. Ibid., p. 151.

58. Ibid., p. 148.

59. Charles Chaplin, "Pantomime and Comedy," *New York Times*, January 25, 1931, sec. 8, p. 6.

60. J. Dudley Andrew, *The Major Film Theories* (New York: Oxford University Press, 1976), p. 33.

61. Arnheim, *Film As Art*, p. 106.

62. Sergei Eisenstein, "Word and Image," *The Film Sense*, trans. and ed. Jay Leyda (1942; rpt. New York: Harcourt, Brace and World, 1947), pp. 3-69.

63. Andrew, *The Major Film Theories*, p. 48.

96   Charlie Chaplin

64. Andrew Tudor, *Theories of Film* (New York: Viking Press, 1974), p. 38.
65. Eisenstein, *The Film Sense*, p. 23.
66. Arnheim, *Film As Art*, pp. 123-124.
67. I studied film theory under Andrew. Parts of this chapter were first done for an Andrew class (1974).
68. Béla Balázs, *Theory of the Film*, trans. Edith Bone (1952; rpt. New York: Dover, 1970), p. 26.
69. Ibid., p. 225.
70. Andrew, *The Major Film Theories*, p. 89.
71. Balázs, *Theory of Film*, p. 237.
72., Ibid.
73. Ibid., p. 63.
74. Andrew, *The Major Film Theories*, p. 99.
75. Balázs, *Theory of Film*, p. 285.
76. Siegfried Kracauer, *Theory of Film: The Redemption of Physical Reality* (New York: Oxford University Press, 1960), p. 86.
77. Ibid.
78. Ibid., p. 307.
79. Ibid., pp. 107-108.
80. Andrew, *The Major Film Theories*, p. 119.
81. Arthur Marx, *Red Skelton* (New York: E. P. Dutton, 1979), p. 245.
82. Bart Andrews, *The Story of I Love Lucy* (1976; rpt. New York: Popular Library, 1977), p. 248.
83. James K. Lyon, *Bertolt Brecht in America* (Princeton, New Jersey: Princeton University Press, 1980), p. 3.
84. Jennifer E. Michaels, "Chaplin and Brecht: The Gold Rush and The Rise and Fall of the City of Mahogany," *Literature/Film Quarterly* 8, no. 3 (1980): 170-179.
85. Frederic Ewer, *Bertolt Brecht: His Life, His Art, and His Times* (1967; rpt. New York: Citadel Press, 1969), p. 386.
86. Gerald Mast, *The Comic Mind: Comedy and the Movies* (Indianapolis: Bobbs-Merrill, 1973), pp. 83-84.
87. Kenneth Tynan, August 1955 *Observer* review of *Waiting for Godot*, in *Samuel Beckett: The Critical Heritage*, ed. Lawrence Graver and Raymond Federman (Boston: Routledge and Kegan Paul, 1979), p. 969.
88. Deirdre Bair, *Samuel Beckett* (New York: Harcourt Brace Jovanovich, 1978), p. 48.
89. René Clair, *Cinema Yesterday and Today*, trans. Stanley Appelbaum, ed. R. C. Dale (New York: Dover, 1972), p. 86.

3

CHAPLIN ON CHAPLIN:
AN INTERVIEW
AND AN ARTICLE

No in-depth examination of an artist would be complete without including some of his own observations. Thus this chapter includes the reprinting of both an interview with Chaplin, Konrad Bercovici's "Charlie Chaplin: An Authorized Interview" (*Colliers*, August 15, 1925), and an article by the comedian, "In Defense of Myself" (*Colliers*, November 11, 1922). These sources were chosen because of the richness with which they demonstrate basic characteristics of the man, and the world around him, during his most acclaimed decade of productivity, the 1920s.

The interview is insightful in at least five key ways. First, the lengthy opening on the influence of Chaplin's gypsy ancestry, while difficult to take seriously today, demonstrates nicely the comedian's tendency to romanticize his life and to influence those around him to do the same.

Second, Chaplin's propensity for rapid mood changes is nowhere better showcased than in this time spent with Bercovici, a close friend. This emotional rollercoaster of an interview varies from the upbeat opening hypothesis on gypsies to the sentimentality of the close, which finds Bercovici and Chaplin tearfully holding hands after the screening of the comedian's then soon-to-be-released *The Gold Rush* (1925).

Third, Chaplin's amazing confession of lying to an earlier interviewer, which the comedian later attempts to qualify—"Maybe in his presence I just felt like telling things differently."—is Chaplin's most bald statement on his lifelong "creative" biographical tendencies.

Fourth, because the interviewer is also a Chaplin intimate (which seemed to help Bercovici to jokingly prod the previous confession from the comedian), he has numerous insights to offer on Chaplin as director, particularly on the production of *A Woman of Paris*. Moreover, late in the interview, which seems to have taken place over several days, the reader is given a lovely taste of Chaplin's frequent tendency to shoot film in sudden movements of inspired improvisation.

Fifth, the interview offers numerous asides on several Chaplin subjects that had been or were about to become controversial, such as his relationships with his mother, his second wife Lita Grey Chaplin, director Joseph von Sternberg, and even Bercovici himself, who would sue Chaplin for plagiarism after the release of *The Great Dictator*. There is also a pleasantly sentimental, yet revealing, view of Chaplin playing with the interviewer's son at the Bercovici home.

Chaplin's own article, "In Defense of Myself," is also very revealing, but in a more indirect manner. For example, the title nicely demonstrates the comedian's need for self-dramatization and the controversial—which are perhaps one and the same—because the article contains nothing remotely close to the provocative situation the reader is led to expect.

Another circuitous message the article contains is that Chaplin's ego is not at all in ill health. While he recounts his rise to fame, nothing is said of Fred Karno or Mack Sennett (though their companies are mentioned), despite the comedy foundation they gave to Chaplin's career. In fact, Chaplin's explanation of his entry into mime and movies is connected neither to Karno nor Sennett, but rather to chance, which again exemplifies his tendency to romanticize.

On a more direct note, the article represents a blueprint for Chaplin's later essay, "Does the Public Know What It Wants?" (*The Adelphi*, January 1924). In both cases he describes the frustrations of trying to read public taste, and how he finally eliminated this by depending upon himself as a barometer of the "average man."

Chaplin posits a third reason for his success, besides chance and his assumption of the role of an average man. It is that the comedian attempts to elicit meaningful, thought-provoking laughter rather than "the guffaws which follow the funny gags which anyone can do." This statement is related to the Progressive issues (such as urban corruption and the plight of the urban poor) that were often highlighted in his Mutual films and anticipates the provocative topics that would dominate his later career.

All in all, the interview and article which follow present an informally insightful look at the comedian at a time when calling himself an "average man" did not seem so incongruous as it now sounds. His greatest triumphs and failures were yet to come. This was Chaplin on the brink.

CHARLIE CHAPLIN: AN AUTHORIZED INTERVIEW

Konrad Bercovici

"I have found out something about myself that has thrilled me as I have never been thrilled before," was almost the first thing Charlie Chaplin said when I revisited him in his studio recently. "But you look hungry, Konrad. Sit down right here," and clapping his hands he called, "Food! Food!"

"Any money in the bank of which you didn't have a record?" I prompted Charlie, who looked happier than I had ever seen him. "Or have you found out that you can act?"

"Wrong. All wrong, as usual."

Charlie leaned forward. His gray eyes glistened, reflecting his intensity, his nervous little hands clasped and unclasped.

"No, I found out from my mother a few days ago I had gypsy blood in my veins. And that has thrilled me more than I have ever been thrilled by anything else. At once a good many things, Konrad, have become clear to me. I now remember little allusions my grandmother made when gypsies passed by our home during the fruit season in England. And I remember many other things that have new meaning for me, now. In those days it was a great blotch on the escutcheon of a family to have gypsy blood. When I questioned my mother the other day for more definite details on the subject of my ancestry, she withdrew within her shell and wouldn't tell me more."

And, as Charlie looked dreamily up at the ceiling and closed the subject by suddenly beginning to talk about something else, it occurred to me that he, too, knew more than he was telling me, and had withdrawn within his shell at the point where he was beginning to give me more information about his ancestry; there were other people present. Charles ("Chuck") Reisner, his assistant, was there. And Jim Tully, and Bergman, and D'Arrast.

And at once a good many details about Charlie became clearer to me. I wondered why I had not thought of it before! So many things pointed to gypsy blood in Charlie's ancestry. Yet, I have speculated a good deal without getting anywhere—and Charlie didn't know or wouldn't tell.

His great love for music, his great gift for improvisation and his instinctive familiarity with musical instruments pointed to gypsy origin. There is hardly an instrument Charlie cannot play more or less well. His gift of improvisation is such that he can sing or play any melody in any mood [Figure 13]. Not only that but he can take any melody and give it a Russian, a Hungarian, or a Jewish twist. He can make it into a French chanson or a jazz tune. Why had I not thought of it before?

Reprinted from *Collier's*, August 15, 1925, pp. 5+.

Charlie Chaplin can take any melody and give it a different twist

13. A John Held, Jr., drawing of Chaplin playing his violin, with the original caption. (From the original Konrad Bercovici article, *Colliers*, August 15, 1925.)

HE SCORNS MILLIONS

And there are a good many other things. Whenever Charlie finishes work he wants to run away from the place where he has been working. Whenever he has an opportunity to go away and live in a tent he abandons his home in Beverly Hills and does so. Like the gypsies, he is unable to stay in the same place without going and coming. Many a time in the midst of the making of a picture he has disappeared from home and studio. As it is, he always has three homes to go to! The big one on the hill, another one in his studio, and a bungalow on the lot. You never know where he is going to eat his lunch, where he is going to have his dinner, or where he is going to sleep!

I had before ascribed these vagaries to his artistic temperament, but now I know that they are to be traced back to the gypsy ancestor whose blood speaks through him. Even his mimicry is absolutely gypsy. Unable to speak the languages of the countries through which they pass, the gypsies have had to learn to rely on sign language to make themselves understood. And the gypsies, it is now definitely known, were a tribe of minstrels, acrobats, and actors in India, before they began to spread over the world.

Charlie's slight figure can contort itself upon itself, and hang and twist in a thousand different ways. It is the figure of the gypsy acrobat and not of the trained actor. He is unable to work unless he feels like it. Although there are hundreds of people in the studio waiting for him, hundreds of people who are being paid huge salaries for waiting time, Charlie cannot be induced to work when he does not feel like it. And the time he loses! Sometimes, when everything is ready and the cameramen are waiting to "shoot," Charlie will suddenly begin to play his violin or dance or sing. Who else would do that but a gypsy?

The artistry and the timing of his pictures as they are being acted is done to inner music which often breaks out in song, sometimes in the studio while the picture is being taken, sometimes in the projection-room where the picture is being shown, sometimes in the cutting room when the picture is being put together. And when the scenes don't harmonize with his rhythm or song Charlie throws them out—and they must be taken anew at a cost of thousands of dollars. His entourage never knows why. Charlie knows.

And there are a good many other things that I know about Charlie which were suddenly explained by what he had told me.

Some time ago I happened to be in Charlie's room on one of the days when he felt depressed. Alf Reeves, his manager, had just shown him the cost sheet of his latest picture. There is always a warm session between Charlie and his manager at the end of the making of a picture, for the cost sheets are not shown to him until the last day. Charlie was in argumentative mood. Why had they not warned him that it was costing so much? Why had he not been cautioned? Why, oh, why, had they not told him?

As if he did not know that all warning would have been in vain! As if he did not know that it had ever been a prearranged thing between him and his manager never to talk to him about the cost of a picture while he was making it! Well, as Reeves says, that, too, is part of the act. It blows over and Charlie will do exactly the same thing next time he makes a picture, although he will start out very, very cautiously and economically.

In the midst of all the turmoil the bookkeeper brought in some bills from a department store. It appeared that Charlie's mother had gone on a buying rampage through the leading department stores of Los Angeles and had bought as many silks of vivid colors as the salesladies had cared to show her. And now the bills had arrived and the figures were way up in the thousands. It was a wrong time for these bills to arrive. Bills always manage to arrive at the wrong time. Charlie grew angry at the sight of the total at the bottom of each bill.

"Good God!" he cried out. "What does she want with these tens of yards of yellow and blue and green and white and black and mauve silk! Thousands of dollars thrown away! Let them take it all back. She has not used it yet—it's all there, somewhere."

But suddenly he checked himself. The tenseness vanished, and he sat down in front of the slowly burning wood in the fireplace. Then, after wringing his hands (at first with fury and then more softly so that presently he was slowly caressing the backs of his hands), he dismissed the bookkeeper. "That's all right," he said. "Don't worry about it. Pay the bills."

And talking to me without taking his eyes away from the burning fire he said, "Let Mother have all that. Let her have that and more—and all she wants of the frippery. The poor soul has been longing for such things all her life. She must have wanted these silks since she was very young to deck herself and show off her pretty figure and beautiful face. Mother was very beautiful, you know. Why . . . she still is, isn't she? And what of it if the silks came thirty years too late? She doesn't know it. She doesn't realize it. [Chaplin's mother had never completely recovered from her mental breakdowns during their poverty years.] Do I? Does anybody realize one's real age sooner than when one has absolutely broken: Will I, will you, ever realize that it is too late? Age comes upon one so steathily . . . suddenly one is old."

And then turning toward me with eyes moist with tears he gripped my arm and said:

"Let her have all that and ten times as much. I should have liked to be with her in the shops when they showed her the silks. How her eyes must have glistened! She has beautiful eyes, the poor old dear! Oh, Konrad, I shall never be able to tell anybody all the poverty and all the misery and all the humiliation we—my mother, my brother and I—have endured. I shall never be able to tell, for no one would believe it. I myself at times cannot believe all the things that we have gone through. Why, at times the work-house in England was a Paradise to us! Why shouldn't she have all the silks she wants, now that we can afford it? For it is 'we' between my mother and me. Let her play with them. I do understand her love for color. She has always loved high colors. She got only rags. Let her have silks now. We shall go out and see her tomorrow. She will be so happy!"

A second later Charlie was dancing to a wild Russian gypsy tune which he played on his violin. He had spoken about his love for color. I knew. I had seen an assortment of Chinese and Japanese robes in his dressing room that rivaled those of an Oriental potentate. Charlie's love for color frequently borders on gaudiness. I did not then understand the reason for that love as well as I understand it now. Now I know. The gypsy ancestry explains that to me.

Down in Hollywood you will frequently hear people talk about Charlie's tightness. Hollywood likes a good fellow who spreads his money like butter on toast. And when the money is gone Hollywood shrugs its shoulders. Never has anybody yet said anything about Charlie's generosity at the beginning of Jackie Coogan's career. How he deliberately let the "kid" run away with a good deal of the picture because he recognized talent in the child. And, though Charlie's managers had Jackie tied up on a long-term contract at a ridiculously low salary (considering what Jackie earned later on), when the elder Coogan came to Charlie and told him about the propositions of other managers, instead of hanging on to his contract and making millions out of it, he just tore the paper up; for he would not stand between the child and his future and the millions that awaited him. Yet he was sorry Jackie was leaving him. He had intended to continue his education and his artistic development. The best in Jackie is what he has gotten from Charlie [Figure 14].

And since I am talking about Charlie's generosities why not also mention the Adolphe Menjou story? Nobody knew about Menjou. [Menjou was actually a well-established performer in the movie capital, but Chaplin made him a star. See Menjou's autobiography, which was done with M. M. Musselman: *It Took Nine Tailors*, New York: McGraw-Hill Book Company, Inc., 1948.] He had played small and insignificant parts on the Lasky lot and elsewhere, until Charlie took him in hand for his "A Woman of Paris." And I know, for I was in the studio during the making of that picture, of Charlie's infinite pains and patience with Menjou. He spent days and days with the actor off the lot, talking to him, explaining details, telling him stories, and making philosophical theories for him, so that he could understand the role of the good-hearted cynic Charlie had created for him in that play.

HE'S A STAR MAKER

And Charlie was forever telling him, "Remember, I don't want you to be a villain" [Figure 15].

Charlie had just gotten hold of Wilde's definition of a cynic: "A man who knows the price of everything and the value of nothing."

"Keep that in mind," he repeatedly told Menjou. "A man who knows the price of everything and the value of nothing."

There were scenes that Charlie "took" over forty or fifty times with the patience of an angel, while the cost of production mounted by leaps of tens of thousands of dollars. Again and again he told Menjou that he was still acting the usual stage villain, that he should have another expression; and to inspire him, played his face for him as one plays one's violin.

And ultimately Menjou reaped and is still reaping all the profits of Charlie's generosity. He has created a new moving picture type, of which all the companies are now trying to avail themselves. Menjou is the busiest man in Hollywood, playing for four or five pictures at one and the same time. It takes some force of character, some inspired generosity, to teach a forty-year-old actor to impersonate a new personality of which he has never thought before.

Who that has seen "A Woman of Paris" will ever forget the actress who played the masseuse! It was one of the finest bits in the picture. But very few know that Nellie Baker—the girl who made it—had been a switchboard operator in Chaplin's studio. How Chaplin drilled and worked with her! How he fired her with an ambition that she had never before possessed, making her dream dreams that she had never dreamed before. Not long ago

The best in Jackie Coogan is what he has gotten from Charlie Chaplin

Charlie was forever telling Menjou, "Remember, I don't want you to be a villain"

14. and 15. Drawings by John Held, Jr., with their original captions, of Charlie and the Kid (Jackie Coogan) based on the 1921 film *The Kid*, and of Chaplin directing Adolphe Menjou, based on the 1923 film *A Woman of Paris*. (From the original Konrad Bercovici article, *Colliers,* August 15, 1925.)

Miss Baker signed a fat contract with a moving picture company, and she is on a fair road to success.

There is the Von Sternberg affair. A former second cameraman with great directorial ambition managed to raise some four thousand dollars and made a picture called "The Salvation Hunters." When the film was ready no company wanted to touch it—until a young English actor who had played in the picture induced Charlie to look at it.

100 CHAPLINS IN 1

After seeing the picture I had my doubts as to what animated Charlie's enthusiasm for it. There were some good things in it, but I doubt whether they were behind his interest. For days and days he talked of nothing but the great Von Sternberg picture. He got Doug and Mary so enthusiastic that they, who admire Charlie very much, talked of nothing but Von Sternberg's

Salvation Hunters. Within a few days the news spread from Charlie's studio that Von Sternberg had made the greatest picture ever.

Needless to say that the film obtained a release immediately. And if it has not revolutionized the moving picture industry it has at least obtained fat contracts for all the participants in the making of it. Von Sternberg does possess qualities of which nobody had been aware; but Charlie went out of his way to point them out. He fought for him. And what Charlie says about picture making is law to many in Hollywood. Everybody admits that he is one of the few who really know.

I could go on repeating such generosities indefinitely. I doubt whether Charlie is conscious of them to the extent I am. I have no doubt that a good many of these things are done without much forethought, just on the spur of the moment and with no intention of being generous. Charlie likes to pick up a person who has never been anybody and make of him a somebody. He has always preferred the association of the inconspicuous to the near-great and the great.

Recently, Charlie, with characteristic sweep, was passing in review the world's literature. Like a child who plays with a new toy until he breaks it, Charlie is constantly exhibiting his literary taste. Suddenly I tripped him up in the midst of a harangue on one of our writers:

"But, Charlie, you were reported in the papers as having told, about that writer, the very opposite of what you are saying now."

"Did he put that in the papers?" Charlie asked, wondering. And then suddenly leaving off the philosophical mood in which he had been, he brought his little hands forward, extending them toward me, and said in a most naive tone, "Well, I lied to him." [This is an interesting admission by one who has often been rather "creative" in recounting his life story.]

"You little liar," I told him. "Perhaps you are lying to me now!"

Instantly Charlie grew very serious. "I don't lie to you. Not to *you*. But why should I spill the beans before everybody? I never show all my feelings to anybody who comes along." And musing again he said, "And maybe I did not lie! Maybe in his presence I just felt like telling things differently."

Knowing the chameleon-like nature of Charlie, I am never surprised when I see him being a hundred different people. I have seen him Charles Spencer Chaplin, Esq., when I wished he would put a monocle in his eye to complete the picture, so grave and so English. I have seen him Charles Chaplin, the European bon vivant—the kind of Charles you might meet on Piccadilly or the Parisian boulevards [Figure 16]. I have seen him, with his shell-rimmed glasses on his eyes, a pessimistic philosopher out of one of the books of Dostoevski. I have seen him as miserable a creature as ever slunk along the Thames River on a clammy night, afraid of the policeman and wishing for one dry place in which to lay himself down for the night. And I have seen him play with my baby, rolling on the floor for her and acting in the silliest way to amuse her, as if he had been engaged for that special purpose.

The Charles you might meet on the Parisian boulevards

16. A John Held, Jr., drawing of Chaplin as a man about town, with the original caption. (From the original Konrad Bercovici article, *Colliers*, August 15, 1925.)

And then one must never forget that besides all these things, besides being an artist, Charlie is also a clever businessman. He has learned business in this country. He did not fall on a bed of roses on landing here. He came here with an act on a vaudeville circuit.

I have frequently heard people say that Charlie is a great mimic because he learned to act in England, where pantomime was at its height in his youth. Charlie himself denies that he learned much in England.

"Everything I know and don't know," he once told me, "I learned here. Not from people who did things as I do them, but from people who did not do what they should have done. And as I watched them do the wrong thing I thought of the right thing. Sir Herbert Tree has taught me many things, but not in England. It was when Sir Herbert and his daughter came here on a contract for Paramount. And he taught me not by acting, for I never liked his acting, but by talking to me.''

Once we had planned to pass a Sunday together, to lunch in haste and loaf the rest of the day, as we had frequently done in the past. I wanted to look over his garden and his home, which I had helped to plan two years ago. That house has turned out so differently from what the original plans were! Charlie had merely wanted a house to live in—"to die in," as he put it. Instead of that it had turned out to be a rather gaudy and pretentious affair. But Charlie's section of it remains as it was planned. His bedroom is severely simple. It is just a large room containing a simple wooden bed, a bookcase, a cheap mahogany dresser, a chair, and a table. But from the large windows one has a magnificent view of the country.

As I said, we had planned to loaf that Sunday, when suddenly Charlie changed his mind.

"I want to work. I want to work. Let's go down to the studio. We must go to the studio. Konrad, I want to work. I have an idea. . . ."

He called up his manager, Alf Reeves, and talked to him for a few moments. Then, still talking feverishly, he dressed himself in great haste.

"Ah, we'll get them all down to the studio."

"You are like all the other lazy people, idling the whole week and working on Sundays," I reproached.

"Sunday. Sunday," Charlie repeated several times. "I want to work. It's always Sunday when I work."

"Please do come down with me to the studio. I want to show you my new picture."

And then pointing to his dresser, to several paintings of still life, he said, "How do you like them?"

They were lovely little things, done in a very naive decorative fashion.

"Not bad, not bad," Charlie said, "Lita, my wife, did them. She has loads of talent, the little rascal. I hope she will develop her talents. I keep on telling her to develop whatever ability there is in her. She'll come to it. Not bad, eh! She has talent."

And then in the projection room I watched the reels of Charlie's new picture—"The Gold Rush"—on which he had been working for more than a year.

Never before had I been moved as much by anything on the screen. There were many questions that I intended to ask Charlie about things that had happened to him recently. But in the darkened room, while the picture was being shown, my hand reached for his. I had no words with which to express myself. And when the light was thrown on we looked at one another, holding one another's hands, and there were tears in our eyes.

IN DEFENSE OF MYSELF

Charles Chaplin

For some reason, which is not clear to me, successful men, whether they be bank presidents or authors of best sellers, are constitutionally incapable of assigning reasons for their success without arrant nonsense.

But of course *I* am capable of telling the truth about myself, and I am going to do it. I can think of three or four points on which my success as a screen comedian hinges, and I am going to set these down in a matter-of-fact way, without any assumption of imaginary virtues or decoration of facts, which are interesting enough, in themselves. A singular piece of luck, a certain discovery about the average man, and a decision to stop throwing custard pies—these reasons may hardly sound like the ordinary structure of framework of success, but they are the best I have to offer.

The year 1913 was my lucky year. I can sketch my autobiography of the years immediately preceding this in a single sentence. Part of the time I was playing in vaudeville sketches in New York and wishing I were back in London, and the rest of the time I was playing in vaudeville sketches in London and wishing I were back in New York. Having thus laid bare my past, I may proceed with the events and discoveries of this remarkable year.

It was spring in Philadelphia—but I will try not to be poetic. I was playing with the Karno Pantomime Company in a sketch called "A Night in a London Music Hall." As I arrived at the stage entrance for the evening performance, the doortender thrust a telegram into my hand. [Alf Reeves, the manager of the Karno company in America, is usually credited with having handed Chaplin the telegram, since Reeves had originally received it because of his position. In fact, that is how Chaplin described it in his later autobiography.] The clerk who addressed this telegram must have been working in the dark or under the stress of powerful emotion, for the name on it sounded like a radio signal. It was addressed to Mr. Crzzxs Okkgdlnx, care of the Fred Karno Pantomime Company. [Though the spellings differ from source to source, "Chaffin" is found most frequently. And Chaplin used this spelling in his autobiography.] Now this mysterious and Slavic-sounding name seemed to beckon toward adventure.

The telegram was from the Keystone Comedy Company, which was beginning to make moving-picture comedies on the Pacific Coast, and since it seemed that Mr. Okkgdlnx had engaged their favorable attention, they invited him to join them at a salary of a hundred and fifty dollars a week—just twice as much as I had ever made in my life. The conflict that took place in my mind was one of the shortest and most decisive battles in history. I went west. [The telegram came in care of Kessel and Bauman of New York, who controlled the Keystone company, among other properties Thus Chaplin did not actually know it was a film offer, nor were salary

Reprinted from *Collier's*, November 11, 1922, pp. 8+.

figures mentioned, until his arrival in New York. Chaplin actually bar-
gained successfully for a slightly higher salary. But he was unable to go west
until late November, due to his Karno contract.]

There was another member of the pantomime company who felt that the
Okkgdlnx telegram was intended for him. He felt that I had cheated him. [I
know of no other such reference.] But he was quite wrong; I found out soon
after my arrival in California that the telegram was not intended for either
of us. [Chaplin has let his embellishments get the better of him. The only
mistake was in the spelling.]

This explains how luck conspired with me and gave me my first great
impetus toward success, but it would be absurd to pretend that luck is
accountable for everything. Luck provides opportunities, but unless you
have some kind of endowment yourself to contribute, it will not do you very
much good. As it happened, I was at the very beginning exceptionally well
fitted for screen acting. This was also, I suppose, largely a matter of chance.

WHERE I KEEP MY EYES

Many years ago [1912] I was playing with a traveling company [Karno]
which was making a tour of the Channel Islands. I discovered that the
audiences in most of the towns we visited did not understand English at all.
Finding words useless, I gradually began to pantomime everything I could.
But although I used this device first as a substitute for words, born of
necessity, I discovered that in many cases the pantomime carried over the
idea more vividly and with more telling effect than words, and I began later
to rely upon pantomime before English-speaking audiences.

Finding that I had some talent in this direction, I soon afterward joined a
pantomime company, and thus more or less by accident received the best
possible training for the screen, on which everything is, or rather should be,
told by pantomime. [This is a reference to the Karno Company, of which he
was actually already a member. "Remembering" things in this order would
seem to place more emphasis on his own natural pantomime inclination,
rather than his Karno training.] It gave me a considerable advantage over
others not trained in this art, for what they sometimes found it necessary to
tell by titles I found it possible to tell by action. Even now I seldom rely for
a comic effect on witty titles. It has always seemed to me a distinct admission that there is something wrong with the presentation of a story or with
the acting when they have to lean so heavily on a crutch of words.

But I want to come to the discovery which I think is chiefly responsible
for my popularity as a comedian. Certainly nothing that I have said yet will
account for the fact that in 1913 I came to the coast a comparatively obscure
actor and that a little more than a year later I was known to more than a
hundred million people, and that I began to receive more notice in the press
than a prime minister. Simply stated, it was because I began to take my eye
off the public and to aim exclusively at pleasing myself. [This comment, and
the elaboration that follows, anticipates his later article "Does the Public

Know What It Wants?'' in the *Adelphi*, January 1924, pp. 702-710, which he devotes entirely to the subject. See also Henry King's reference to the *Adelphi* article in '' 'Movie' or 'Talkie'?'' (Chaplin's views) *The New Adelphi*, March 1929, pp. 248-250.] This formula sounds so easy that I am afraid everyone will be tempted to try it. But let me explain.

There is one malady to which nearly all actors, producers, and playwrights are victim—this is an inordinate concern over the way in which audiences will receive their best efforts. This, you will understand, is a form of apprehension and misgiving almost unrelated to the merits of the thing you are doing—an unaccountable tradition that a play or a picture may be almost a masterpiece and yet fail to satisfy the taste of the audience. It seems to argue that the audience is a fickle and erratic quantity which, moved by some perverse taste, may miss what is good and exhibit a preference for what is commonplace and inferior.

Perhaps I have an exalted opinion of the intelligence of the average audience, but I think that this old-fashioned notion that a play may be good and completely satisfy the conscience of the producer, but for some mysterious reason fail to go over with the public, is one of the silliest fallacies that sensible people have ever entertained.

MY BOGEY MAN

But in the early days I used to worry a great deal about that mythical person—the Average Man. Some few discerning people, I used to figure, might like my work, but I was never quite sure how it would appeal to the average. I used to imagine this terrible bogey—the average man—seated somewhere about halfway down the orchestra wearing an unfriendly scowl and an expression which challenged me to make him laugh against his better judgment.

I never saw him very plainly, but he had pale, watery features and was usually dressed, I think, in a ready-made blue serge suit which fitted him too loosely, patent-leather shoes with cloth tops which had weathered several seasons, and a narrow four-in-hand tie which he had bought at a department store sale. He was the kind of man who had come to see the show on the recommendation of one of his wife's relatives and was prepared to dislike it thoroughly. I used to fear this fictitious person and wonder if it was in me to please him.

Then, during my first year of screen work, I made a startling discovery. Gradually the vague and indeterminate features of this average man began to merge into a face and personality very familiar to me. He was no longer a hostile person about whom I could have any further misgivings, but a rather friendly man with whom I had had long acquaintance. This average man, in short, whom I had feared and nervously sought for in so many audiences, was myself!

Indeed, I can think of no one with a better claim to the title. My life has brought me into familiar contact with every kind and class of people, and I have absorbed a little of the viewpoint of each. I have played with crown princes, diverted myself with the company of eminent scientists, sociologists, and historians, and prosecuted long inquiries into the mystery and meaning of life with London cabmen. I feel equally at home with clergymen and prizefighters; both have put me to sleep. I have been entertained by bootleggers and British peers. In fact, it is established without a doubt in my mind that I am that long-sought person, the average man.

YOURSELF AS HERO

This decision simplified things very much. It enabled me to banish for all time my morbid concern about audiences, for the audiences were made up of people just like me. All I had to do was to please myself and I couldn't go wrong, for I would be pleasing the average man. In some fifty or sixty pictures which I have made, there is no exception to the rule that when I have satisfied myself, the picture has been a success, and that when I have not, it has been a failure. I am probably one of very few actors on the screen who acts primarily for his own entertainment. This in itself has been a great asset, for it does not take a highly developed perception to note the difference between a comedian who laboriously and painfully works his way through mechanical gags and conventional formulae in order to get a laugh and one who thoroughly enjoys what he is doing.

One of the happy consequences of electing myself to this post of the average man is that the public has unconsciously confirmed me as a kind of unofficial representative. The average man naturally finds great delight in seeing himself on the screen. Dashing and romantic heroes may provide him with a momentary thrill, but they sooner or later fill his soul with despair. Their ways are far from his ways. He will never come vaulting tempestuously into romantic situations, dressed immaculately in evening clothes, silencing men with a proud glance while fair women almost swoon at the gallant spectacle he makes.

He is not that kind of man and he knows it. He is much more like me. He does not cut a very dashing figure as he blunders through a drab and commonplace existence. Adventure means to him stealing home late at night and trying to evade or pacify his wife, and heroism with him has never soared to greater heights than his interviews with the landlord. He is a rather undersized, pathetic figure, this average man, not able to afford very elegant clothes, but trying his best to appear decent and proper, slightly bowed with a sense of his own limitations and almost resigned to the fact that fate never intended him for a Don Juan or a captain of industry.

I would like to write more about this poor average man, for I feel that I know him very well. His fortunes always drag a little behind his expectations and fulfillment lies always just out of his reach. Somehow, he never quite seems to make things go. He tries hard, much harder than some who succeed, but he never goes over the top. And as he goes shambling along, with dwindling hopes, he is smitten more than ever with a sense of his own unfitness and inadequacy when he sees on the stage or screen the romantic hero who sweeps through life like a whirlwind, leaving in his path a lingering gust of admiration and applause. The distance between him and this heroic figure grows into an unnavigable gulf.

Then he spots me shuffling along in my baffled and aimless manner, and a spark of hope rekindles in him. He begins to straighten up and take heart. Here is a man like himself, only more pathetic and miserable, with ludicrously impossible clothes, in every sense a social misfit and failure, at whom it is hard to look without laughter and pity. And yet this impossible person, without the build, the air, or any of the usual equipment of the hero, seems through sheer blundering and circumstance to get on very well indeed. He has a protective air of mock dignity; he takes the most outrageous liberties with people, as if they were the commonplace customs of an ordered life; and he wears adversity as if it were a bouquet. These are his sole possessions, but he finds life full of interest and adventure. He circumvents policemen, gets entangled in strange happenings, blunders into brilliant social gatherings and the company of charming women—and, in short, enters portals which the average man had always imagined were closed to him. And in spite of the most painful and obvious shortcomings, he manages to acquit himself fairly well. In emergencies he even triumphs over those imposing characters whom the average man has always viewed with so much awe. It is the successful rebellion—the long-delayed triumph of the mediocre and ordinary person, who without physique, finery, or the grand air, nonetheless begins to extract some of the rewards of life. It is a gratifying picture of the average man coming at last into his own.

He stirs in his chair and glows with a new confidence in himself. He is not so inferior and useless as he had thought. If the reader has been able to follow this little exploration into the mind of the average man, he will see that in a way I have become perhaps a kind of champion of the public, a glorification of the commonplace, a sop to that eternal human desire to show ourselves superior to our associates and our circumstances, and that my popularity is not the result of being different from other people, but of being so much like other people.

THE PART THE PIE PLAYS

I have already mentioned that the third reason for my popular success as a comedian was the decision to stop throwing custard pies. I do not mean this to be taken too literally. It was a discovery about the nature of humor itself—an article which I had been dealing in for a long time without knowing as much about it, I am afraid, as I should. If I state that there has not always been a very close relationship between humor and moving-picture comedies, I think that the reader will not be disposed to argue with me.

The comic spirit meant to me at the beginning of my screen career, as it still means to many people, a series of "gags" and funny business of a not very high order—anything to capture a moment's laughter or to stir the most elementary sense of the ridiculous. Now, this broad and slapstick kind of comedy, compounded mostly of boisterous spirits and physical violence, has about the same relation to humor as tickling a man on the soles of his feet with a wisp of straw. He laughs, but it is hardly a sign of fine humorous appreciation. Throwing sticky and gelatinous substances at unsuspecting victims, or falling into barrels of water or whitewash, will, I suppose, always get a laugh, but the laughter comes from no deeper than the throat—a kind of physical reflex at which the mind revolts. I began to realize very soberly that if I were to attain a reputation as a humorist, I would not travel very far by falling down manholes or throwing custard pies.

The true spirit of humor, I began to realize, does not revolve about physical mishaps or even incongruities of dress and behavior. These may be the outward paraphernalia of humor, like the motley of the fool, but humor itself is woven deeper into the fabric of life. I began to look upon humor as a kind of gentle and benevolent custodian of the mind which prevents one from being overwhelmed and driven to the point of insanity by the apparent seriousness of life.

TRUTH IN BAGGY TROUSERS

It finds compensation in misfortunes, detects in tragedy a note of gaiety, turns pathos wrong side out and sees it lined with unexpected bright colors. It says: "Look here, this hardship which you are taking so seriously is only a colossal joke which life is playing on you. You haven't any monopoly on hardships, anyway. They are common property." Looking at life from a new and unaccustomed angle, it finds the accepted values entirely changed. Worldly success and prosperity, authority and dignity lose a considerable part of their impressiveness and one begins to wonder if a meeting of bankers or a political campaign is any more worthy of attention than the figure of a tramp watching the sun rise on a May morning.

I did not intend to embark on an essay on humor, but since my ideas of humor have been so widely explained and discussed by other people, it seems only fair that I should have a word to say on the subject myself. [In all of Chaplin's copious writing he seldom explores the subject of his comedy. Even here, beyond the suggestion of a rational control or understanding of it, he adds little.] I have sought to show humor as a sympathy with the common troubles of mankind, a gentle amusement at the vast distance between its great aims and its petty achievements. If I can sometimes stir this inaudible laughter of the mind and incite an audience to a whimsical contemplation of life itself—to a spirit of mockery in which there is no sting, since it is aimed at everyone and everything, I would rather have it a thousand times than the guffaws which follow the usual funny gags which anyone can do.

I am afraid it is rather a shock to the reader for a comedian to speak so seriously of his work. But the humorist is just as much in search of truth and beauty as the poet or philosopher. He is aiming at his own interpretation of life, which he contends is just as sensible as the grim and frowning mien with which it is customary to attack the problems of living. And if it seems that there is a vast distance between this gentle philosophy and the crudities of some of my pictures—between truth and beauty and baggy trousers—I would remind the reader that in this spirit of mockery which I have mentioned, in this amusing contrast between our aims and our results, I include myself.

4

A CHAPLIN
BIBLIOGRAPHICAL ESSAY

Late in his career Chaplin closed an interview with this comment about his intensity of involvement in film comedy: "And so this thing that I've got, whatever it is, whether it's creativeness or whatever it is, I care. I really care."[1]

This bibliographical essay is an attempt to organize, in a logical manner, those key reference materials which are most helpful in studying Charles Chaplin's life and career. All the works are divided first by length and then by subject. Unless reference is made to a specific quotation, source notes are omitted from the text of the essay. The pivotal works discussed will also be found in the bibliographical checklist in Chapter 5.

The first section is devoted to book-length sources, written about and/or by the comedian. The materials are then subdivided into four categories: Chaplin critical biographies, Chaplin on Chaplin, Chaplin viewed by insiders, and Chaplin references.

The second section is comprised of shorter works and includes articles, interviews, book chapters, and monographs. It is subdivided into four categories: Chaplin critical analysis, Chaplin on Chaplin concerning comedy theory and pantomime, Chaplin's working style, and Chaplin's world view.

There is a brief account of existing Chaplin archives and film sources.

BOOKS

Chaplin Critical Biographies

From 1951 to 1978, *the* text on Chaplin was Theodore Huff's *Charlie Chaplin*, though it had been published before the end of the comedian's career. The 1978 publication of John McCabe's *Charlie Chaplin* broke but did not take away from Huff's domination of the subject. The McCabe book should be seen as a companion volume rather than as a successor to the earlier work. In his introduction McCabe himself notes that "my principal task, as I see it, is to update and amplify Huff in view of recent scholarship, and to draw from some remote corners a fuller overview of Chaplin as man and artist."[2] It is gratifying to note that McCabe has generally achieved that goal.

Both Huff and McCabe were able to sift through a large body of material, managing to balance the affection for their subject necessary to any good biographer with the analytical distance of the good historian. This is no easy task for a subject matter in which many people feel expert. Because McCabe's book is more a companion than a successor to Huff's, this Chaplin pantheon of two will be examined jointly.

McCabe's construction of the text, as promised in the introduction, follows the Huff pattern. Chaplin's early Dickensian years are examined in detail, followed by the music hall years with the Karno troupe. Moving to films, individual chapters are devoted to the early companies that predated Chaplin's United Artists years (Keystone, Essanay, Mutual, and First National), and then focus on the individual feature films.

Each book periodically divorces itself from the career man of "Charlie" fame in order to make forays into Chaplin's private life, often keying upon his stormy relationships with women. For example, each text devotes a full chapter to Chaplin's marriage to second wife Lita Grey (whose real name, Lolita, aptly describes his preference for child-like women). McCabe adds a chapter focusing on the comedian's messy Joan Barry paternity suit of the 1940s and the period that led up to it.

McCabe has been assisted greatly in his examination of the complex interactions in the personal life of the comedian by being able to draw upon two excellent biographies of Chaplin done in the 1960s—that by his son Charles Chaplin, Jr., *My Father, Charlie Chaplin* (1960) and Lita Grey Chaplin's *My Life with Chaplin* (1966). Weaving these and other sources together, McCabe gives the reader a balanced look at an often sphinx-like artist (who, McCabe reminds us, covered the events told in Lita Grey's book in only three sentences in his *My Autobiography*, for the sake of the two boys, Charlie Jr. and Sydney, born of the union.)

A relationship with Chaplin could be difficult even in the best of times, as both Huff and McCabe suggest in reference to his controversial third marriage (if indeed they were married) to Paulette Goddard, the lovely gamin of *Modern Times* (1936) and the equally lovely Hannah (his mother's name) of *The Great Dictator* (1940). Goddard, the only Chaplin acting protégé to sustain a successful career after her split with the comedian, had two particular crosses to bear. First, there was Chaplin's domestic view of the role of a wife, outside his own professional utilization of her, which he could make binding by way of Goddard's contractual obligations to Chaplin Studios. Second, there was the very nature of the "marriage" itself, which has never been officially documented. One or the other of these two points is often noted as having cost Goddard an opportunity for the role of Scarlett O'Hara in *Gone With the Wind* (1939). Huff subscribes to the latter, more frequently cited, cause—the taint of scandal this apparently unrecorded marriage represented for Hollywood and America during the heyday of the censorship code—while McCabe points to Chaplin possessiveness as not allowing her to take the opportunity.

The meat of both the Huff and McCabe books is to be found in their chapter-length examinations of the Chaplin features. Opening critical remarks on each film's background are followed by a detailed synopsis of the work in question. Errors are rare, though not unknown. For example, in the description of the snowball scene with the saloon girls in *The Gold Rush* (1925), both authors have Charlie opening his door to watch the girls, when in fact their off-target throwing has made him think someone is knocking. Only then does he open the door, to become an accidental target himself.

Huff's critical comments are generally the stronger of the two. One might liken his approach to the funniest film title in *Shoulder Arms* (1918), if not to Chaplin's whole career. After Charlie has performed a Sergeant York-style capture of seemingly half the German soldiers in uniform, he is asked how he did it. His simple reply is delightfully complex: "I surrounded them." Huff is able to surround each subject with the most thorough of overviews. He is able to enlighten without leading the reader into some preconceived critical corner. Each time I read the Huff biography, I am amazed at the foundation it has provided for Chaplin study since 1951. For example, his comments on the magic of Charlie's "comic transpositions" and Charlie's ability to bring inanimate objects to life 180 degrees from their standard usage would lead to Charlie's ability to "metamorphosize" objects in Gerald Mast's *The Comic Mind: Comedy and the Movies* (1973).

It is in McCabe's favor that when he does comment critically on a film, he is not adverse to countering standard views of Chaplin's work, such as the generally panned speech that closes *The Great Dictator*—most critics find it inappropriate for Chaplin's character of the Jewish barber.

> The last speech, despite its strident clichés, is ultimately moving not only because it is beautifully acted but also because, like any good homily, it makes sense. And more. It is in retrospect a haunting reminder that because there was no little Jewish barber to deflect them Germans set forth to erect Auschwitz, Buchenwald, and Treblinka.[3]

Though one might not agree with this or other analysis by McCabe, it encourages reexamination of old approaches, always a healthy exercise in scholarship. My strongest disagreement with McCabe comes, in fact, not when he expands in new directions but rather when he expands on what I feel is an already misleading critical position—negating the endings of those Chaplin films that conclude happily, which represents a goodly number of films, despite the stereotype of the sad tramp going down the road.

It seems as if so much has been made of the traditionally sad elements of Charlie that it is now necessary to question the too-happy tramp film endings for inclusion in the "superior" listing of tramp films with pathos. Though McCabe notes revisionist comments by Stanley Kauffmann (*Living Images*, 1973), the classic model until now had been Mast's statement, from *The Comic Mind*, that the happy conclusion of *Easy Street* (1917) was a "pollyannaish hoax."[4] That is, when a comedy deals with a generally negative situation, any sort of happy conclusion is not realistic and therefore is not appropriate. McCabe expands upon this tactic by questioning the happy endings of four other Chaplin films: *The Vagabond* (1916), *A Dog's Life* (1918), *The Kid* (1921), and *The Gold Rush* (1925).

This is a dangerous precedent to continue because it ignores the basic pattern of the comedy genre itself, which moves toward the happy ending after overcoming some initial problems, just the opposite of the tragedy. The very origins of comedy are tied to ancient fertility rituals and rites of spring, events that are commensurate with rebirth, with marriage, with a new world, and with the happy ending. As Northrop Frye has so nicely articulated in his *Anatomy of Criticism* (1957), the comedy happy ending is not there to impress the audience with truth or reality but rather to give them what is desirable—a happy ending. No matter how unlikely the manipulation, it is inseparable from both the comedy genre and the audience anticipation of that genre. Huff's only observation on the subject was that the happy close of *A Dog's Life*, one of the films in question, was "perfectly logical."[5]

Critical differences aside, the Huff and McCabe books are the place to begin or review one's Chaplin study. And though the absence of footnotes in both texts is disappointing, the authors often cite references within their material (McCabe is better about this). The books also contain valuable supplemental index material. Huff includes a filmography and synopsis through *Monsieur Verdoux* (1947) and brief biographical sketches of people with whom Chaplin worked. McCabe's index includes both an extensive bibliography (books and articles) and a complete filmography, compiled by Denis Gifford, author of *Chaplin* (1974).

Two additional "must" books for this section are Raoul Sobel and David Francis, *Chaplin: Genesis of a Clown* (1977), and Donald W. McCaffrey's anthology, *Focus on Chaplin* (1971).

Chaplin: Genesis of a Clown is the best book available focusing on the comedian's career in short subjects. It begins with almost a sociological look at the London of Victorian England, the London of Chaplin's youth.

Placing these extremes of class existence in perspective makes for a very effective framing device in telling the story of film's greatest clown, with the most provocative observation being that Chaplin's early years were not nearly so bad as those of the real London poor.

Sobel and Francis often examine Chaplin and his films in conjunction with basic Victorian values, from male mores on sexuality to the value attributed to the countryside in late nineteenth-century England. At their best the observations are compellingly fresh and insightful. It is only late in the book that their analogies become somewhat simplistic, such as one broad list of music hall characteristics that also show up in Chaplin's short subjects. The list is so general that the items noted would be equally at home with Aristophanes or Spike Jones.

At points such as these, while still generally maintaining an interesting, though questionable, hypothesis, the argument can become somewhat forced, not unlike moments in Siegfried Kracauer's celebrated but often controversial *From Caligari to Hitler* (1947) where the sociological and psychological approaches sometimes become a bit too pat.

Sobel and Francis do an excellent job of placing the Chaplinitis that swept the Western world during the teens into more of an historical perspective. With this they make *Charlie Chaplin: Early Comedies* (1968), Isabel Quigly's equally detailed yet less historical account of the Charlie marketing bonanza, a more valuable research tool. This is no small task, since the Quigly book is often considered a pivotal work on the early years.

Chaplin: Genesis of a Clown is also very impressive in both its historical overview of the commedia dell'arte and in the most logical placement of Chaplin's Charlie within this cornerstone of comedy tradition. Many Chaplin books at least briefly touch base with this. David Madden's disappointing *Harlequin's Stick—Charlie's Cane* (1975) focuses on it, as well as dealing with other silent comedians. But no Chaplin work examines commedia dell'arte quite so straightforwardly and thoroughly, from Charlie's ties with the pathos of Pedrolino (who becomes Pierrot to the French), to the complex and often cunning Harlequin.

As in both Huff and McCabe, the Sobel and Francis text is rich with references, references strengthened by the numbered footnotes at the close of each chapter, and a strong annotated bibliography. Particular attention is placed on Thomas Burke's *City of Encounters* (1932) essay on Chaplin, described in the bibliography as "A penetrating study of Chaplin's erratic creative processes by a novelist and life-long friend who experienced the same social origins."[6] I dwell on this source description because it nicely articulates a possible cause for the refreshingly varied, even iconoclastic, insights of *Chaplin: Genesis of a Clown*, as well as a suggestion of its sometimes slightly forced sociological or psychological criticism.

Though the book does not deal with the possibility that some early material by Chaplin was ghostwritten, as both Huff and McCabe suggest, it inadvertently offers a legitimate reason for the continued significance of any written work on which Chaplin was assisted. That is, Chaplin has always been rather creative in his writing, from his first book, *Charlie Chaplin's Own Story* (1916, McCabe suggesting it was ghostwritten), which often seems to parallel the story of *Oliver Twist*, to *My Autobiography* (1964), which Sobel and Francis demonstrate as equally capable of romantic, Dickensian flights of fantasy. For example, the comedian relates in the latter volume that when his father died the Chaplin side of the family was saved the humiliation associated with charity when a visiting Uncle Albert from Africa offered to pay the burial expenses.

Sobel and Francis are able to document, however, that Chaplin's father was buried in a pauper's grave, thus undercutting the magic of Uncle Albert's opportune arrival as well as the mildly eloquent funeral also described in *My Autobiography*. My point is that although no one has suggested the latter book is ghostwritten, it does demonstrate a certain creative flair consistent with Chaplin's earlier, sometimes questioned writings, though not to the degree of *Charlie Chaplin's Own Story* (withdrawn from print by the actor apparently because of its extreme variance with reality). More than one review of the autobiography did, in fact, deal with the dramatic "artifice" of the story. (See especially John Houseman's critique in *The Nation*, or Brendan Gill's in the *New Yorker*).[7]

This suggests that not every discrepancy in the early writing of Chaplin was due to someone else's narration or taking of the comedian's dictation. Chaplin himself defends dealing with history "poetically" in his autobiography. "A poetic interpretation achieves a general effect of the period. After all, there are more valid facts and details in works of art than there are in history books."[8] Thus, it might be posited that a romantic lie can be just as significant as some first-time revelation, which McCabe somewhat suggests by his observation of *Charlie Chaplin's Own Story* as at times "accurate in spirit if not in detail."[9] (See also Chaplin's admitting to a lie in the interview included in Chapter 3 of this book.) I have paused on the subject of ghostwriting not because Huff and McCabe have overreached themselves in comments concerning the subject but rather because of the semantics involved. The term "ghostwriting" is too often seen today as a total negation of a work. But in Chaplin's case a ghostwriter, if there were one, can hardly be seen as the source of his occasional romantic tall tales.

Two excellent companion works for *Chaplin: Genesis of a Clown* and the prefeature years are the aforementioned Quigly book and Henry Poulaille's early *Charles Chaplin* (1927, in French). Quigly's volume is briefer than Sobel and Francis's, but is more direct in dealing with each of the early films; for this reason it might be preferred by some readers. Pulaille's biography is still considered by some to be *the* French work on Chaplin's early years.

McCaffrey's *Focus on Chaplin* is an often excellent collection of essays and excerpts from longer works on the comedian. Editor and contributor McCaffrey has divided the twenty-four pieces among four subjects: Chaplin's career, his working method, pro and con essays dealing with his art, and reviews of specific films, this last category containing half the entries.

As is to be expected in a work of this nature, a number of its contributors had, or went on to make, reputations based upon Chaplin or film comedy scholarship. Material is excerpted from editor McCaffrey's *4 Great Comedians: Chaplin, Lloyd, Keaton, Langdon* (1968), John Montgomery's *Comedy Films: 1894-1954* (1954), and Louis Delluc's *Charlie Chaplin* (1922, generally considered to be the first serious analytical examination of the comedian's work).

Other contributors who would go on to write major studies in the area include Roger Manvell, the biography *Chaplin* (1974); Gerald Mast, *The Comic Mind: Comedy and the Movies* (1973); Walter Kerr, *The Silent Clowns* (1975); and Timothy J. Lyons, *Charles Chaplin: A Guide to References and Resources* (1979).

Additional key entries include five essays and excerpts by Chaplin himself; Minnie Maddern Fiske's milestone 1916 article "The Art of Charles Chaplin," which gave him his first recognition by the intelligentsia; a generally insightful essay written in 1935 by none other than statesman Winston Churchill; and a series of additional reviews.

Despite this "who's who" collection, all is not well in Chaplinville. I find McCaffrey's excerpt from *4 Great Comedians* unnecessarily negative in two ways. First, it is overly harsh on the episodic nature of Chaplin's storytelling, completely neglecting the tramp's ties with picaresque heroes such as Don Quixote and Huck Finn mentioned by Gerald Mast. Though McCaffrey is correct in saying Chaplin contemporaries like Buster Keaton and Harold Lloyd (on whom McCaffrey did his excellent Ph.D. dissertation) produced tighter narratives, he does not give adequate credit to the unifying nature of the Charlie comedy persona, an area where Keaton and Lloyd have to take a back seat.

One might add that comedy, by its very nature, tends to put less emphasis on narrative in order to focus on characterization. And the loose or non-existent comedy story line has always found especially fertile ground in America. For example, Mark Twain, the country's foremost humorist, opens his most celebrated work, *Huckleberry Finn*, with the warning: "Persons attempting to find a motive in this narrative will be prosecuted; . . . persons attempting to find a plot in it will be shot."[10]

The second negative aspect is that McCaffrey continues a trend which seems to have hounded Chaplin almost from the beginning: that of applauding the comedian despite what is seen as his technical limitations. It required André Bazin's milestone essay, "The Virtues and Limitations of Montage" (1958), to make it clear that Chaplin's decision to film in long shot and long take was wise technically and represented the comedian's production awareness of the most effective form of presentation for his comedy art.

These exceptions taken with *4 Great Comedians* should not distract from a truly excellent Chaplin anthology, though it has always marred my study of the work; as Roger Manvell so delicately described it in his own Chaplin biography, *4 Great Comedians* is "an analysis, more sharply critical than usual, of Chaplin as filmmaker."[11]

The strength of *Focus on Chaplin* falls clearly in the review section, particularly the pieces by Mast, comparing *The Gold Rush* and Keaton's *The General* (excerpted from *A Short History of the Movies*); Lyons's examination of pathos-humor in *The Gold Rush*; and Kerr's affectionately critical look at *Limelight*. In each case the authors have created study models full of insight and readily applicable to other Chaplin and/or comedy situations. This is especially true of the Mast piece, which is quite possibly the best essay ever done comparing Chaplin to another comedian.

McCaffrey has done a good job in his selection of Chaplin-authored materials, choosing interesting though not readily available items. There are two career excerpts from the controversial *Charlie Chaplin's Own Story* (1916) and three articles dealing with his working method, all but one having originally appeared before 1919. My only qualifier is that the more familiar one becomes with Chaplin's pen, the more one is aware of the contradictory nature of his writing; Philip G. Rosen's commentary points up the comedian's war against any plan of rational thought.[12]

My own research on Chaplin's comedy theory position, in *Charlie Chaplin's World of Comedy* (1980), posits the same contradictions, as well as a surprising neglect of the subject (comedy) in general, though the comedian does not consciously embrace intuition until the close of his career. Thus it is a tribute to McCaffrey's insight that the excerpt from *Charlie Chaplin's Own Story* entitled "Creating the Role of Dr. Body in *Casey's Court Circus*" contains one of the few meaningful comedy comments in Chaplin's longer works.[13] This delightful reminiscence, which is elaborated on in Chapter 1 of this book, taught him how to intensify audience response by feigning dignity regardless of the comic humiliation his character was suffering.

McCaffrey is also to be commended for selecting two early Chaplin articles which originally appeared as "How I Made My Success" (1915) and "What People Laugh At" (1918), because despite Chaplin's continued proclivity for writing—more than any other silent performer—these pieces would constitute the core of what he had to say on comedy. The final Chaplin entry, drawn from "Pantomime and Comedy" (1931), is the comedian's celebration of the universality of pantomime art and the silent screen, which, as McCaffrey notes, stayed much the same throughout his life—a rare example of consistency in the comedian's writing.

Focus on Chaplin also includes scenario extracts from *Shoulder Arms*,

The Kid, and *Modern Times*; a filmography, and an excellent annotated bibliography, both of books and articles. It is a truly versatile work, but due to the crunch of Chaplin material, it should be volume one in a series of Chaplin anthologies, instead of the only one.

Persons interested in further critical biography reading are best advised to seek Peter Cotes and Thelma Niklaus' *The Little Fellow* (1951, revised in part in 1965), Manvell's *Chaplin* (1974), and Robert F. Moss's thin but provocative *Charlie Chaplin* (1975). As in the order of their publication, Manvell's book is the most middle-of-the-road in attitude toward the subject, while the Cotes-Niklaus work tends to worship and the Moss text is more iconoclastic.

Chaplin on Chaplin

Charles Chaplin is credited with having written five books: *Charlie Chaplin's Own Story* (1916), *My Trip Abroad* (1922), *A Comedian Sees the World* (1933), *My Autobiography* (1964), and *My Life in Pictures* (1974). The autobiography is clearly the most important of these and will be the focus of my comments on Chaplin's longer written works. But the other volumes merit some passing observations.

Charlie Chaplin's Own Story is the book the comedian took off the market when the critics found his life history a bit too creative. His deprived childhood is transformed into something very close to Charles Dickens's *Oliver Twist*, a volume his autobiography tells us he was moved to buy when he could "hardly read," noting that he "felt like Oliver Twist."[14] Though certain parallels can be drawn between Charles's and Oliver's childhoods, Chaplin seems to be literally writing his book with an open copy of *Twist* before him. Chaplin's story even has a nasty Fagin (Mr. Hawkins) who steals a child (young Chaplin) away to slave for him, as well as an Artful Dodger (Snooper) who, of course, steals purses.

However, it is unfair to slur this first book, because there is a certain naiveté (his flights of Dickens notwithstanding) that can be most revealing—for example, the childhood anecdote on comedy mentioned earlier, which was reproduced in *Focus on Chaplin*. There is a freshness here (again, this is 1916) generally missing from his other works.

Discarding his "literary" aspirations, in *My Trip Abroad* Chaplin merely records the significant events of his 1921 trip to Europe. The result is a seemingly endless repetition of the important books he read or took along, the important people he met, and the generally unprecedented public response he received. Both *A Comedian Sees the World* (Huff and McCabe suggest this was ghostwritten) and *My Autobiography* follow the same "who's who" format, with the latter applied to a lifetime. Ironically, one would be almost hard pressed to name Chaplin's occupation from the mere reading of these three volumes.

Of the travel books, *My Trip Abroad* is to be preferred to *A Comedian Sees the World*, because in 1921 international adulation is still something new for him. Consequently, between name dropping lists there is still something of the freshness of *Charlie Chaplin's Own Story*, from the praise he lavishes on Thomas Burke's *Limehouse Nights* and the parallels of their backgrounds (which no doubt encouraged the significance Sobel and Francis placed upon Burke's later essay about Chaplin), to the bubbling innocence of a new celebrity: "I drew a picture of my hat, cane, and boots, which is my favorite autograph."[15]

At one point Chaplin, a man now far removed from the poverty of his youth, even finds himself passing out money among London tramps outside his homecoming hotel. And it seems a genuine gesture, not unlike the later moving scene in Preston Sturges's *Sullivan's Travels* (1941), where the wealthy but socially conscious filmmaker passes money out among the tramps, one of whom he had so recently been.

My Life in Pictures is a visual treat for scholar and fan alike, with many insightful captions accompanying the photos, though there are occasionally recycled observations from his autobiography. The pictures provide an interesting look at Chaplin both on and "behind the screen"—to quote one of his early film titles. The book includes everything from sharp film enlargements and candid private snapshots to lush color reproductions of early Charlie posters, "Movy-Dolls," comic strips, comic books, cigarette cards, and playing cards.

My Life in Pictures, while not the most important book by Chaplin, is probably the most satisfying in terms of the reader's prebrowsing expectations. If it whets your appetite for similar collections of Chaplin pictures and the assorted iconography his tramp character inspired, two classic volumes are Gerald D. McDonald's *The Picture History of Charlie Chaplin* (1965) and Denis Gifford's *Chaplin* (1974), with its often striking color reproductions. These works have a better balance between text and the printed page than *My Life in Pictures*.

These are the other books by Chaplin, but the key volume, despite its name-dropping tendencies, is *My Autobiography*. This rambling, 500-page-plus work, like a Hitchcock film, starts with extreme specifics—"I was born on April 16, 1889, at eight o'clock at night, in East Lane, Walworth [London]"—and then gradually succumbs to the general, as Chaplin tries to play too many roles in proving his all-around genius. Consequently, we get further and further away from the specifics of comedian *Charlie* Chaplin and must meet Renaissance man *Charles* Chaplin, who talks socialism with H. G. Wells, economics with John Maynard Keynes, the plight of India with Ghandi, and so on. And whereas Hitchcock's movement from specific to general helps an audience relate to a character, Chaplin's potpourri of generalities only alienates. In an autobiography of film's greatest clown, the audience very much wants to stay focused on that specific clown.

It is therefore necessary to look deeper into the book, once the poignantly written early chapters about the Dickensian childhood are past. Certain patterns soon emerge that in and of themselves seem inconsequential but when considered in total represent a much more strongly Victorian value system than has ever before been linked with Chaplin.

To start with, there is his propensity for name-dropping. Is this merely the wish fulfillment of a poor, neglected boy who has become rich and famous? While this is certainly a part of it, no Chaplin author seems to have addressed the point that Victorian culture was obsessed with hero worship. Walter E. Houghton, in his celebrated *The Victorian Frame of Mind*, makes the point that for the Victorian

> in actual life to meet a great man, or look on anything he possessed, was an overwhelming experience. "One man is so little," a lecturer told his audience, "that you see him a thousand times without caring to ask his name; another man is so great, that if you have exchanged a word with him while living, or possess 'a hair of him' when dead, it is something of which you are proud."[16]

This captures nicely Chaplin's sense of awe at meeting the famous. For example, while socializing with actor Sir Herbert Beerbohm Tree, Chaplin confessed: "I never thought of you as existing offstage. You were a legend. And to be dining with you tonight in Los Angeles overwhelms me."[17] Ironically, as Arthur Knight notes, "it never seems to occur to him that the people he has met were, in all probability, no less impressed at having met the great Charlie Chaplin."[18]

If Chaplin's interest in the famous can be linked to this Victorian characteristic, it certainly received assistance from Chaplin's mother, the most influential force in his young life. As Chaplin himself notes, she had had a life-size painting of Nell Gwyn (the English actress and mistress of Charles II) in their sitting room and was wont to do imitations of everyone from Gwyn and Napoleon to the famous of fiction. And though she often brought parody to her mimicry, there was also a balance of respect; for example, this was his description of her rendition of Wilson Barrett in *The Sign of the Cross*: "She acted with a suspicion of humor, but not without an appreciation of Barrett's talents."[19]

Chaplin's lifelong fascination with Napoleon (at one time there were even plans for him to star in a serious film about the leader) can be traced to the same source. Houghton notes that Napoleon was one of the pantheon heroes of the Victorian era.[20] And the first few of several references to Napoleon in his autobiography are attributed to his mother, with the most telling involving the father Chaplin hardly knew: "Mother said he looked like Napoleon."[21] As an adult he would visit Napoleon's tomb and report, in *A*

Comedian Sees the World (which was serialized in *Woman's Home Companion*), that the French general "was the most dramatic mortal that ever lived."[22]

An extension of Victorian hero worship can be seen in the period's interest in self-development, to become all that is possible. Chaplin notes that after he read Emerson's "essay on 'Self-Reliance' I felt I had been handed a golden birthright."[23] And the dropping of book titles therefore joins that of names, a characteristic that was starting to surface as early as *My Trip Abroad*. His autobiography constantly finds him haunting bookstores. And when his comedic fame allowed him to converse with some of the very authors he was reading, it is not surprising that he should dwell on, even celebrate, such a metamorphosis.

Further encouragement for this infatuation for the famous no doubt came from the fact that Victorian society did not place that much significance on comedy. For example, America's greatest humorist, Mark Twain, died believing his most important book was the sentimentally serious biography of another Victorian hero/heroine, Joan of Arc. Chaplin mirrors this in his autobiography by seldom talking about comedy and the nuts-and-bolts construction of his films. Apparently he started to link comedy with a second-class identity as early as 1922, when the article "Charlie Chaplin, as a Comedian, Contemplates Suicide" reported his preference for tragedy.[24]

He does, however, have time for a Victorian fascination with the macabre. The autobiography is full of grizzly tales: the murder scene of a Japanese prime minister; an acquaintance who develops leprosy; a clinical examination of what the electric chair does to its victim; often vivid descriptions of the suicides of several friends; a chance meeting with a man condemned to hang; the story of a Buddhist monk who, because he had spent a lifetime floating in oil, had skin so embryonically soft that a finger could be put through it; and on and on.

Charles Chaplin, Jr., suggests that the comedian's interest in the macabre was very much like that of Charles Dickens, and invariably his bedtime stories were extracts from the novelist with a "macabre cast to them."[25] Later Chaplin's son theorizes that the reason his father's favorite fiction writers were Dickens and Maupassant was "because of the peculiar combination of the humorous and the macabre in their works."[26] Interestingly enough, though he does not extend the analogy any further, each of the other fictional writer favorites of his father (Edgar Allan Poe, Oscar Wilde, and Mark Twain) also often combine the "humorous and the macabre."

Charles Jr. also notes that his father's friendship with Dr. Cecil Reynolds, who later committed suicide, was largely based on the fact that Chaplin Sr. was "attracted to the macabre, and as a surgeon, Dr. Reynolds had plenty of this kind of fare to serve him."[27] These observations are consistent with those of his prodigal son from his fourth marriage, Michael

Chaplin, in *I Couldn't Smoke the Grass on My Father's Lawn* (1966), right down to more grizzly bedtime stories. Except, now the tales are of Chaplin's own invention and fall under the general heading of the "Nice Old Man" stories. One of Michael's favorites ends with a baby falling in the sea and the "Nice Old Man pushed the pram in after him and went off to spend the money the parents had given him to look after the baby."[28]

It seems appropriate, however, that the most macabre story in Chaplin's autobiography manages to find its way back to the subject of comedy, though only briefly. The tale in question involves the ill-fated Donner Party, a group of mid-nineteenth century pioneers who found themselves stranded in the mountains by snow and had to resort to cannibalism. Chaplin drew heavily upon this real-life tragedy for *The Gold Rush*, his most celebrated comedy. Charlie plays a starving miner in the frozen North, with an equally hungry partner who hallucinates that the little fellow is a chicken. Charlie must do comic battle for his life until they compromise by cooking and eating Chaplin's boot. (Some members of the Donner Party had eaten their moccasins.)

Unfortunately, Chaplin's autobiography spends little time on this interest in the mixture of the macabre and comedy beyond observing the paradox "that tragedy stimulates the spirit of ridicule. . . . We must laugh in the face of our helplessness . . . or go insane."[29] Yet this observation is enough to suggest the secret of Chaplin's ability to create films full of pathos—the comic is mixed with scenes realistically rooted in the tragic or the macabre. And though he does not expand upon this formula, it could be applied to a number of his films, from the abandoned baby of *The Kid* to the blind girl in *City Lights*. For those interested in further analysis along these lines, Timothy J. Lyons's essay, "The Idea in The Gold Rush: A Study of Chaplin's Use of the Comic Technique of Pathos-Humor" is an excellent resource; however, similar analyses are rare.[30]

The Chaplin heroine was very much the idealized Victorian woman, and though the comedian does not directly address this in his autobiography, his every female interaction seems pointed in that direction, be it the boy who fell in love with a girl playing Cinderella, the famous screen comedian describing a brief romance as "like the last chapter of a Victorian novel," or the retired artist still romanticizing about Hetty Kelly, his first real love.[31] And as Francis Wyndham suggests, "Hetty Kelly, and her delicate but incomplete image seem to recur throughout his creative work . . . [as] objects of distant worship."[32] Poor Hetty even seems to follow the scenario of that classic Victorian poem idealizing the divine woman—Dante Gabriel Rossetti's "The Blessed Damozel." As with Rossetti's heroine, Chaplin's Hetty dies young, before their love can be consummated. This "idyllic dream of Hetty continued to haunt him through the years."[33]

It seems appropriate that Chaplin's second wife, Lita Grey Chaplin, notes in her *My Life With Chaplin* that the comedian often remarked that she reminded him of the girl in the *Age of Innocence* painting.[34] Eventually

Chaplin had a company artist "paint a likeness of her . . . in the *Age of Innocence* pose."[35] The original painting, which was done by Sir Joshua Reynolds in 1788, is a touchingly romantic rendering of a young girl by an artist more often associated with the classical tradition.[36] The hardback editions of Grey's memoir include a photograph of her posing for the *Age of Innocence*-inspired portrait, in which she is remarkably similar to the girl of Reynolds' original. It makes it all the more believable that at the height of their romance Chaplin should tell her, "There are many things attractive about you, Lita, but the most appealing is your virginal innocence."[37]

Chaplin's fascination with a portrait of his love brings to mind two similar instances of image worship. One was of the Victorian era; the other continued those values, as did Chaplin, well into the twentieth century. A celebrated element of Mark Twain's courtship of his beloved wife, Olivia, was his falling in love with her picture in an ivory miniature years before they met. D. W. Griffith uses this same romantic idealization in *The Birth of a Nation* (1915), when his central character, the Little Colonel (Henry B. Walthall), falls in love with the miniature of Elsie Stoneman (Lillian Gish), years before they are to meet. Twain was one of Chaplin's favorite authors, and the comedian is said to have seen *The Birth of a Nation* weekly during its initial long run in Los Angeles. While Chaplin detractors might be more likely to search the comedian's archives for a Dorian Gray-type picture, Chaplin was in love with at least the Victorian idealization of love sketched above.

The general mission of the Victorian woman was to maintain civilization in the sanctuary of the home, to counterbalance and even save the male from the debasing materialism of the world marketplace. And again and again Chaplin's autobiography delineates the breakdown of a relationship because the woman wanted to begin or continue a career. This was most specifically the case with first and third wives, Mildred Harris and Paulette Goddard. Charles Jr. described the final conflict between Chaplin and Goddard as "that perennial Hollywood plaint between married players: career."[38] Close family friend R. J. Minney, in his affectionate biography *Chaplin: The Immortal Tramp* (1954), described the Harris conflict in the following manner: "He wanted her to stay at home and be his wife; she could not be a film actress and look after him at the same time."[39]

It was only with his fourth marriage, to Oona O'Neill, that Chaplin found real happiness. And not surprisingly, he notes that "soon after we married Oona had confessed she had no desire to become an actress on the screen or the stage. This news pleased me, for at last I had a wife and not a career girl."[40] Chaplin had at last found the Edna Purviance of his private life.

More than one reviewer of the autobiography was surprised at the relative silence of Chaplin on his many amours.[41] Yet this is also perfectly consistent with Chaplin's Victorian perspective on idealized womanhood— women were heavenly symbols meant for worship, not for the debasement of sexuality, at least not in print. For as Houghton suggests, the Victorian male had to constantly fight the sexual "tempest of passion," or else be reduced to a "wild beast."[42] After all, that is why he put the female on such a high pedestal.

Chaplin suffered from more than a modicum of this duality, as the telling juxtapositioning of his heavenly screen romances and the messy sex scandals of his private life so vividly demonstrates, not to mention Grey's tell-all autobiography. This is made all the more complex by the fact that the same woman was sometimes involved in both worlds, private and professional. This was the case with Edna Purviance (without scandal), Lita Grey, Paulette Goddard, and Joan Barry. Even Oona O'Neill was originally contacted on a professional basis for a part in a film.

One might even say life imitated art in the dream fantasy of *The Kid*, where the lovely angel tempts Charlie into a damning sexuality. This angel, who is literally made heavenly by way of the story line, is played by Grey. Their subsequent marriage and divorce would be second only to the Barry case in terms of scandal affecting Chaplin.

Though Chaplin avoids commenting on this Victorian male duality in his autobiography, there is an almost provocative tongue-in-cheek reference to it in *My Life in Pictures*. Midway in the volume is a beautiful full-page picture of Harris which faces a far from complimentary full-page picture of an unshaven, completely disheveled Chaplin. He labeled the pictures "Beauty and the Beast."[43]

The same romanticism Chaplin aspired to in his heterosexual relationships can be found in the male friendships, though they were decidedly fewer in number. Douglas Fairbanks was easily Chaplin's best friend, and every reference to him in the autobiography tends to describe Fairbanks as "incurably romantic," or words to that effect.[44] Fairbanks, like the swashbuckler of *Robin Hood* and *The Mark of Zorro* or the dashing all-American of *His Majesty the American* and *Wild and Woolly*, seemed the same nonstop romantic dynamo off screen as well. Chaplin refers to the Fairbanks lifestyle as including everything from serenading wife Mary Pickford with a Hawaiian orchestra at three in the morning to convincing Chaplin to go horseback riding before dawn, though no one else could even get the comedian on a horse.

Chaplin's romanticism is even a more likely reason for his fascination with William Randolph Hearst, whom he described as the personality that had "made the deepest impression on me."[45] While Stanley Kauffmann's excellent review of the autobiography makes a logical suggestion that tight-fisted Chaplin's interest in Hearst was monetary (the comedian does, in fact, note the newspaperman's net worth),[46] a more logical *romantic* reason can be found in a later autobiography reference to Hearst. Chaplin describes Hearst's periodic visits to Hollywood as a time when "the film colony enjoyed an era of *Arabian Nights*."[47]

For a Victorian romantic like Chaplin, Hearst (the man who built a

California castle by the sea in San Simeon) had the irresistible ability to bring a bit of the fairy tale to modern society. Moreover, he successfully compartmentalized the Victorian male's Jekyll and Hyde stance on the female by having an East Coast wife and a West Coast mistress, film star Marion Davies. Chaplin was impressed by the civilized manner in which all parties (Hearst, wife, and mistress) played an adult game of musical chairs around what would be scandal for anyone else, particularly Chaplin. And certainly the provocative complexity Hearst brought to the enterprise by starring mistress Davies in epic costume romances like *When Knighthood Was in Flower* was not lost on the comedian, who as already noted, often found himself utilizing a private favorite in public film projects, though never quite so flamboyantly.

These, therefore, have been some of the more subtle Victorian points of reference with which Chaplin interlaces the book. In contrast, the opening chapters on childhood are much more direct in their homage to a Victorian value system. References to Dickens, by Chaplin and critics alike, run rampant here, but they are seldom applied to the values of the time. Dickens was merely the quality tip of the literary iceberg among Victorian novelists and playwrights, who often specialized in the cult of the child, especially the orphaned child, mixed with a healthy dose of sentimentality.

Chaplin's real childhood, or negation of one, with a father dead from drink and a mother institutionalized for insanity, was certainly a prime candidate for this popular Victorian genre, especially since he was also institutionalized in the orphanage-like setting of Lambeth Workhouse. And as with his friend and contemporary Mary Pickford, who was made to sacrifice much of her childhood for a career, this Victorian cult of the child often reappeared in their later work, though Pickford usually appeared as one of the children (as in *Sparrows*, 1926), while Chaplin was the surrogate parent (as in *The Kid*).

If *My Autobiography* is read from this somewhat sociological standpoint, it still is capable of giving the patient reader some insight into film's greatest comedian. Otherwise, Brendan Gill's observation about Chaplin and the tramp could be applied to Chaplin's whole life, as described in the autobiography: "Having read elsewhere of the tradition of the tramp, . . . we appear to know more about the Tramp than Chaplin himself knows."[48]

Chaplin Viewed by Insiders

Considering the magnitude and length of Chaplin's career, the stormy marriages, the scandals, and the numerous children, it is somewhat surprising that so little has been written about him by Chaplin insiders. The key books of this type are only five in number: Charles Chaplin, Jr.'s *My Father, Charlie Chaplin* (1960); Lita Grey Chaplin's *My Life with Chaplin*

(1966); Michael Chaplin's *I Couldn't Smoke the Grass on My Father's Lawn* (1966); Gerith von Ulm's *Charlie Chaplin, King of Tragedy* (1940), which drew heavily upon the memory of Toraichi Kono, Chaplin's secretary and general man Friday during the 1920s and early 1930s; and close family friend R. J. Minney's *Chaplin: The Immortal Tramp* (1954).

As if by special arrangement, the first three of these volumes cover succeeding decades of Chaplin's personal life, while the Ulm and Minney books attempt general overviews, with the former continuing a personal focus and the latter attempting to balance the comedian's life and career.

More specifically, with regard to the family authors, Lita Grey focuses her chronicle on the late teens and twenties, when she went from Chaplin child performer to the role of Mrs. Chaplin. Lita and Chaplin's son Charles Jr. next examines the thirties and forties, when Junior and his brother Sydney managed to become as close as anyone has to their father. Michael Chaplin, one of eight children from Charles Sr.'s fourth marriage, gives the reader a flower child's perspective of his father in the fifties and sixties.

Lita Grey Chaplin's memoir is a very underrated book, largely because of a marketing campaign that catered to the lowest common denominator; for example, the paperback edition had cover blurbs like "The shockingly candid account of a marriage that became one of the most infamous scandals of all time," and "He had taken her under his wing at twelve—and into his bed at fifteen."[49] Yet the first half of the book, before the ugly divorce proceedings, presents interesting insight into the thoughts and working philosophy of cinema's premier clown, from his ideas on spontaneity to those of director Joseph von Sternberg, who was something of a Chaplin protégé after his *The Salvation Hunters* (1925).

For a parallel outside the Chaplin milieu, Lita Grey's book could be compared with the later biography of W. C. Fields penned by his mistress Carlotta Monti, *W. C. Fields & Me* (1971).[50] The Monti book was also marketed in a sensational manner, yet it offers excellent insight on Chaplin's greatest comedy contemporary.

Unfortunately for Lita Grey, as well as for the reader, she did not have direct access to Chaplin for anything approaching Monti's fourteen years with Fields. The Lita Grey-Chaplin marriage lasted a scant two years. But what is often neglected is the fact that she had a longer professional association with the comedian, going back to *The Kid* and *The Idle Class* (both 1921). And as she tells us, Chaplin's fascination with her even then inspired him to add the dream sequence at the close of *The Kid*, with her occupying the pivotal role of the lovely tempting angel. Grey was also the original leading lady of *The Gold Rush* (1925) and remained so well into the production, until her pregnancy.

Her descriptions of Chaplin on the set in these productions is most revealing, including the touchingly warm description of Chaplin's habit of allowing time to play with the child performers, in a "genuine and passionate" manner.[51] There are also excellent capsule descriptions of key members of the Chaplin entourage interspersed throughout the book. For example, "Henry [Bergman] was Charlie's studio sidekick, an upbeat, perennially jolly man who ran errands, worked in big parts, sat in on the few story conferences held and served in general as a kind of court jester."[52]

As John McCabe has suggested, since Chaplin avoids commenting on his personal relationship with Grey, her remarks on the subject, however true or provocative they may be, must be read accordingly.[53] Yet, the controversial relationship notwithstanding, her book is surprisingly even-tempered toward Chaplin. The darker side of the comedian that is sketched in the biography's second half is often balanced by unexpected positive references, such as her comment about the court action Chaplin took after their divorce to block Grey's agreement with Warner Brothers to star their two boys and herself in a film. She refers to the actual court battle as a "legal tug-of-war" but then adds: "He was right, of course, and I was wrong. I'll always be grateful to him for refusing to let me do it."[54]

The biography is also of special interest in dealing with Chaplin's often idealized conception of women, both on and off screen. As noted earlier, his initial response to his second wife as a contemporary *Age of Innocence* girl says a great deal about his romanticism, as do the cloak-and-dagger methods Chaplin enjoyed in planning their secret rendezvous. (Grey was underage and always chaperoned by her mother.) He was even willing to go so far as to establish a fake engagement with someone else (Thelma Morgan Converse) as a cover for including Grey in their outings.

Some shorter tales of Chaplin's romantic exploits are to be found in Clare Sheridan's *My American Diary* (1922) and *Naked Truth* (1928); Carlyle R. Robinson's "The Private Life of Charlie Chaplin," in editor Frank C. Platt's *Great Stars of Hollywood's Golden Age* (1966; Robinson's essay originally appeared in the early 1930s, after he lost his position as Chaplin's jack-of-all-trades press agent); and Pola Negri's *Memoirs of a Star* (1970). In 1935 May Reeves' *Charles Chaplin Intimé* appeared, based on a short affair she had had with the comedian during his 1931-1932 circling of the globe.

A chronological examination of the insider biographies by family next brings one to the volume by the oldest child of the Lita Grey-Chaplin union, Charles Jr.'s *My Father, Charlie Chaplin*. This is easily the best book done in this category, as well as ranking with any other Chaplin biography. Its superior status is a result of the perceptive insights of a son often saddled with his father's sensibility (but without the iron casing into which Charles Sr. so often retreated in times of stress), as well as its beautiful writing, which often makes arresting metaphorical points before establishing them in fact.

The best example of poetic insight occurs early in the work when the child Charles Jr. first sees his father in the tramp costume and is badly frightened.

The Little Tramp who had made millions laugh had frightened his own small son to tears—frightened him with the thought that the father whom he saw so seldom but still loved . . . had been metamorphosed into something alien. For how completely that familiar face had changed before my very eyes . . . a nature to which I couldn't cling . . . something unreliable that was there and gone again.[55]

Unlike that delightful sense of comic "metamorphosis" that Mast later so aptly used in *The Comic Mind* to describe the meaning Chaplin the performer brought to inanimate film objects, Charles Jr.'s use of the word is directed at the dark, personal side of the character, which could so easily turn the man into a stranger.[56] It is a story of a son who, despite later closeness, always called his father to see if he could visit—even as a child.

Ironically, Charles Jr.'s childhood was at times reminiscent of his father's, from his unstable mother and famous but often missing father to childhood enrollment in a military school that bears a number of parallels with Charles Sr.'s workhouse days, including a traumatic separation from his brother (also named Sydney) and the strict discipline inherent in most institutional upbringings. *My Father, Charlie Chaplin* does not play upon these similarities; in fact, the general tone of the book is both upbeat and pro-Chaplin, but the parallels exist just the same. Because of this, there is an added poignancy in the telling, as if Charles Jr. had applied his father's filmic gift of mixing pathos and comedy to the biography itself.

Chaplin's oldest son, who had the longest direct access to the great comedian among the relatives turned authors, also provides thoughtful commentary on a number of questions often merely touched upon, or given pat answers, in other Chaplin material, from numerous insights on his father's interest in Dickens and in the macabre to some refreshingly new observations on why the tramp remained silent as long as he did. The latter subject concerned a number of perspectives, from Chaplin's concern over his own voice and hesitancy about direct competition with the sound comedians to the trauma of merely "contemplating the death of a very dear though imaginary relative—his alter ego," the tramp.[57] Such additional commentaries on sound give an emotional side to Chaplin's well-taken yet dry intellectual soundings on aesthetics found in his 1931 article "Pantomime and Comedy," from which McCaffrey has excerpted "A Rejection of the Talkies."[58] Charles Jr.'s ability to more fully flesh out such subjects is what makes *My Father, Charlie Chaplin* an exciting book.

Six years after the appearance of Charles Jr.'s book, Michael Chaplin told a rather different story in *I Couldn't Smoke the Grass on My Father's Lawn*. It is a difference that occupies two levels. First, unlike Charles Jr.'s volume, Michael's work is more his own autobiography than a treatise on his comedian father. Second, it presents a somewhat negative (by neglect) view of Chaplin, a father who was not giving enough of his time and who ran a dogmatically disciplined home. These faults are not absent from the oldest son's book, but there they are balanced by the unique status of being Chaplin's child. Michael, Chaplin's first son by fourth wife Oona O'Neill, spends little time on such a balancing act.

If Chaplin often wrote as if he had an open book of *Oliver Twist* before him, Michael was certainly familiar with J. D. Salinger's *The Catcher in the Rye.* As with that novel's central character, Holden Caulfield, Michael Chaplin's story chronicles the flight of a boy-man away from what he sees as the phoniness and injustice of the modern world, which in his case were accented by being the son of a celebrity. Unfortunately, Michael's writing has neither the comic vitality nor the stinging poignancy of Salinger's work, though both focus on the same character—the neglected rich kid "institutionalized" in private schools. In fact, because of Michael's droning, nonstop negativism, Mr. Antolini's attempted pep talk to Caulfield, with its "You'll find that you're not the first person who was ever confused and frightened and even sickened by human behavior,"[59] would be much more appropriately applied to Chaplin's son.

There is an interesting irony at work here, however, in the nature of the rebellion upon which Michael's book is based. Like Caulfield, or Mark Twain's Huck Finn (to whom Caulfield is so often compared), Michael is a child of nature, anxious to leave the phoniness of civilization, a condition that would never merit notation as "Civilization." (Salinger had a predilection for accenting importance by extra capitalizing.)

Without trying for a pun, Michael Chaplin is quite literally a "flower child." (His large dust jacket portrait even finds him sprawled out among the flowers.) "Flower children" is often applied to the pastorally romantic youth of the 1960s who rejected society's "hypocrisy" (an updated word for phoniness, just as "society" was for civilization) by dropping out and returning to nature, via communes or more specialized urban living arrangements. As was often the case in the 1960s, this life-style caused divisions between parents and children; this was the case with Michael and his father.

The irony of the situation derives from the fact that Chaplin's tramp figure is also a pastoral romantic, forever undercutting the hypocrisy in the assumed civilization of the urban setting, particularly among members of high society. The tramp, so often associated with Pan, the figure from Greek mythology who was the god of fields and forests, might also have been called a flower child, both because of his inherently rural view of the city (as something negative and ugly) and his persistent use of a flower motif in the films, forever a sign of the purity and innocence of nature.

Chaplin the father does not, however, seem to share the flower child perspectives of his "child," be this a reference to his biological offspring or to the cinematic one he gave to the world. Thus the Chaplin enigma receives another wrinkle, tempting the reader to describe him with the biographical title "The Mask Behind the Mask," which was originally applied to Peter Sellers.[60]

Because it does not generally provide the background material expected of it—a candid look at the later years of his father—Michael's biography also could be called ironic in the sense that it has a negative affinity with much of Chaplin's own autobiography, which often managed to skirt areas of key interest. This accent on the independent ego is also reflected in the fact that both father and son are billed as the sole authors of their works, while the generally more informative and traditionally constructed texts by Lita Grey Chaplin and Charles Chaplin, Jr., were done in conjunction with professional writers.

While Michael always avoids the big names with whom his father constantly held court, Gerith von Ulm's *Charlie Chaplin: King of Tragedy* returns the reader to the name-dropping tradition of Chaplin's writing. However, unlike the comedian's own travel book, von Ulm's biography allows us a closer personal look at Chaplin the celebrity. This is made possible largely through the assistance of long-time Chaplin secretary Toraichi Kono. The book even opens with a lengthy biographical note on the servant.

In von Ulm's foreword she quotes from Chaplin's March 20, 1939, advertisement in the *Los Angeles Daily News*, where he expressed his determination to produce the controversial *The Great Dictator*. "I wish to state that I have never wavered from my original determination to produce this picture. . . . I am not worried about intimidation, censorship, or anything else."[61] Ulm then appropriates this as her own credo in writing the book, leading the reader to expect the most damning of exposés.

Such a brave stance is hardly necessary, since her writing is generally sympathetic throughout to the point of being in awe of Chaplin. And though there are no single eye-opening revelations, the book is of significance as a composite picture of Chaplin at leisure, from further insights on such diverse people as Thomas Burke and Edna Purviance to some rather comically pointed observations, such as that Chaplin "loves children in the abstract."[62]

While von Ulm, with the assistance of Kono, has written an overview of Chaplin's personal life often steeped in near mythic awe of his creative genius, the biography by the comedian's friend Minney, *Chaplin: The Immortal Tramp*, goes in the opposite direction. That is, while balancing views of both home and career, it seemingly attempts down-to-earth perspectives on just about every Chaplin subject under the sun. In fact, the description "down-to-earth" is pivotal, because the thrust of Minney's book is to present neutralizing, or demystifying, insights on the life and times of Chaplin through 1954. This is best exemplified by both the high number of actual events claimed to have been recycled in his films, such as the celebrated David and Goliath scene from *The Pilgrim* (1923), which was "one of Chaplin's most hilarious private party pieces,"[63] as well as Minney's more straightforward, less dramatic, telling of the comedian's story.

Written by a friend at the height of the McCarthy era and only two years after the United States had rescinded Chaplin's reentry permit, sending him into self-imposed exile, it is not surprising that this is easily the most one-sidedly positive Chaplin biography of the five insider volumes. Its provocatively simplistic and direct style is marred only by the vagueness of Minney's relationship with Chaplin and the absence of any supportive references.

When a biography is done by a friend or family member, formal footnotes are hardly expected. However, it is standard procedure for the author, who enjoys this status due to his unique access to the subject, to include himself in the storytelling framework—to have shared, or even precipitated, common experiences in the individual's life. This is what gives special credibility to the work of Lita Grey, Charles Jr., and Michael Chaplin—a very necessary commodity for someone who is not a professional writer. Minney has no doubt foregone this route in order to focus on a total life and times overview of the comedian and thus not limit the book to whatever was the abridged period of his friendship. While this is perfectly valid, it leaves the reader uneasy at times over the sources of observations, since the author has forfeited his first-person status for the invisible presence of the standard biographer, without the equally standard references this usually includes. As if to underscore the reference problem, there are also periodic minor errors in the book, from wrong dates, such as when *Tillie's Punctured Romance* was released, to a handful of mistaken scene descriptions, like the patrol wagon escape of *Modern Times*, where Minney incorrectly credits the tramp, instead of the gamin, for their joint escape.[64]

Despite these qualifiers, the book is well worth reading, if only to acquaint oneself with the aforementioned insights on the possible origin of several key Chaplin film scenes. And at this level the reader can actually mine his or her own background on some possible inspirations for Chaplin's work, because Minney's wealth of facts is not always linked to a specific film scene. For example, there is a description of Chaplin's early Hollywood interest in boxing, to the point of his even serving occasionally as a second in the ring, but there is no follow-up connection to the comedian's later often brilliant use of the sport in his films, especially the choreographed magic of the fight in *City Lights*.[65]

Chaplin References

There are three key reference texts: Timothy J. Lyons's outstanding *Charles Chaplin: A Guide to References and Resources* (1979); *The Films of*

Charlie Chaplin (1965), which was edited by Gerald D. McDonald, Michael Conway and Mark Ricci; and Uno Asplund's *Chaplin's Films* (1971, translated by Paul Britten Austin).

Lyons has done an excellent job on the most ambitious of projects—a book-length bibliography of Charlie Chaplin. Building upon Glauco Viazzi's *Chaplin e la critica* (1955), the first such book-length collection on the comedian, Lyons has followed the Viazzi model in limiting himself to those works (approximately 1500 in number) in which an in-depth focus is given to both Chaplin's personal life and his work.

The book is divided into six sections, with the meat of the work (114 pages of the work's 232) coming in the annotated guide to the writings on Chaplin (Section 4), which stretch from a 1914 review of *Making a Living*, Chaplin's first film, to McCabe's 1978 biography. Citations are arranged by year, and each annotation is kept "brief and descriptive" (a sentence or less) to encourage further research by interested scholars.

It should be kept in mind, however, that any time you have a selective bibliography (even when the size goes to 1500 annotations) there will be some disagreement about what is chosen. I was reminded of this as I went through the Lyons book and noted a few absent works I had found interesting in my own Chaplin research. For example, in the early years there is a fascinating sociological look at the cultural impact of the comedian, called, appropriately enough, "Chaplinitis," which appeared in two parts in *Motion Picture Magazine* (July and August 1915). More recent is a Spring 1970 Mast article, "The Gold Rush and The General," in the *Cinema Journal*, which is a strong extract from his then forthcoming *A Short History of the Movies*. I note these not as a criticism of Section 4 but as a reminder of what selective implies. (Curiously, the *Cinema Journal* Mast piece is cited in a later reprinting, in McCaffrey's *Focus on Chaplin*.)

The book's five other components are broken down in the following manner: in Section 1 Lyons has given the reader a chronological overview of the 1,500 citations to follow (partly in terms of national biases), as well as expounding on the dual nature of the text—differentiating between Charlie the creator and Charlot the creation.

Section 2 is a time line of the comedian's life; Section 3 is a Chaplin filmography. In Section 5 Lyons lists Chaplin's musical compositions, his writings, and his often neglected other film appearances (usually as himself), as in King Vidor's *Show People* (1928).

The final section is a look at Chaplin's archival sources and distributors, which Lyons calls "notes" because there appears to be neither "one complete source" of Chaplin films nor one archive with a really comprehensive collection of Chaplin literature. By closing in this manner, Lyons is able to further underline the challenge of the opening pages: that further Chaplin work remains to be done, something he expanded upon more fully in a special 1979 Chaplin edition of *The Journal of the University Film Association*.

Lyons also posits, quite justifiably, the sheer size of this bibliography as evidence of Chaplin's unique and ongoing impact not only on film but on world culture in general. Lyons further demonstrates that merely stockpiling information can unlock further Chaplin insights. For example, the time line accents the interesting fact that the initial Chaplin film to appear after the death of his first son (July 7, 1919) was *A Day's Pleasure* (December 7, 1919), which is the comedian's most domestic comedy, where he is in the rare situation, for Charlie, of having a wife and two little boys. This brings added poignancy and insight to what is a rather atypical work.

Preferences on what should or should not appear on a subject time line vary from author to author. But in my opinion two omissions had to do with Academy Awards. Though an entry is made for Chaplin's special "homecoming" Oscar (1972), no mention is made of the other special Oscar he received (1929) for "versatility and genius in writing, directing, and producing *The Circus*" (for the 1927-28 season, the first year for which awards were given). And there is no reference to the only Oscar he won (with Raymond Rasch and Larry Russell) for Best Original Dramatic Score for 1972, from *Limelight*. (The 1952 film was eligible for belated consideration because a Los Angeles theater had never previously shown the film—an Academy rule.)

There are also two time line mistakes concerning Chaplin's father, Charles Sr. The first lists his death as occurring in 1894; yet the general consensus among Chaplin historians of the last decade makes the date 1901 (though *My Autobiography* is rather lax about noting years). The second error concerning Charles Sr. has Charles and his half-brother Sydney living with Sydney Hawks (Sydney's father) and his mistress Louise in 1898. In actuality the two boys were living with Charles Sr. and *his* mistress Louise, though most recent historians hedge on the date.

The book's persistent reference to Charlie as incompetent is equally bothersome, especially in the film synopses: the "inept" laborer of *Pay Day* (1922), the "inept" waiter of *The Rink* (1916). Though Charlie is not without frustrations, each of his films usually provides him with a sizable number of accomplishments. In *Pay Day* he is so handy at stacking bricks that it takes two assistants working at top speed to keep up with him. And as the waiter in *The Rink*, he is able to construct a customer's bill brilliantly by deciphering the various bits of food the diner has broadcast on himself. But these are small concerns in a bibliographical work that brings so much crucial Chaplin material together.

With credentials like these, the Lyons book would seem to cover all options, but such is not the case. *The Films of Charlie Chaplin*, edited by McDonald, Conway, and Ricci, adds a much more thorough synopsis for each film (up to 1,200 words, vs. the former book's 20 to 200 range). *Films* also offers numerous stills from each production, something the Lyons work misses, and, what is possibly of the most importance, includes credited extracts from several of the original reviews for every film.

Editors McDonald and Conway open the text with separate short essays on Chaplin, the former examining the early years of the tramp in sociological and comedy theory terms, while the latter concentrates on a basic career overview. A coauthored essay, entitled "Chapliniana," falls midway in their text and chronicles both the additional film appearances of Chaplin via the editing bench (from legitimate anthologies to counterfeits constructed of old film and new filler) and those of out-and-out imitators who attempted to pass for the comedian.

Uno Asplund's *Chaplin's Films* is on the same order as *The Films of Charlie Chaplin*, with most of its space also devoted to detailed plot synopses and occasional still enlargements. But Asplund's book is more apt to have that additional observation that can make a synopsis such a helpful tool. For example, the commentary on Chaplin's satire of World War I, *Shoulder Arms*, compares his fresh recruit to the good soldier Schweik, the wise fool comedy character of the same period created by Czech writer Jaroslav Hasek.[66] Though the reference is made merely in passing, Charlie/Schweik is a much more appropriate pairing than the standard silent comedy linking of Chaplin contemporary Harry Langdon to Hasek's Schweik.[67]

Asplund's book and *The Films of Charlie Chaplin* are not without occasional errors in the plot synopses, however. For example, both volumes fail to note that the competition for Edna Purviance between Charlie and the city slicker in *Sunnyside* (1919) takes place in a dream, thus negating our hero's apparent loss at love.[68] But such discrepancies are hardly frequent enough to handicap use of the references.

Asplund offers several additional short essays on a multitude of Chaplin subjects: a career overview (with a time line), his imitators and rivals, early censorship, unknown films, false "Chaplin" films, Chaplin film anthologies (legal and otherwise), Chaplin collaborators (with biographies of fellow actors), costumes and comedy types, and footages and running times (with charts) for all eighty-one Chaplin films.

Other reference works that might be of special interest would include John Mitry's detailed *Tout Chaplin* (The Complete Chaplin, 1972, often considered the definitive French text on the comedian), Joe Hembus's *Charlie Chaplin und Seine Filme* (1972), and Lennart Eriksson's "Books on/by Chaplin" (1980), which is an international Chaplin bibliography, arranged by country. Eriksson, who is presently updating his reference, also notes Chaplin books in progress.

Numerous Chaplin books provide additional career data in notes and/or index sections, from Gifford's *Chaplin*, which includes recordings by Chaplin, to the excellent annotated bibliographies of Sobel and Francis's *Chaplin: Genesis of a Clown*; Manvell's *Chaplin*; and McCaffrey's *Focus on Chaplin*. The McCabe bibliography, though not annotated, contains more items than any other biography of the comedian and is a good cross-reference for use with Lyons's *Charles Chaplin: A Guide to References and*

Resources. See also Marcel Martin's *Charles Chaplin* (1966); Pierre Leprohon's *Charles Chaplin* (1970); and Tino Balio's *United Artists: The Company Built by the Stars* (1976), which presents a closer look at the business side of Chaplin and his associates.

SHORTER WORKS

Chaplin Critical Analysis

Any number of essay-length critical works might have been chosen for this section. I have focused on one or more pieces by each of eight different writers who have had a major effect on shaping the study of Chaplin through largely mainstream publication outlets: James Agee, Gerald Mast, Walter Kerr, André Bazin, Robert Warshow, Charles J. Maland, Andrew Sarris, and Stanley Kauffmann. A special bonus of this particular grouping is the often ongoing consistency of tone and style each writer brings to his Chaplin insights. (And though these are the focus authors, I have periodically referred to additional work by other writers.)

James Agee's often anthologized essay, "Comedy's Greatest Era," has been the starting point for serious study of silent film comedy since it appeared in the September 3, 1949, issue of *Life*. It is only logical that a section devoted to shorter pieces on Chaplin should follow suit, since Agee was always strongest in his praise of Chaplin.

It also seems appropriate that the first piece in this section should be from the hand of a poet (as well as a screenwriter, film critic and Pulitzer Prize-winning novelist), because poetry so often comes to mind when studying the art of Chaplin, who was indeed poetry in motion (Figure 17). Moreover, poets have that unique talent of so concentrating praise that it is often only in their hands that we feel secure in the praise of our favorite subjects. Thus Vachel Lindsay once described Chaplin's tramp as "an etching in the midst of furious slapstick," while Carl Sandburg labeled Charlie's unorthodox stance as "east-and-west feet."[69] Agee's celebrated essay often reaches equal heights of description, with none more winsome than his word picture of Charlie's delightful antics as a drunk in *One A.M.* (1916): "the delicately weird mental processes of a man ethereally sozzled."[70]

It was "Comedy's Greatest Era" that firmly established the silent film comedy pantheon of Chaplin, Buster Keaton, Harold Lloyd, and Harry Langdon—a grouping that continues to be reflected in more recent overviews of the period, such as McCaffrey's *4 Great Comedians: Chaplin, Lloyd, Keaton, Langdon* (1968), which, at book length, is the most sustained comparison of the four.

Inclusion of the Agee article in this section is unusual only in the sense that the majority of the other selections focus entirely on Chaplin, or make a more pointed comparison, than the four-part breakdown of "Comedy's

17. The ballet-like grace of Charlie on roller skates in *The Rink,* 1916. (Courtesy Museum of Modern Art/Film Stills Archive.)

Greatest Era.'' But the unique status of this piece, both in terms of its historical precedent-setting credentials and the long-celebrated quality of its prose, make its inclusion a foregone conclusion.

A final key in using Agee as a starting point for this section comes from the fact that though ''Comedy's Greatest Era'' is the highlighted work, this poet-critic wrote a number of other essays on Chaplin that are most valuable, especially his three-part defense and celebration of *Monsieur Verdoux* (examined in Chapter 1), which originally appeared in *The Nation* during May and June of 1947. (See also other articles included in Volume 1 of *Agee on Film.*) I draw attention to this because several of the authors under review in the following pages have also contributed multiple pieces on Chaplin. And though I will focus on what seem to be their most valuable contributions, as I have done with Agee, the selected material will, on occasion, also serve as an acknowledgment of their cumulative contributions to Chaplin scholarship.

An excellent companion piece to Agee's ''Comedy's Greatest Era'' and a logical extension of its focus is Mast's ''A Comparison of the Gold Rush and The General'' (1970). The work originally appeared in the Spring 1970 issue of *Cinema Journal*; it also has been included in *Focus on Chaplin* and Mast's own *A Short History of the Movies*, where it surfaced in expanded form as Chapter 6, "Movie Czars and Movie Stars."

Mast reduces the Agee pantheon to two, comparing Chaplin to his only real artistic rival of the three: Keaton. After opening the essay with general insights into the basic contrasts between their comedy persona, from character goals to their most frequent types of antagonists, Mast narrows his focus to each comedian's most celebrated work: *The Gold Rush* (1925) and *The General* (1926).

The key to their variation finds the former a "comedy of character" and the latter a "comedy of narrative."[71] That is, Chaplin's tramp is allowed any number of minor distractions on the comic journey to the close, regardless of whether the tale is momentarily relegated to a back burner. In contrast, nothing occurs in the Keaton world that does not advance the narrative. With this working dichotomy established, Mast proceeds to drive home his comparison of the two poles of silent comedy, using a descriptive style again reminiscent of Agee.

Also, as for Agee, this focus piece is merely the tip of the iceberg for Mast, who probably has written more valuable criticism on Chaplin, short of actually doing a book on the comedian, than any other scholar in film today. Thus *A Short History of the Movies* also boasts an excellent companion piece to the expanded Chaplin-Keaton comparison in Chapter 5, "The Comics: Mack Sennett and The Chaplin Shorts," which does for the early two-reelers what Chapter 6 did for the features. This proves most insightful when Mast differentiates the uses to which Chaplin and Sennett put four key motifs—cops, the ocean, the chase, and the bum.[72] In each case the Chaplin utilization has a more serious or political flavor, which heightens the comic intensity of Charlie's adventures by accenting the real dangers to which he could succumb, if his comedy magic were to fail him.

To grant Chaplin special status in a general film history text is consistent with earlier watershed overviews of cinema. For example, Terry Ramsaye's provocatively entertaining *A Million and One Nights: A History of the Motion Pictures through 1925* (1926 originally published in two volumes) focuses two chapters on Chaplin, while Lewis Jacobs's long-celebrated *The Rise of the American Film: A Critical History* (1939) devotes a sizable chapter to the comedian.

Mast further expands his Chaplin analysis in *The Comic Mind: Comedy and the Movies*, easily the best comedy overview available on film history. He devotes three detailed chapters to the artistry of Chaplin, examining his career in chronological order, as the titles suggest: Chapter 6, "Chaplin: From Keystone to Mutual"; Chapter 7, "Chaplin: First Nationals and Silent Features"; and Chapter 8, "Chaplin: Sound Films." Rich and varied as these Chaplin soundings are, Mast is the most brilliant in his introduction to the three periods, where he briefly examines the comedian's career, while also pricking some clichés that have long distracted from it, such as the claim that his work suffered from weak stories.

> Chaplin's structures are not stories but thematic investigations—putting the wandering *picaro*, the homeless tramp (or some variation of him) in juxtaposition with a particular social and moral environment. . . . As such, Chaplin's film structures are as "good" as anybody's and better than most.[73]

Just as Mast's *The Comic Mind: Comedy and the Movies* is the best book-length overview, Kerr's *The Silent Clowns* is *the* history of film comedy before sound. And Kerr devotes nine chapters (of thirty-seven) to the tramp figure, one of which indirectly acknowledges a debt to Mast by focusing on a comparison of *The Gold Rush* and *The General*. A complete breakdown of the other Chaplin material reveals the following organization: two chapters on the short subjects for Keystone, Essanay, and Mutual; two chapters on the transition period between shorts and features at First National; and single chapters on *The Circus*, *City Lights*, and *Modern Times*, in which an ever-increasing amount of time is spent on the approaching end of the tramp and the sound deployment that helped precipitate it.

As is the case with Agee and Mast, Kerr is strongest when presenting his views through close analysis of individual scenes in a given work. For example, he notes that at Keystone Chaplin developed "two profitable personal strains. One was the power to confide in the audience directly. The other was the insistence—perhaps it was the first realization—that the best comedy would always be played seriously."[74] Then Kerr proceeds to demonstrate these Chaplin traits in several affectionately detailed examples from various early films, such as *Kid Auto Races at Venice* (1914) and *His Trysting Place* (1914). The reader invariably derives a double pleasure from this approach, enjoying both Kerr's telling and his teaching.

Film theorist and teacher André Bazin was not so prolific in his Chaplin writing as Mast and Kerr, but his essays on the comedian deserve the same kind of recognition granted Agee's "Comedy's Greatest Era." Bazin was the film theorist who rescued Chaplin from being labeled a technically limited artist. Thus the close of Bazin's essay, "The Virtues and Limitations of Montage," is the seminal statement on Chaplin's comedy production techniques.

> If slapstick comedy [early Chaplin] succeeded before the days of Griffith and montage, it is because most of its gags derived from a comedy of space, from the relation of man to things and to the surrounding world. In *The Circus* Chaplin is truly in the lion's cage and both are enclosed within the framework of the screen.[75]

Only with Bazin has Chaplin's comedy of space, his use of long shot and long take, become legitmate in film theory. Chaplin's film world would not exist with traditional editing, which would distract both from the unique ability of his mime and the equally unique setting. This can be seen in Bazin's example from *The Circus*, where Charlie and the lion occupy the same film frame. The comedy is heightened because we know Chaplin is performing the routine or actually taking the risk, as in entering the cage. Editing would have made us question this. Chaplin's decision to film in long shot and long take was wise technically and represents Chaplin's production awareness of the most effective form of presentation for his comedy art. Bazin thus reverses a trend that seems to have started with Rudolf Arnheim in *Film As Art* (1933): to applaud Chaplin despite what was seen as his technical limitations or applaud him for his relatively rare formalistic techniques, such as the apparent seasick scene from *The Immigrant* (1917), where the comedy is derived from camera placement rather than mime.

A large emphasis of Bazin's writing on Chaplin focuses on the myth of Charlie and how a huge public relates to him as a twentieth-century Ulysses.[76] Bazin even applies his thesis to Chaplin films in which the comedian did not play the archetypal Charlie, such as the iconoclastic *Monsieur Verdoux*, discussed in Bazin's "The Myth of Monsieur Verdoux."[77]

Bazin's concept of the "Chaplin myth" has much in common with film theorist Béla Balázs's interest in true personalities of the screen (*Theory of the Film*, 1952), those who consistently play themselves while generating great viewer identification. But whereas Balázs sees this cult of personality as an end in itself, Bazin attempts to expand his cult of myth into less-studied Chaplin territory—the post-Charlie/tramp films, such as *Monsieur Verdoux* and *Limelight*. By doing so, Bazin is able to produce a greater perspective on these late Chaplin characterizations, as well as to explain audience identification. This is no small accomplishment, since one of the characters, Verdoux, is a very active Bluebeard.

> It is the character [of Charlie in *Verdoux*] that we love, not his qualities or defects. The audience's sympathy for Verdoux is focused on the myth [of Charlie], not on what he stands for morally. So when Verdoux, with the spectator on his side, is condemned, he is doubly sure of victory because the spectator condemns the condemnation of a man "justly" condemned by society. Society no longer has any emotional claim on the public conscience.[78]

Like Bazin and Agee, celebrated genre critic Robert Warshow ("The Gangster As Tragic Hero" and "Movie Chronicle: The Westerner") was moved to write an insightful defense of *Monsieur Verdoux*, which originally appeared in the July-August 1947 edition of the *Partisan Review*. And like Bazin's essay, Warshow's is most valuable in terms of observations that can be applied to the whole of Chaplin's career.

> The satiric point of the relationship [the conflict between Charlie and society] lay precisely in this element of fortuitousness and innocence: it *happened* that the Tramp and the society were in constant collision, but neither side was compelled to draw any conclusions from this. . . . After 1933, it became increasingly more difficult to maintain such a picture of the relationship between the individual and his society.[79]

Beginning with the major social changes of the 1930s, this essentially "live and let live" relationship, as Richard Schickel so nicely described it, was at an end.[80] The individual was no longer free to shuffle along oblivious to the actions of a once indifferent state.

It is therefore quite appropriate, as Warshow suggests, that Chaplin's first complete break with the tramp figure produces the murderous Verdoux, who

> carries the world inside him. . . . The opposition between the individual and society has lost its old simplicity. The society has flowed into the individual, and the two have in a sense become co-extensive; the struggle is now an internal struggle, full of ambiguities and contradictions.[81]

Thus, while the tramp is the popular figure, Verdoux is the more challengingly complex, as well as being better adapted to the sinister modern world, even though it will eventually destroy him.

Warshow's "A Feeling of Sad Dignity," which draws its title from a Chaplin quote in *Limelight* (1952), and originally appeared in the November-December 1954 issue of *Partisan Review*, takes a more bittersweet look at Chaplin's career, based upon the hypothesis that the comedian has, until near the end, been asking his audience to ". . . love me, love *me*, poor Charlie, sweet Charlie. . . ."[82]

Though an entertainer's need for love, especially that of a comedian, hardly seems like news, Warshow makes this the basis for a provocative reading of Chaplin's late career. He posits the theory that Chaplin's "feeling of sad dignity" in *Limelight* is thus the result of his having "grown reluctant to submit directly to humiliation" (a Warshow necessity for all "love me" comedian types), because he "is anxious to be accepted as something 'more' than a clown."[83] Consequently *Limelight* actually presents Charles Chaplin "in person" rather than as his normal screen persona, Charlie.[84] Bazin draws the same conclusion about the close of *The Great*

Dictator where the Jewish barber, mistaken for the dictator, gives his impassioned speech. "Underneath [Charlie's mask], as if it were a super-imposition, appears the face of . . . Charles Spencer Chaplin."[85]

Both Warshow essays deal in part with the social nature of Chaplin's work, a subject the comedian was always reluctant to recognize in his films. "There are those who always attach social significance to my work. It has none. I leave such subjects for the lecture platform. To entertain is my first consideration."[86] Yet, author after author has been drawn to issues in Chaplin's work that are difficult to pigeonhole as purely entertainment, from the Progressive Era stance of his Mutual films (see my "Chaplin and the Progressive Era: The Neglected Politics of a Clown," in the Fall 1981 issue of *Indiana Social Studies Quarterly*), to the overview stance of Harry A. Grace in "Charlie Chaplin's Films and American Culture Patterns," in *Journal of Aesthetics & Art Criticism* (June 1952).

The most sustained examination of Chaplin as social critic, however, can be found in Charles J. Maland's Ph.D. dissertation, *American Visions: The Films of Chaplin, Ford, Capra, and Welles, 1936-1941*, published by Arno Press in 1977. This work is in the best sociological tradition of Siegfried Kracauer's *From Caligari to Hitler* (which focuses on German Expression-ism and culture of the 1920s) and Andrew Bergman's *We're in the Money: Depression America and Its Films* (originally written as a doctoral disserta-tion at the University of Wisconsin). Maland's main difference from these two other social historians is the auteur slant he brings to his work—sifting the period through the work of Chaplin, Ford, Capra, and Welles.

Maland's key focus on Charlie is in Chapter 2, "Chaplin: The Tramp Turns Social," in which he analyzes *Modern Times* and *The Great Dictator*. After a detailed look at the former film, Maland is at his most provocative when he suggests that Chaplin's reluctance to retire the "tramp's panto-mime" (silent film in general) was eventually more than balanced by "his desire to say things and make stands almost impossible to convey without talking pictures."[87]

Maland has in part built his argument upon Warshow's premise of the lost innocence in the relationship between the tramp and society, but he draws a lovely quote from the often aesthetically nebulous Parker Tyler to summarize this position:

> Gestures without speech, without sound—this was the fate of the Little Tramp; a fate accepted without protest. Silence was, finally, the supreme armor against the reality of the world. And yet, because a certain professional ego grew strong in Chaplin, the hermetic silence of the Little Tramp became hatefully irksome.[88]

Maland's study examines in depth a number of other issues that have long remained controversial about *Modern Times* and *The Great Dictator*, such as the closing speech of the latter film. Maland questions Chaplin's comment that the speech is the one "the barber would have made," feeling it is completely out of character for this figure.[89] After examining the finale from several perspectives, he concurs with Bazin that the only "reasonable" explanation for the final speech is that "Chaplin himself" is on the platform.[90]

Maland's book, with its high praise of Chaplin (to Maland, *Modern Times*, which originally drew mixed reviews at best, "remains one of the great film comedies ever made"), represents part of the increased critical praise that would again come the comedian's way in the 1970s. Though Chaplin had almost continuously occupied the first chair of American comedy since the 1910s, numerous controversies had obscured that significance in the following decades.

Chaplin had been hurt by the sexual and political scandals of the 1940s and 1950s, especially since he was no longer making films with his most popular comedy persona—Charlie the tramp. (The popularity of Charlie seemingly had helped Chaplin weather similar scandals in the 1920s.) His new, more personalized, film projects were meeting with much less critical and commercial success. And silent comedy contemporaries like Buster Keaton and Harold Lloyd were being given increased critical attention in the 1960s, sometimes at Chaplin's expense. (For example, it should be remembered that McCaffrey's sometimes coolish stance toward Chaplin in his 1968 *4 Great Comedians* is predated by his 1962 dissertation on Harold Lloyd.)

Two contemporary critics whose writing during the 1960s and 1970s no doubt helped reverse the Chaplin critical slide were Andrew Sarris (The *Village Voice*) and Stanley Kauffman (*New Republic* and *Horizon*). Their insightful commentary was in the high journalistic tradition of Agee and Warshow. And like Agee, they wore more than one creative hat: Sarris was a teacher and author of several film books (besides his review collections), while Kauffmann was a teacher-novelist-playwright as well as a film critic. I cite these two critics not because of individual essays but rather because of the cumulative effect of their Chaplin writing.

Sarris is probably the better known, largely through his association with the auteur theory. And as if to counterbalance Kauffmann's preference for the early Chaplin, Sarris is more apt to praise the post-Charlie films, much as Agee and Bazin did. In fact, in a two-part article on *Monsieur Verdoux*, which originally appeared in *The Village Voice* (July 16 and 23, 1964), he refers at length to Agee's earlier defense of the film. He opens the essay with a lovely wish for poetic justice for the late critic, a wish that is both appropriate to, and reminiscent of, Agee's gift for writing.

If this were the most fitting of all possible worlds, Chaplin
would have dedicated the current revival of *Monsieur Verdoux*
to the late James Agee in the generous spirit of Renoir's dedication of the restored *La Règle* to the late André Bazin.[91]

It is a wish that would not have been outside the realm of possibility, since
Chaplin had dedicated the 1942 reissue of *The Gold Rush* (with spoken
narration) to Alexander Woollcott for his high praise of the film during its
initial 1925 run.

Sarris does not entirely agree with Agee's position on the film, "but I
admire the force and lucidity of his arguments."[92] More importantly,
however, Sarris credits Agee's *Monsieur Verdoux* piece with keeping the
film alive during the seventeen years it was not available for exhibition, as
well as for the fact that Agee's once lonely critical stance on the project has
now become the norm.

Later in Sarris's article, when he describes contemporary (1964) Chaplin
by paraphrasing Cocteau—"it is the fate of iconoclasts to become icons"—
he approaches Warshow's *Limelight* commentary on the difficulty for
Chaplin the artist of separating himself from the comedy persona of
Charlie.[93] As if acknowledging this, he suggests that "we consider *Verdoux*
as Chaplin's last dialogue with a drifting audience, and *Limelight* as his first
soliloquy before a departed audience."[94]

The year 1964 also saw revival reviews by Sarris of two other post-Charlie
films: *The Great Dictator* and *Limelight*. He praised "the remarkable
duality of Chaplin as the Dictator and the Barber" in the former film, while
he likened him to "an actor capable of playing Lear, Falstaff, and Prospero
all at the same time" in *Limelight*.[95]

Sarris's best overview of Chaplin came in his provocative later auteur
study, *The American Cinema: Directors and Directions, 1929-1968*. The
comedian is placed in the pantheon group, and once again the post-Charlie
period merits special attention. "Chaplin has been criticized for
abandoning the Tramp, a creature who had engulfed his creator in the
public's mind. Chaplin might be criticized with equal justice for having
grown old and reflective."[96]

In contrast, Kauffmann is uncomfortable with Chaplin's film comedy
persona after the *Modern Times* retirement of the tramp. The duality Sarris
praises in *The Great Dictator* represents more of a breakdown for Kauffmann. He finds the same thing true of *Monsieur Verdoux*; in both films
Chaplin "attempted to play a quite different character but had to fall back
on the tramp to help him."[97] As a true celebrant of Chaplin's tramp films,
he finds the best moments in *The Great Dictator* and *Monsieur Verdoux* to
be throwbacks to earlier works. But since the later films were not originally
conceived with the tramp in mind, his actions are strikingly out of place.

Writing later on a 1973 revival of *A King in New York* (1957) Kauffmann finds the post-tramp duality of Chaplin to be more a schism between the "serious" filmmaker and the clown (shades of Warshow). But whereas Warshow saw this occurring most specifically in *Limelight*, Kauffmann charts the schism as growing ever wider between *The Great Dictator* and *A King in New York*. Yet regardless of which moment, or moments, are pinpointed, there remains the irony that Chaplin had divorced himself from a clown "as if in fear that the clown, whose very persona had won his claims to seriousness, was no longer serious enough—or not explicitly serious."[98]

This schism in Chaplin's work was, for Kauffmann, a result of the coming of sound; therefore it is not surprising that he focused his praise on the comedian's earlier work. And appropriately, his most ambitious essay on this period examines *The Gold Rush*, the film still generally considered to be Chaplin's greatest. Kauffmann feels the film "exemplifies two of the Tramp's most important qualities—innocence and an unwitting faith in the power of innocence"[99] (shades of Warshow once again).

Kauffmann even addresses those revisionist historians that would elevate other silent comedians at the expense of Chaplin. In a 1970 review of a Buster Keaton festival in New York, he labels such action as "nonsense."[100] While he highly praises Keaton (which mirrors Sarris's auteur inclusion of Keaton, with Chaplin, in his pantheon group), the highlight of the essay is his comparison of the two comedians, which complements Mast's previously noted juxtapositioning of the duo in the same year, without rehashing any old points. In fact, Kauffmann's most refreshing observation comes when he examines the more often praised tighter narrative style of Keaton.

> Many of Chaplin's long films have better structures than Keaton's: Chaplin would never have let a film run ten minutes or more, as does *Our Hospitality*, before we get the first hint that it's a comedy. Most of Keaton's pictures are more obviously carpentered together than most of Chaplin's; they build toward a big climax, but they also deliberately delay it.[101]

My only Kauffmann qualifier concerning Chaplin's tramp period pertains to his questioning of *The Gold Rush*'s happy ending, which was alluded to in the McCabe material. Kauffmann hypothesizes that since heroine Georgia is most certainly a prostitute, what kind of post-happy ending life can she give Charlie? But besides the Northrop Frye genre response—that the comedy happy ending is not there to impress the audience with truth or reality but rather to give them what is desirable, a happy ending —the Kauffmann theory is vulnerable to being turned against itself. For example, one might hypothesize that the sad ending of *The Circus*, where Charlie and the troupe part company, cannot last for the tramp because he has proved himself to be a circus clown drawing card. Ironically, it is really the circus that has a sad future ahead, since it was going broke before Charlie joined the troupe and it seems safe to assume it will return to that state now that he has left.

Possibly Kauffmann's greatest tribute to the tramp period of Chaplin's career comes in the anthology he edited (with assistance by Bruce Henstell) entitled *American Film Criticism: From the Beginnings to Citizen Kane* (1972). It is a collection of reviews of important films from the time they initially appeared, covering the first forty-plus years of cinema.

Within this time frame, which encompasses the evolution of the tramp, Kauffmann has selected one, and sometimes two, reviews of every Chaplin feature, from *The Kid* through *The Great Dictator*. Moreover, the earlier short films receive a general celebration through the inclusion of a 1917 *New Republic* essay by playwright Harvey O'Higgins entitled "Charlie Chaplin's Art."

The book represents an excellent collection of early writing on Chaplin, the majority of the articles not having been previously anthologized. For example, only two (from a total of twelve) pieces in the Kauffmann collection appeared earlier in the excellent review section of McCaffrey's *Focus on Chaplin*. Moreover, by reading through the non-Chaplin reviews the reader is given added cultural-critical insights toward the response generated by major filmmaking contemporaries of the comedian.

My comments on Kauffmann represent the last author in this section that I have chosen to examine in some detail. This by no means comes close to the total numerical possibilities on a subject so immense as Chaplin. I would therefore like to briefly suggest *some* additional analytical works of possible interest, starting with material originally written in the silent era.

George C. Pratt's outstanding anthology, *Spellbound in Darkness: A History of the Silent Film* (1966), is a key source for early Chaplin film reviews and behind-the-screen articles on the comedian. Material related to the early short subjects of Chaplin, as well as Sennett, are the focus of Chapter 10, while Chapter 15 is entirely devoted to Chaplin in the 1920s.

Louis Delluc's monnograph-length *Charles Chaplin* (1922) is often cited as the first serious in-depth examination of the comedian, just as Minnie Fiske's essay is consistently given that credit among the shorter works. Delluc's criticism has about it a stream-of-consciousness poetry, such as his labeling of Chaplin as "a genre of his own."[102] But what is most important today is that the work is partially an anthology, drawing commentary on the comedian from such sources as Max Linder, Chaplin's production secretary Elsie Codd, and the comedian himself. (McCaffrey includes material from Delluc in *Focus on Chaplin*.)

My long-time favorite among the early Chaplin literature remains Gilbert Seldes's touchingly insightful essay "'I Am Here Today': Charlie Chaplin," in his equally winsome *The 7 Lively Arts* (1924). The title of the piece is a reference to the caption on the cardboard Charlies that theater owners used to put out to announce a new Chaplin film.

Seldes wrote with the same loving detail—especially about *The Pawnshop* (1916)—that would later characterize the work of Huff and Mast. In fact, it seems most appropriate that in one of the 1957 postscripts, which Seldes has scattered throughout the new edition, he refers to Huff's biography of Chaplin.

Seldes's original text also returns a resounding no to Stark Young's famous "Dear Mr. Chaplin" open letter in the August 23, 1922, issue of *The New Republic* (which is included in Pratt's *Spellbound in Darkness*), where Young suggests that Chaplin retire the tramp figure and essay such classics as *Peer Gynt* and *Liliom*. Seldes responds, "If the literary side conquers we shall have a great character actor and not a creator; we shall certainly not have again the image of riot and fun."[103]

Two early antecedents for Agee's "Comedy's Greatest Era," which in no way detract form its significance, are to be found in Chaper 8 of Iris Barry's *Let's Go to the Pictures* (1926), and Caroline Alice Lejeune's essay on Chaplin in *Cinema* (1931). Barry calls Chaplin "the everyman of the twentieth century," while comparing him with numerous silent comedians but especially Lloyd and Keaton (Langdon is omitted, no doubt because he did not enter feature production until 1926).[104] Barry also manages a brief survey of Chaplin's career to this point, from *Kid Auto Races at Venice* (1914, which Barry describes but does not refer to by title) to *The Gold Rush* (1925).

Lejeune's essay focuses on Chaplin, while referring briefly to the three comedians around whom Agee built his pantheon. The piece is also nicely complemented by a second Lejeune essay entitled "Slapstick," which examines the physical comedy losses sustained by the coming of sound, while including numerous references to Chaplin.

Two additional early articles that represent more tightly drawn Chaplin comparisons with pantheon silent comedians include Harry Carr's psychological study "Chaplin vs. Lloyd, A Comparison" (*Motion Picture Magazine*, November 1922), and Edmund Wilson's contrasting of Chaplin's use of a gag with that of Keaton and Lloyd in "The New Chaplin Comedy" (*New Republic*, September 2, 1925).

Film theorists have been probing the artistry of Chaplin since the silent-film days of Vachel Lindsay. Bazin has received the critical focus in this chapter because of the seminal nature of his commentary on Chaplin's use of film space and the consistency with which Chaplin's artistry matches Bazin's realist theory. But there are other, often formalistic, views of the comedian, some of which have already been touched upon in the first two chapters of this book.

A good starting point for further reading on the subject would be the third chapter of my Chaplin monograph, where I examine his film comedy in relationship with, and its impact on, the theories of the five most influential film theorists: Arnheim, Sergei Eisenstein, Balázs, Kracauer, and Bazin. As sketched earlier in this book, each theorist could be very "creative" in finding ways to include the Chaplin comedy milieu in his film theory structure, such as *realist* Kracauer's surprising selection of Chaplin *fantasy* scenes for special praise in *Theory of Film: The Redemption of Physical Reality* (1960). Consequently the study also provides an example of "Chaplinitis" at the highest level of film scholarship.

Final additions of special interest to this section might include Raymond Durgnat's *The Crazy Mirror: Hollywood Comedy and the American Image* (1969); *Film Comment*'s Chaplin homecoming issue (September-October 1972); and Stuart Byron and Elisabeth Weis, *The National Society of Film Critics on: Movie Comedy* (1977).

Durgnat's *The Crazy Mirror* is an often insightful, often disjointed collection of chapters loosely huddled around the subject of American film comedy. Chaplin's name appears frequently, but the key analysis occurs in Chapter 11, "Aimless Odysseus of the Alleyways." Durgnat's musings on Chaplin are among the best in an often uneven book.

The special issue of *Film Comment* opens with a Chaplin overview by the always insightful Charles Silvers, who runs the Film Study Center at the Museum of Modern Art in New York. Each of Chaplin's features, as well as the feature-length *Chaplin Revue* (a 1959 anthology, released by the comedian, of *A Dog's Life, Shoulder Arms*, and *The Pilgrim* is then examined by a different writer, including such prominent film authors as Stanley Kauffmann, David Robinson, David Denby, and William K. Everson. Unfortunately, because of the then recent appearance of a *Film Comment* piece on *The Circus*, ("David Bordwell on *The Circus*," Fall 1970), this Chaplin critical compilation skips the film. Otherwise the pieces are uniformly good, though Everson seems overly harsh on *A Woman of Paris*, while Emily Sieger, in her essay on *Limelight*, mistakingly suggests that the tramp films portrayed defeat after defeat for Charlie.

The Byron and Weis *Movie Comedy* anthology contains five Chaplin essays, with an overview by Richard Schickel; pieces on *City Lights* and *The Great Dictator* and a comparison with W. C. Fields, all by Roger Ebert; and a piece on Chaplin's films by Bruce Williamson. Schickel's essay is the most lengthy, the most well-known, and the most critical. Written the year of Chaplin's 1972 homecoming, it was possibly too ambitious in its attempt to counterbalance the otherwise nonstop stream of hosannas to the tramp. Schickel's overview originally appeared as "Hail Chaplin—The Early Chaplin" (*New York Times Magazine*, April 2, 1972).

*Chaplin on Chaplin Concerning Comedy Theory
and Pantomime*

"Whenever I meet people who ask me to explain the mystery of 'making people laugh' I always feel uncomfortable, and begin to edge away."[105] In this manner Charles Chaplin begins his 1918 article "What People Laugh At." The apparent trepidation of these lines is quickly denied by Chaplin. His comedy magic, he claims, is merely the result of knowing "a few simple facts about human nature."[106] An examination of his writing, as well as comments attributed to him by his family, finds Chaplin rather reticent, to say the least, on the subject of comedy. That comments on humor were occasionally made by Chaplin even the rather egotistical "What People Laugh At" title implies. But considering his position as film comedy's greatest artist, the longevity of his career, and his propensity to write, Chaplin has left few comments on a personal theory of comedy. Those comments he did make are too often fluctuating, schoolboyish platitudes instead of moments of personal insight. His only consistency lies with his undiminished celebration of pantomime.

Chaplin on comedy is to be the focus of this section for two reasons. First, additional themes that might have been addressed, from his Dickensian childhood to his interaction with the celebrities of every continent, have already been dealt with in the section on books authored by the comedian. Second, through an in-depth examination of the comedian's writing in Chapter 2 of my Chaplin monograph, it was concluded that his views on comedy were best expressed in his shorter works.

The meat of what Chaplin would say on comedy seems to appear early in two magazine articles. The first, which originally appeared as part of "How I Made My Success" (*Theatre* magazine, September 1915), is reducible to the most basic of comedy statements: Comedy is made "by studying my characters and situations in real life."[107] This observation is definitely a good start; one can even link it with Aristotle's "Comedy is imitation of baser men." But the article then ends there instead of marching onto higher ground. Except for an interesting anecdote about studying a real hobo, it is short on comedy and flat on explanation. The article was intended to be an extrapolation upon success, not comedy, so it should not be judged too harshly. (See also Victor Eubank's March 1915 *Motion Picture Magazine* interview/article, "The Funniest Man on the Screen" reprinted in Pratt's *Spellbound in Darkness*, for related material.)

More should be expected of the second key article, "What People Laugh At," especially since it has appeared so often under different titles, without acknowledgment. The May 3, 1919, *Literary Digest* published an edited reproduction of this article as "Charlie Chaplin Says Laughs Are Produced by Rules," while Delluc nearly reproduces the piece verbatim in his celebrated *Charles Chaplin*. And before the English translation of the Delluc monograph was available, *World's Work* ran the material (crediting Delluc) in its February 1922 issue as "How Charlie Chaplin Does It: His Theory of the Comic."

"What People Laugh At" is more informative than "How I Made My Success," quite possibly containing Chaplin's most sustained comedy comments, but it still seems somewhat lacking in personal insights. The strength of the article is in its continuation of the real-life focus of the earlier article, for example, his discovery of a department store escalator, which produced the focus of *The Floorwalker* (1916), or his attendance at a prizefight, which would eventually result in *The Champion* (1915).

The article also touches on another basic comedy tenet: "it strikes people as funny when they see someone else placed in an undignified and embarrassing situation."[108] Probably the hoariest of all comedy tenets, this one is merely a variation of the incident of the man slipping on a banana peel. Henri Bergson noted that philosophers often even took their basic comedy definition from this loss of dignity. "They described the laughable as causing something to appear mean [lowly] that was formerly dignified."[109]

For Chaplin this loss-of-dignity tenet would seem to represent recycled Mack Sennett. It was no doubt a law of comedy drilled into Chaplin during his 1914 film apprenticeship under Sennett at Keystone. That one of Chaplin's examples for this fall from dignity involves "policemen falling down coalholes, slipping into buckets of whitewash, falling off patrol wagons and into all sorts of trouble" would seem to point all the more to Sennett and shades of the Keystone Kops. (At the same time this article appeared—November 1918—a Sennett piece in *Motion Picture Classic*, "The Psychology of Film Comedy," expanded fully on this fall-from-dignity tenet.) Chaplin puts a more personal stamp on this tenet when he takes it a step further: the ridiculous man becomes all the funnier when he "refuses to admit that anything out of the way has happened, and attempts to maintain his dignity."[110] In this explanation he strikes upon the underlying theme of Bergson's *Laughter*, that man becomes comic when his actions become mechanical, whether the fierce physical contortions of Harpo's face every time his ire is raised or the eternal repetition of Jack Benny's verbal "Well . . ." in times of stress.

Again Chaplin has reached a high point in an article, only to close with a letdown. Beyond this he simply notes the use of contrast, such as the physical disparity between the tramp and his personal nemesis Eric Campbell, and that of surprise. Chaplin is once more recycling Sennett. This fact he lets drop years later in his autobiography: " 'The element of surprise and suspense' was a phrase dropped every other day on the Keystone lot."[111]

Chaplin's comment on surprise, though again hardly a new comedy observation, would still have been significant if surprise played a more important part in his work. That is not to deny the humor involved in Chaplin's example, from the beginning of *The Immigrant* (1917), where the tramp is leaning over a ship's rail as if seasick, only to reveal upon turning around that he has been fishing. However, a high proportion of Chaplin's humor is a product of anything but surprise and is instead dependent upon a camera placement that guarantees the audience a full view of Chaplin's ingenuity at every task and with every object. Examples abound: his poker-shuffling finesse in the very same *The Immigrant*, the wrestling match with the Murphy bed in *One A.M.*, the balancing ladder act in *The Pawnshop*, his ability to carry a limitless number of chairs in *Behind the Screen* (1916), his grace on roller skates in *The Rink* and *Modern Times*, his cake-stuffing charm in *A Dog's Life*, his dance with the forest nymphs in *Sunnyside*, the brick-stacking magic of *Pay Day*, his "sermon" on David and Goliath in *The Pilgrim*, the cowardly finesse by which he avoids boxing in *City Lights*, his attempt to serve a chicken on a crowded dance floor in *Modern Times*, his ballet with the globe in *The Great Dictator*, the money-counting dexterity of *Monsieur Verdoux*, ad infinitum. In each case, to deny the audience the full reality would be to deny the humor.

There is, of course, more to surprise than mere camera placement. But even in those Chaplin scenes where camera placement does not make any difference in a comic "surprise," the audience is usually either forewarned of the "surprise" gag or recognizes the routine soon after its onset; for example, the trapdoor scenes of *Behind the Screen*, the abandoned baby in *The Kid*, the cliff-hanging cabin of *The Gold Rush*, as well as the same movie's "Back up, please" photographer who causes Chaplin's fall into steerage, the streamers that resemble spaghetti in the nightclub of *City Lights*, the open basement that the blindfolded roller-skating Chaplin is unaware of in *Modern Times*, the inability of the train to stop precisely at the red carpet in *The Great Dictator*, and in the same film, Chaplin's failure to get rid of the coins in his meal that will "volunteer" him for danger.

Later on Chaplin himself undercuts his remarks on surprise, while championing the use of quickly recognizable material.

> "You can use the unexpected to some extent to get a laugh," he used to say. "But the gag that is sure to go over is the one where the audience has been tipped off in advance. That's why I like to use old gags. . . . [Chaplin then relates the dive into shallow water from *Modern Times*.] It's been done so many times everyone is already familiar with what is going to happen. All you have to worry about is your interpretation."[112]

In the Chaplin exceptions to this theory—for instance in *The Immigrant*—he had no doubt dealt with camera placement that confuses the viewer to prove himself an artistic director as well as a performer. Though Chaplin was almost universally acclaimed as a performer from the beginning, his use of film technique, most specifically long takes and long shots that negate surprise, was generally seen as primitive until the 1960s and the assimilation of realist film theory, as in André Bazin's aforementioned "The Virtues and Limitations of Montage." When film theorist Rudolf Arnheim wrote his formalist *Film As Art*, which indirectly negates realistic silent comedy, in order to praise Chaplin, Arnheim found it necessary to use the same formalistic example Chaplin uses, the scene of apparent seasickness from *The Immigrant*, which is so atypical of his films.

"What People Laugh At," therefore, does have some rocky spots, but for that point in Chaplin's career it seems a most promising early comedy articulation. Ironically, this was to be *the* articulation. Comments on the nature of comedy from his books are not merely disappointing, they are generally absent, or measurable in paragraphs instead of pages.

Quite possibly Chaplin felt justified in claiming to have articulated some personal comedy theory, despite his failure to reveal one publicly, by his opinion that the audience has even less of a grasp of the mechanics of humor. In an article he wrote a few years later (1924), he gives a resounding "no" to the question posed in the article's title, "Does the Public Know What It Wants?" Though he does not take the derogatory opinion of the public that such comedy contemporaries as Mack Sennett and Fatty Arbuckle did, Chaplin is clearly suggesting that while the public does not have an answer, he does. But the closest he gets to disclosing it is, "I prefer my taste as a truer expression of what the public wants."[113] Before it received his full attention in 1924, Chaplin had briefly referred to the audience's inability to articulate a preference in the 1922 article "In Defense of Myself," which is reproduced in Chapter 3 of this book.

Chaplin never really articulated a comedy theory. He either avoided comments on the nature of comedy, while writing voluminously on other subjects, or he touched lightly on the most basic of comic platitudes, often relating them to personal techniques he used but rarely. The answer no doubt lies in the fact that his production technique was anchored in day-to-day improvisation. Though this observation is hardly new, Chaplin himself noted his need for spontaneity in both "The Funniest Man on the Screen" and his first book, although this need was later often downplayed by Chaplin. The downplaying eventually even embraced denial, from the self-confident title of his 1918 article "What People Laugh At" to his 1964 memories of 1918 in his autobiography. "I was beginning to think of comedy in a structural sense, and to become conscious of its architectural form. Each sequence implied the next sequence, all of them relating to the whole."[114]

Chaplin's approach to comedy theory did not openly embrace intuition until his career was over, in contrast with Rosen's observation on Chaplin's general sociopolitical thought, for example, that the comedian consciously opposed a strong use of reason.

This smokescreen on the subject of comedy was the case, anyway, until an interview he gave after his last film, *A Countess from Hong Kong*. For *Life* magazine, it was called "Chaplin: Ageless Master's Anatomy of Comedy," but a more logical title, in light of this chapter, would be "Chaplin: Ageless Master's Confessions on Comedy." From the first page, with "Comedy is essentially something that just comes out of you," Chaplin for once neither avoids the subject nor talks double talk on it.[115] He even admits what could earlier have been read between the lines. "I'm not too interested in why people laugh—only that they do. A lot of my comic business was ad-libbed."[116]

The whole tone of the interview suggests that Chaplin was merely an inspired vessel of comedy, instead of a creating artist. His language at times parallels that of Socrates's dialogue with Ion on inspiration. "In like manner the Muse first of all inspires men herself. . . . For all good poets . . . compose their beautiful poems not by art, but because they are inspired and possessed . . . under the power of music."[117] Chaplin says, "I think creation comes initially out of a mood—music, a calm sea. . . . You don't just come down one morning and begin, because the muses don't work that way. You have to open the gates for them by mood."[118]

Is this just Chaplin playing one more role? No, I think it is a unique revelation by film's most unique clown. There is no real way, of course, of proving it, even by the examination of such nebulous material by Chaplin as I have outlined. But later in this interview is a bittersweet reminiscence pointing in the same direction. Chaplin is discussing the mystery of performing comedy and slips back into his music hall days. He recalls a week when he could do no wrong and performers gathered in the wings each night to watch. "And then I lost it. They said, 'What's the matter? You weren't as funny tonight.' I could give no answer."[119]

Further support for the Chaplin intuition position can be found in the work of the comedian's close friend, poet-critic Max Eastman, whose comedy theory text *The Sense of Humor* (1921) was actually written at Chaplin's elbow. "I used to hang around Charlie's studio and watch him make pictures, learning much of what I put in my book on humor there."[120] And the position Eastman endorses in his theory is, "The sense of humor is a primary instinct of our nature."[121]

While Chaplin's position on comedy theory seemed to fluctuate forever before coming to rest on intuition, his thoughts on the uniqueness of pantomime were consistent throughout his career. Once again, his key observations on the subject seem to be lodged in two early journal pieces that appear at the beginning of the sound era, when pantomime was being unceremoniously retired.

The first is an interview article by Gladys Hall entitled "Charlie Chaplin Attacks the Talkies," which appeared in the May 1929 issue of *Motion Picture* magazine. It is an often overlooked reference, generally going unnoted in Chaplin bibliographies. In the article Chaplin is quick to note how "I loathe" the talkies. "They are spoiling the oldest art in the world—the art of pantomime."[122] He goes on to imply that pantomime is the foundation of all screen art, regardless of the genre. There is also shock that "anyone who can possibly avoid it [sound], does use it, Harold Lloyd, for instance.''[123] (Chaplin no doubt is referring to Lloyd's having completed *Welcome Danger* in 1929 as a silent film, only to extensively reshoot it for release as a talkie later in the year.)

Closely connected to the loss of pantomime were two other pictorial casualties. ''Beauty and sex-appeal'' were being ruined, what he would describe as the appeal of the star system, anticipating Norma Desmond's (Gloria Swanson) *Sunset Boulevard* remark: ''I am [still] big. It's the pictures that got small,'' by twenty-plus years. Sound, by making the performer realistic, did decrease the uniqueness of the star. Cinema would continue to have stars, but after they started to sound like the audience, part of their bigger-than-life mystique disappeared.

''Charlie Chaplin Attacks the Talkies'' was a blueprint for Chaplin's later, better known ''Pantomime and Comedy,'' which appeared on January 25, 1931, in the *New York Times*, and is the second key Chaplin article on mime. Coming almost two years after the first piece, and coinciding with the release of yet another Chaplin silent film, *City Lights* (though there was a synchronized score and sound effects), the comedian again balanced praise of pantomime with an attack on ''talkies.'' McCaffrey's inclusion of the essay in *Focus on Chaplin* is even entitled ''A Rejection of the Talkies.''

''Pantomime and Comedy'' is, however, more methodical in its examination of mime and more realistic in its appraisal of sound. While Chaplin expands upon the universality of silent film and on the history of pantomime in general—both free of the limitation of any one language—he does grant the talking film a certain legitimacy. But it is a legitimacy of ''addition'' (another option for cinema), not a substitution for mime.

His earlier implication that mime is the foundation of all screen art was now boldly expanded to make mime ''the base of any form of drama.''[124] The balance here comes from the recognition that ''I am a comedian and I know that pantomime is more important in comedy than it is in pure drama.''[125]

Chaplin would best illustrate these same points the following month (February 1931) with the successful release of *City Lights*, a film that includes both direct and indirect attacks on talkies, from the sheer audacity of releasing a silent film this far into the sound era to the film's statue unveiling sequence, where Chaplin parodies the frequent voice distortions of early talkies.

The emotional range of *City Lights*, which is actually subtitled ''a comedy romance in pantomime,'' underscores most movingly the center stage Chaplin grants mime in the history of drama. In fact, the haunting close-ups of Chaplin that end the film, when the formerly blind girl first sees the tramp, is the epitome of mime gone beyond laughter. Agee, Mast, and McCabe call it cinema's most memorable moment, a point on which I would concur.

Chaplin's references to pantomime do occur more frequently than those on comedy theory, possibly because of the comedian's career-long consistency on the subject. Thus one of Chaplin's most revealing comments on pantomime occurs in Henry King's brief article, " 'Movie' or 'Talkie'?" (1929).

> I can say more with a gesture than I can with words, because the audience finishes the gesture for me. Where I can only look sorry they will supply for me all the words that were ever said when they were sorry, all the sad things in their lives, and all the sad things they ever read; and I can have them crying not because of anything I do so much as because they see me sorry and begin to feel sorry for themselves.
>
> For the word "sorry" you can substitute the word "happy" or "frightened" or "worried"—or what you wish."[126]

Because Chaplin more frequently touched upon pantomime, the most accessible source for his references on the subject is the comedian's auto-biography, especially the sections on the productions of *City Lights* and *Modern Times*. But even the Chaplin article included in Chapter 3 of this book, "In Defense of Myself," has an anecdote about pantomime and a non-English-speaking audience (the Channel Islands).

As with the focus articles on comedy theory, Chaplin's writing on pantomime is best placed in perspective when compared with the Meryman interview, "Chaplin: Ageless Master's Anatomy of Comedy." But in this case the interview demonstrates Chaplin's long-time consistency on the subject. "Pantomime to me is an expression of poetry, comic poetry. I knew that in talking pictures I would lose a lot of eloquence."[127]

Chaplin's Working Style

As a comedy theory based on intuition suggests, the key to the Chaplin production story is his day-to-day improvisation. His off-the-cuff approach is usually not absent from film histories, but is often buried under an avalanche of materials on the huge Chaplin shooting ratios or his sporadic shooting schedules. Ratios and schedules are rather misleading because Chaplin's excess film footage was not limited to multitakes of the same scene with miniscule differences; he often pursued several different potential directions for his character, just to end up using one. This point Chaplin indirectly dealt with from time to time when he spoke of someday releasing an anthology of never before seen outtakes (a project on which film historians Kevin Brownlow and David Gill are currently working). The Chaplin production approach might best be equated with that of documentary filmmaker Robert Flaherty; both shot film to an excess, but their shooting usually followed a wide panorama of possible alternatives.

The most revealing comments on Chaplin's productions and spontaneity are those made by his family and/or coworkers; for example, second wife Lita Grey Chaplin, who was part of the production of *The Kid* and *The Gold Rush*, noted that "he extemporized a great deal, having learned from experience that spontaneous thoughts for a scene can sometimes be the best ones."[128]

The spontaneous Chaplin could, at times, even take on mysterious qualities; for example, his son Charles Jr.

> noticed how he always spoke of himself in the third person, as though he were two people—one just the commentator, the other the real person who did the things and won the applause, and who was the Little Tramp.[129]

On rare occasions Chaplin might even be made to extrapolate about what could be called these gifts of inspiration.

> For me he [the tramp character] was fixed, complete, the moment I looked in the mirror and saw him for the first time, yet even now I don't know all things there are to be known about him.[130]

And at the height of his career, just after the release of *The Gold Rush*, he even confessed to journalist Harry Carr that his filmmaking was "pure instinct. . . . I don't figure it out: I just know it is right or wrong."[131]

A number of sources examine Chaplin as director, with his "pure instinct approach," but four sources would seem to be of primary importance. These include the comments of his secretary Elsie Codd in Chapter 5 of Delluc's *Charlie Chaplin*, "The Method" (see also Codd's *Charlie Chaplin's Methods*, 1920); Adolphe Menjou's observations on *A Woman of Paris* in his autobiography, *It Took Nine Tailors* (1948); the periodic Chaplin production references by film pioneers in Kevin Brownlow's *The Parades Gone By* (1968), particularly in Chapter 44, "Chaplin"; and Timothy J. Lyons's masterful weaving of two previous interviews with long-time Chaplin cameraman Totheroh into the lengthy *Film Culture* article in Spring 1972 entitled "Roland H. Totheroh Interviewed: Chaplin Films."

Codd's general observations on the comedian present a host of Chaplin characteristics that changed little in the ensuing years. His comedy ideas came slowly; he was even apt to go "fishing" until an "inspiration" struck. During such periods it was hard to live with him. But once an idea was decided upon, he was impatient with any production delays, such as set construction, that kept him from his work. Chaplin's mood fluctuations during productions earned him the nickname "Melancholy Dane." (See Henry F. Pringle's "The Story of Two Mustaches," in the July 1940 *Ladies' Home Journal*.)

He was happiest directing the players and demonstrating all their actions. "Without exaggeration I think I can say that he has played every character in every one of his comedies."[132] His key instruction was "Don't act—be "sincere," which coincides nicely with Menjou's more poetic reminiscence of director Chaplin saying, "Don't sell it! Remember, they're [the audience is] peeking at you."[133]

Chaplin checked rushes the morning after the film was shot, and then again in a week or ten days to measure his first impression. (See Robert Van Gelder's "Chaplin Draws a Keen Weapon" in the September 8, 1940, *New York Times Magazine*). He disliked using titles, feeling the public paid to see, not read, film. Totheroh later revealed that the titles that did appear often covered continuity gaps.)[134]

Codd closes with Chaplin's use of the unannounced sneak preview, what was then called "trying it on the dog," to see how the film might be improved prior to going into general distribution. (In the days before a sound track was physically part of the finished print, it was technically and financially much easier to make changes.)

Trying it on the dog would seem to represent a mild contradiction for a filmmaker who, in articles such as "Does the Public Know What It Wants?" found it more appropriate to follow his own everyman tastes in the construction of his comedies. Nevertheless, giving the public a chance to react to his film was evidence of his instinctive production approach.

Menjou's comments on *A Woman of Paris*, which made him a star, provide excellent insights from a performer subjected to the directing intensity of Chaplin. To Menjou the comedian had the ability to "inspire other actors to perform their best."[135] The inspiration was reinforced by "Chaplin's devotion to perfection. It was not as though we were working for a salary; it was do or die for alma mater. The actors and the crew became a team trying to make the best picture it could."[136] Menjou was also impressed by the almost "country store" look and feel to the Chaplin studio, which was so much more humanistic than the already factory-like settings of the other Hollywood production centers.

Chaplin's demands for perfection often necessitated dozens of retakes for a scene, besides rehearsals—one more apparent contradiction of the instinctive comedian as director. Yet, as Elsie Codd noted, this often meant "he has merely recorded a certain number of variations on a single theme, . . . [seemingly from being] struck with a sudden new idea when the cameras have finished recording a scene."[137]

When no ideas would come, Chaplin either came in late or not at all. Described by Codd as "fishing" trips, these times were not at all uncommon. Menjou even described a color chart guide Chaplin's staff applied to the comedian's clothing each morning to measure his mood. For example, green was bad, gray was in-between, and blue with pin stripes was good. Menjou felt this color psychology was overrated, but similar clothing guide stories are found in other Chaplin material.

Terry Ramsaye's comically insightful "Chaplin—And How He Does It" (in the September 1917 *Photoplay*) probably described best a production setup in which assistants were reduced to charting potential shooting efficiency via the daily haberdashery selectons of the boss. "Mr. Chaplin himself does not know when the next one [tramp film] will happen. If he knew how to make one he would quit waiting and do it. Chaplin comedies are like the rare jewels of earth, they are to be found but not made."[138]

An instinctive director is more open to happenstance during production; thus accidents are sometimes mentioned in these Chaplin filmmaking commentaries. Menjou remembers one such incident during *A Woman of Paris*, when his unintended dropping of a shirt collar "gave Charlie an idea for a later scene in which the maid accidently dropped a collar and thus disclosed to the girl's former sweetheart that she was living with Revel [Menjou's character]."[139] Kevin Brownlow later called this the "most celebrated scene" in the film.[140]

Chaplin also utilized accidents during actual shooting. "In the making of a comedy I usually leave the mistakes in, as there is a certain spontaneity, and sometimes the very recorded annoyance that the wrong thing caused proves funny."[141] He uses as his example a scene from *The Pilgrim* where his flat-brimmed clerical hat is blown off unexpectedly. Initially upset, Chaplin had the scene reshot with the hat made to stay in place. But the subsequent comparison of the two favored the unexpected laugh generated by the displaced hat. Chaplin might have added that since his role had him masquerading as a dignified man of the cloth, the accident was consistent with a key satirical theme of *The Pilgrim*: the sometimes pompous nature of both churchmen and overly religious people.

Menjou's comments on the comedian as director are consistent with the observations of Chaplin leading ladies, from Edna Purviance in the early years to Dawn Addams in *A King in New York*, the last heroine of a film with whom he would star. Purviance, who starred in more Chaplin films (thirty-five) than any other heroine, noted both his improvisational method and the learning experience the performer was privy to while working with him. (See especially Maude S. Cheatham's article about Purviance, "A Star Who Longs for Pretty Clothes," *Motion Picture Classic*, November 1919.) As with Elsie Codd, Purviance describes Chaplin acting out each performer's role. Nearly forty years later Addams would second each of these points. (See John Francis Lane's interview with her, "My Life as Chaplin's Leading Lady," *Films and Filming*, August 1957.)

Brownlow's work, with its lovely metaphorical title, *The Parades Gone*

By, covers numerous Chaplin items I have dealt with already, from his use of the spontaneous to his taking time off from a production to obtain ideas. But the most intriguing segment is Gloria Swanson's 1966 reunion with Chaplin on the set of *A Countess from Hong Kong* (1966), where she observed him directing Marlon Brando and Sophia Loren. Chaplin's direction was just as it was in Codd's 1922 description: he tutored the performers' every action. But unlike the vast bulk of his earlier work, he neither starred in this film nor directed a cast of young, eager, about-to-be-molded Chaplin "team" players. Swanson nicely captured the inherent tension being emitted by Academy Award-winning method actor Brando as Chaplin closely instructed him in the taking of an Alka Seltzer. Chaplin's striving for perfection had created periodic tensions in earlier films; for example, Menjou reported a kissing scene in *A Woman of Paris* that required 150 takes. (With kissing take after kissing take Menjou's thoughts had quickly turned from delight to disillusionment as he began to question his credentials as a screen Don Juan.) But incompatibility between a Chaplin player and Chaplin direction had never been quite so apparent on the screen as it was with Brando in *A Countess from Hong Kong*.

Of the four highlighted production sources, Lyons's interview is the most arresting, because Totheroh was with Chaplin from Essanay days (1916) through *Limelight* (1952). After Chaplin's 1952 exit from this country, Totheroh spent two additional years doing special assignments for the comedian before retiring.

Totheroh contributes both new and old material and often adds more detail to the most familiar stories. For example, when dealing with Chaplin's weakness for improvisation, Totheroh notes that everybody had to be on the set through the complete production, because the comedian never knew just when he would need someone or even whom.

One of the most surprising Totheroh revelations also qualifies as another apparent Chaplin contradiction—the comedian's often cavalier attitude toward continuity, even though everything else had to be perfect.

> We would shoot thousands and thousands of feet of film; but if it wasn't just right, we'd shoot it all over again. [Yet] sometimes he'd make mistakes, continuity mistakes. I'd say to him, "You left with the cane in your right hand instead of your left," and he'd say, "They're not paying attention. That's a lot of nonsense. Doesn't mean anything."[142]

It is hardly news to a Chaplin viewer that continuity mistakes exist in his films. Even his scene of scenes, the close of *City Lights*, suffers from a continuity problem regarding the correct location of the flower. It is more his superiority to the mistakes, than the mistakes themselves, that is surprising. Yet there is a Chaplin defense. During the production of *Sunnyside*

Totheroh had informed Chaplin of a continuity problem, only to receive the reply: " 'Take it, Rollie, they'll never notice it; they'll be busy watching me.' Sure enough, he was right."[143] I myself must confess that I have rarely caught a Chaplin continuity problem on the first screening. This does not make Chaplin's toleration of such mistakes legitimate, but it does put his production priorities in sharper focus.

Totheroh surveys a host of other Chaplin subjects: Henry Bergman, yes-man and frequent actor in the comedian's films; Chaplin's need to always have someone with him, like a "bodyguard"; his lack of patience with mechanical devices; the expanded role of the cameraman in silent cinema; variations in film speed for Chaplin's silent comedy; a highly critical view of half-brother Sid Chaplin; the cloak-and-dagger intrigue of keeping the negative of *The Kid* from being attached, with Chaplin's other assets, during his divorce from Mildred Harris; the special effects Totheroh devised for the cabin scene in *The Gold Rush*; the use of miniatures in *Modern Times*; and Chaplin's need to be a "teacher" in private life as well as in production.

A number of other production sources help flesh out the topic. Early examples include James E. Hilbert's "A Day with Charlie Chaplin on Location" (*Motion Picture Magazine*, November 1917), which chronicles the frustrating efforts of the comedian and crew to get the opening footage for *The Adventurer* (1917). The article is meant to be comic as well as revealing, and thus closes with the topper that it is Friday the thirteenth. The difficulties connected with location shooting on a film where such footage will be of minimal use also anticipate the much more arduous location work necessary for the opening of *The Gold Rush*.

Harry Carr's "How the Great Directors Work" (*Motion Picture Magazine*, May 1925) is a not always complimentary look at the comedian, as a director steeped in emotional perfectionism. Chaplin is just one of several directors surveyed.

Egon Erwin Kisch's "I Work with Charlie Chaplin" (*Living Age*, October 15, 1929) is an entertaining yet modest look at a Chaplin production. The title promises more than is delivered, since Kisch is actually a German visitor to the Chaplin set whose views are solicited during the production of *City Lights*. For example, over a week is spent on the subtleties of putting across the reason why the blind girl thinks Charlie is a rich gentleman after their first meeting.

Mack Sennett's autobiography, *King of Comedy*, provides insightful commentary on Chaplin's 1914 Keystone beginnings. The main Chaplin focus is to be found in Chapter 14, "Discovering Charlie Chaplin" and Chapter 16, "Poetry in Slapstick." Sennett praises the comedian's dedication to his work, while noting his independence even then. "He would agree to a scene as I outlined it [where Sennett directed], then discombobulate me by doing everything some other way."[144] However Sennett agreed that on the whole I think he was correct in omitting our three main trademarks, the Bathing Beauties, the chase sequences, and the pies. Anything that diverts the camera's eye from Chaplin himself is likely to be a waste of celluloid. His style is intimate, not panoramic—the one-shot instead of the crowd scene. We understood that early in the game.[145]

How "early in the game" this difference was recognized remains rather nebulous, but there is no doubt Chaplin's comedy depended on a slower pace and a much more deliberate characterization. Still, the year with Sennett represented Chaplin's production apprenticeship. The comedian was able to make a large number of films (thirty-five) in a short period, giving him the experience to move from film novice to director relatively early in his tenure with Sennett. And Chaplin was able to draw some production habits directly from the comedy producer, from the use of improvisation to focusing upon everyday events for subject matter.

Two years prior to the Sennett book, several articles appeared heralding a unique behind-the-screen look at a Chaplin production. The work in question was *Limelight*, and two of the best pieces were "How Mr. Chaplin Makes a Movie" by Thomas M. Pryor (*New York Times Magazine*, February 17, 1952), and "Chaplin at Work: He Reveals His Moving-Making Secrets" (*Life*, March 17, 1952), both of which boasted large photo layouts.

Such sessions always had been at a premium, since Chaplin was ever afraid of having material stolen, especially since his films were usually in production so long. A comic scene he might have originated could have been incorporated into someone else's quickie picture and appear on screen prior to the Chaplin film.

The more serious tone of *Limelight* no doubt minimized Chaplin's stolen gag fears. But more importantly, this open house gesture by the comedian was certainly an attempt to dissipate some of the political and sexual controversy that had been overshadowing the public's reception to his work since the 1940s. (One example was the shocking treatment he was accorded at a 1947 press conference for *Monsieur Verdoux*, reprinted in *Film Comment*, Winter 1969).

The criticism had been so severe that the *Life* article in question saw fit to protect itself with an opening page disclaimer. "It is with Chaplin the filmmaker that these 11 pages of LIFE are almost entirely concerned—not with Chaplin the public figure, whose political views and personal life have in past years scandalized many people."[146] The *New York Times* piece did not carry a disclaimer, but it did hypothesize about Chaplin's need to "ingratiate himself with the public."[147]

Despite these opening qualifiers, both articles are insightful in three ways. First, they document that Chaplin was continuing a number of production techniques first employed in silent cinema. For example, as *Limelight* producer and director, he still attempted to keep a production finger in every pie. And just as he was still interested in improvisation, continuity continued to be a lesser concern.

Second, the articles provide new input into some of these same long-standing Chaplin production habits. Thus he confesses, "I wouldn't do all this work myself if I didn't enjoy it. I am naturally pedagogic. It's not the nature of the beast to let someone else do it for me."[148] (This takes one beyond the mere bared ego of a rare previous workaholic explanation: "I can't shake off the belief that no one I can employ knows as much about making a picture as I do.")[149] Chaplin's de-emphasis on continuity also merits further explanation.

> At one point in the ballet sequence [of *Limelight*] his assistant director, Robert Aldrich, called to an aide before the cameras started to turn: "If anything goes wrong technically give me a signal." To which Chaplin promptly appended: "We'll stop if anything is *esthetically* wrong." Chaplin later told his visitor [author Thomas M. Pryor] that "if the audience is so intent on watching technique that people become disturbed if you come into a scene from the left in one shot and from the right in the next, then you are not entertaining them. If the picture is good enough they should be too absorbed in the story to notice."[150]

Third, some production information is provided on less-documented material, such as the laborious process of composing a score when you cannot read music—Chaplin hired a musician who could transcribe his hummed melodies into notes. And his first manuscript of the *Limelight* story ran 750 pages; this followed a procedure often recommended now in texts on script writing: "He found himself writing full biographies of his main characters, describing their childhood and their family life. Most of this material was discarded in the final version. 'Yet,' Chaplin explains, 'I was able to build my characterizations on those pages thrown away.' "[151]

There are moments in each of these articles when enthusiasm for the unfolding comedy almost makes the reader forget those somber openings. For example, the *Life* essay is delightful when it describes the magic moments of "patient improvisation" as Chaplin and Buster Keaton develop a musical skit as an acrobatic violinist and a nearsighted pianist. There is even an appropriately whimsical close to this historic event (their first and only teaming), as one reads, "Stagehands, dancers, musicians sat in bemused groups breaking into laughter, applauding as they watched a show no one else would ever see."[152]

It has often been observed that the real treat of a Chaplin production was what did not get recorded: the comedian rehearsing, whether he was playing his own part or that of another character. Gloria Swanson's Brownlow piece called it a loss to film that such moments were never recorded, while Dawn Addams described the opportunity to witness such an event with detailed fascination.

> Chaplin rehearsing his own part was a joy to watch. I used to go on the set every day, even when I was not working—something, I might add, I have never done before. I did not want to miss a single moment of Charlie at work. Although he had worked out most of his gags beforehand, he still kept on improvising and changing moves till he was satisfied.[153]

Chaplin had a special magnetism when it came to directing and inspiring his actors. But it has sometimes been suggested that he did not adequately share the credit for the success of his films with his production assistants. Some articles have implied that for a non-Chaplin idea to be accepted by the master, it had to first be refused by the comedian (planted, as it were, in his mind), so that he could "think" of it later.

The most ambitious revisionist look at the subject occurs in Jack Spears's "Chaplin's Collaborators," which originally appeared in *Films in Review* (January 1962). It was later revised and expanded into chapter seven for inclusion in Spears's *Hollywood: The Golden Era* (1971).

Ironically, Spears undercuts the key focus of his work on the first page, noting that Chaplin was most dependent upon his assistants during his rare ventures into drama, while

> His assistants on his tramp comedies, an area in which he felt completely sure of himself, were, by and large, a court jesterate of yes-men who merely catered to his ego—but who absorbed his comedy techniques for use later in their own careers.[154]

Spears's piece is important, however, for its excellent capsule overviews of key Chaplin assistants, and their film activities after leaving the comedian. His best and most detailed look at what the article would consider Chaplin production limitations concerns *Monsieur Verdoux* and the assistance of Robert Florey. Florey, also the subject of the book's final chapter, was a Chaplin friend amazed at the comedian's disregard of many standard production conventions. From a production textbook stance, much of what Florey imparts is valid, and Chaplin seems to have treated him shabbily in the film's final credits. But there is also a sometimes limited understanding of Chaplin's comedy. For example, when shock is expressed that Chaplin still often photographed actors in full figure, the comedian's reasoning, "I act with my feet as much as my head," is referred to in a deprecating manner.[155] Yet the comedian is merely articulating in a pedestrian way what Bazin would later recognize as the unique demands of Chaplin's comedy of space. And as Sarris observed, "the apparent simplicity of Chaplin's art should never be confused with lack of technique."[156]

Chaplin's World View

Terry Ramsaye once closed a Chaplin article with the following tongue-in-cheek summation:

> True to my promise I have set forth the complete science of Chaplinism. Do not think that Mr. Chaplin knows all these things. He can not and does not. Mr. Chaplin is not an organized thinker or worker. If he had a correct system of mental operation and knew how to run himself as a producing machine he would be a failure. Science knows a lot about proteins and carbohydrates but the hen still controls the egg market. It is so with Chaplin comedies.[157]

Ramsaye's hypothesis on Chaplin anticipates by decades the chicken story celebration of the irrational with which Woody Allen chose to close *Annie Hall* (1977): a man tells a psychiatrist that for years his brother has believed he could lay eggs, and when the doctor asks why the brother has not been institutionalized, the man says they needed the eggs. Chaplin, like the man who needed the eggs, had a world view very much based in the irrational.

Much of the already reviewed Chaplin literature has suggested this, from the improvisational shooting methods to the heart-on-the-sleeve romanticism. But there are numerous writings that further document this view. One of the more interesting actually offers a title that might be the subheading for this section: "A Man with Both Feet in the Clouds."[158]

There are two key works, however, that offer unique credentials as a framing structure for the subject: Thomas Burke's celebrated Chaplin essay "A Comedian," from the 1932 *City of Encounters*, and Philip Rosen's "The Chaplin World-View," from the Fall 1969 *Cinema Journal*.

The first is an early account by a Chaplin friend whose similar London childhood initially drew the two together. Like the Chaplin philosophy, or lack of a philosophy, that it chronicles, the essay wanders freely over the private side of its subject, enriched by the artistic kinship of author Burke, whose writing had already inspired Chaplin hero D. W. Griffith. (Burke's *Limehouse Nights* was the source of Griffith's much-praised *Broken Blossoms*, 1919.)

"The Chaplin World-View," which did not appear until after the close of the comedian's career, was written by a young, scholarly American student of film. The essay is as rationally methodical as Burke's is disjointed. Not privy to direct subject access nor able to trade upon an established writer's persona (both of which Burke utilizes), Rosen sifts through a wide assortment of key public (published) Chaplin philosophical references. But despite such different gestations, both pieces document the generally irrational nature of the comedian's world view.

Early in Burke's essay is the observation that Chaplin "does not yet know himself; he has found nothing in life to hold onto. This might explain some of the puzzling points about him. It might explain why he is unknowable."[159]

Burke proceeds to describe this twentieth-century sphinx:

> He is often as kind and tender as any man could be, and often inconsiderate. He shrinks from the limelight, but misses it if it isn't turned upon him. He is intensely shy, yet loves to be the centre of attention. A born solitary, he knows the fascination of the crowd. He is really and truly modest, but very much aware that there is nobody quite like Charles Chaplin.[160]

Burke's Chaplin collage presents an artist whose only consistency seems to be inconsistency itself. In fact, Burke hypothesizes that the comedian "deliberately tried" to create a "splendid tangle of Chaplin Legend."[161] Others have suggested much the same, notably Charles Chaplin, Jr., in *My Father, Charlie Chaplin*. But it is also between the lines in Chaplin's own writing, such as the provocative title he chose for the article "In Defense of Myself," which is reprinted in this book. While the title implies "I am different" and seems to anticipate the Chaplin controversies of the 1940s and 1950s, when an article of defense would seem most fitting, "In Defense of Myself" is an interesting but innocent 1920s look at his career in comedy, miles from the controversial.

Burke's lengthy essay also chronicles many other elements of Chaplin duality, from the capitalist who flirts with the Left to the humorist who likes being "morbid." ("It does me good. I thrive on it.")[162] Eventually the comedian's affinity for the irrational seems best summed up by a Chaplin reference from something Burke had already written about him: "I live on my emotions."[163] Burke later fleshes this out by observing: "Not only has his life been a drama to the onlooker; he does his best to make it a drama to himself. . . . He dramatises every event of the day. He stands in the wings watching his life."[164]

This ability to step outside of himself for personalized drama would later be echoed by Sarris in *The American Cinema*, when he would note the "sublime egoism" of Chaplin imagining his own death in *Limelight*. And one of his many lovers, Pola Negri, would describe Chaplin's attitude in terms of the same personalized drama in her *Memoirs of a Star* (1970).

Rosen's reinforcement of Burke's assessment of the irrational nature of

Chaplin is posited in a most scholarly, methodical manner, with thirty-seven years of additional material from which to draw, often directly from Chaplin's own writing. Though Rosen does not explore the comedian's long-time facade of rationalism toward comedy theory, his work is the most definitive examination of Chaplin's often irrational outlook.

Rosen's thoroughness traces the comedian's inconsistencies and dependence upon intuition through several world-view "isms," from his romantic distrust of the intellect to his periodic flirtations with determinism (sympathetic concern with the effects of poverty) and individualism (the everyman ability to rise above that poverty). And while Burke eventually lodges the Chaplin menagerie of inconsistencies in the comedian's proclivity for personalized emotional drama, the key for Rosen lies in Chaplin's persistent demand for freedom.

> The only socio-political (as opposed to artistic) ideal which Chaplin seems to have actively, consistently, and consciously pursued throughout his turbulent life is that of personal independence—for himself. And as many critics noted of his famous tramp, it was an independence so extreme as to possess anarchic overtones.[165]

Thomas M. Pryor nicely describes the same demand for freedom in Chaplin's professional life.

> He simply has an innate contempt for anything he believes to be interfering with his complete freedom of expression. All his life Chaplin has been in revolt against restricting forces, and his comedies, even in the days when he played The Little Tramp, exemplifed this spirit of rebellion.[166]

There were also comic sides to this rebellion; for example, because of the rigidly scheduled time-clock nature of his early theater and film work, he later "refused to be told what day of the week it was. . . . He would not carry a watch."[167]

While an irrational stance (intuition) was the key to the general Chaplin world view, certain subjects to which it was applied were of consistently more importance than others: his number-one priority for work, his idealization of the woman-child, his expression of power through a teacher-student relationship, and his self-consciously "loner" pose. For example, ranking his work above all else was often the source of his seemingly irrational relationships with friends and lovers, especially the latter. After subjecting his normally young, impressionable romantic object to the considerable Chaplin between-production charm, he would all but abandon her once he returned to a film project. "When I am working, I withdraw absolutely from those I love. I have no energy to give them."[168] Though often the subject of rather somber retellings by those involved, such as Lita Grey Chaplin, there were comic sides here, too. Alistair Cooke recounts a Chaplin lecture to Paulette Goddard on the "decadence of night life," after which

> Paulette saw her [party] vision collapse like the Ghost of Christmas Present. A tear ran down her enchanting face and her eyes fairly popped in frustration as she said, "What are we going to do evenings—stay home and *write theses*?!" "Well," Chaplin replied, "One night a year is enough of that [nightclub] rubbish."[169]

This workaholic nature even represented part of his block against letter writing, as he once confessed to Upton Sinclair. "You know I don't write letters! I think one reason . . . is the spirit of the merchant in me—the thought that if I have to exert the energy to write a letter, I might as well do something creative."[170]

As the Victorian duality of his autobiography suggests, the idealized woman was a second constant focus of the Chaplin philosophy, be it the inspiration of a film or the boon to his leisure life. Two excellent articles on the subject are Adela Rogers St. Johns's early, forthright look at the private side in "The Loves of Charlie Chaplin" (*Photoplay*, February 1923) and René Micha's career examination in "Chaplin As Don Juan" (*Sight and Sound*, January-March 1954).

For a more theoretical, thorough, sometimes fuzzy look at the idealized woman as a source of Chaplin inspiration, see Parker Tyler's "Chaplin: The Myth of The Immigrant" (*Western Review*, Autumn 1953). Jackie Coogan notwithstanding, Chaplin's interest in young girls is reminiscent of an observation by Lewis Carroll, a Victorian who also found inspiration, though of a platonic nature, in female children: "I am extremely fond of children, except boys."[171]

Chaplin's devotion to work and the idealized woman seem to combine in a third key subject to which he often applied his sense of intuition—the need to be the teacher. Whether it be the virgin in the bedroom or the novice on the film set (sometimes one and the same), he needed the sense of control.

Long-time Chaplin cameraman Totheroh so links the comedian's stance as teacher to both Chaplin's private and public life that he even manages to combine the two subjects during the detailed Lyons interview. Totheroh slides without transition from a description of Chaplin as sexual teacher to that of Chaplin as film directing teacher.[172] One is tempted to think of the comedian as an X-rated Professor Henry Higgins, in an *adult* version of George Bernard Shaw's *Pygmalion*, an analogy Chaplin fan Shaw might very well have appreciated.

Chaplin the teacher was not limited to sex and film comedy, though he was probably the most secure in them. The vast bulk of Chaplin literature, especially that authored by the comedian himself, is full of social engagements where he "lectured" dignitaries from every conceivable discipline. And though sources differ as to the skill he brought to these educational exercises, they are nearly uniform in their praise of his quick study abilities. Will Rogers provides an amusing 1930s observation on Chaplin as Renaissance man.

> I was talking to the "Old Economist" [Chaplin] the other night. . . . Did you know that Charley is just about the one of our best minds on all these deep subjects, well what that little rascal knows will just surprise you.
> Yes, sir, if you want to get yourself a loaf of economics, with a side car of theories, why Charley can give em to you.[173]

Samuel Goldwyn's excellent *Behind the Screen* (1923) suggests two key reasons for Chaplin's perpetual interest in playing teacher. First, "Chaplin loves power—as no one else whom I ever met loves it."[174] Just as money helped him calm the fears of his early poverty, a teacher-to-student relationship with those around him (invariably referred to in the writings of both friends and detractors) was more salve to the wounds he had suffered as a youngster from martinet workhouse and theater people. And of course it gave him the power he had not had before.

Goldwyn's second teacher-related statement foreshadows Burke's "I live on my emotions" quotation. "His reaction to life is, you see, intensely personal, intensely emotional. . . . Chaplin loves to talk about government and economics and religion. Mention of a new 'ism' or 'ology' brings him loping from the farthest corner of a room."[175]

Chaplin's quick assumption of the teacher-lecturer stance at a social gathering would allow him a perfect setting from which to project the aforementioned personalized emotional drama. And as Goldwyn later noted:

> One could see it was not really abstract truth which he desired. It was the theory which most successfully represented his own prejudice . . . against anything which interferes with his own personal freedom, . . . hateful to him in the degree to which they infringe upon that coveted sense of power.[176]

A fourth and final key subject in the Chaplin philosophy of intuition is the self-consciously loner pose he assumes, what Goldwyn called his "enduring isolation." This can, of course, lead one back to further study of his youth along the "ism" trail of one's choice. But more interesting than this is the fact that Chaplin eventually became used to and then thrived on being alone. Twice in his autobiography he even observed, "I like friends as I like music—when I am in the mood."[177]

This preference for the loner stance might also be seen as the corollary that holds each of the other three subjects together. That is, his recognition as a unique and gifted artist encouraged Chaplin to further place his work above everything else. And whereas such self-imposed artistic autonomy destroyed the career of comedy contemporary Harry Langdon, who was attempting to emulate the creator of Charlie, Chaplin thrived on it.

Also, as cinema's eccentric comedy loner, his continued pursuit, both personally and professionally, of the idealized child-woman was somehow understood by an adoring public in the 1920s and 1930s, a public that had ended several other careers for indiscretions much closer to standard norms. While he was not free from earlier controversy, it took the woman-killing *Monsieur Verdoux* to destroy that public understanding.

And again, his loner position forever guaranteed his assumption of the teacher-student stance on those rare occasions when he surfaced for a professional or social engagement, because the public had never gotten enough of him, on screen or off. For that reason *New Yorker* book reviewer Brendan Gill regretted the appearance of the Chaplin autobiography because it detracted from the mystique of comedy's answer to Garbo's "I want to be alone." "I had assumed [Chaplin] chose early in his films to remain permanently hidden from us behind a series of beautiful masks: the mask of the Tramp, . . . Don Juan, . . . the smiling patriarch posed on a green Swiss hillside. . . . My assumption was wrong."[178]

CHAPLIN ARCHIVES AND FILM SOURCES

Unfortunately, Timothy J. Lyons was only too correct when he observed in his watershed Chaplin reference guide that there was no "single library with a really comprehensive collection of writings on and by Chaplin. . . . Research into the literature . . . will depend greatly on chance and perseverance."[179]

Lyons goes on, however, to suggest six libraries with sizable Chaplin holdings: the Library of Congress (Washington, D.C.), the University of California Theatre Arts Library (Los Angeles), the Academy of Motion Picture Arts and Sciences Library (Los Angeles), the University of Southern California Cinema Library (Los Angeles), the University of Iowa main library (Iowa City), the Wisconsin Center for Film and Theatre Research (Madison), and the Museum of Modern Art Film Study Center (New York).[180]

My experience in preparing both this text and my Chaplin monograph would strongly second those suggestions, though Lyons's initial reference to "chance and perseverance" is well taken, because just as he found resource material in unusual places, so did I. For example, I came across several fascinating Chaplin letters (see source note 170 of this chapter for a reference to one such letter) in the manuscripts department of Indiana University's Lilly Library (Bloomington, Indiana).

Happily, Chaplin films are much more accessible. The majority of his short subjects from Keystone, Essanay, and Mutual are available from several film rental houses (Chaplin did not possess their copyright), while RBC Films controls all his work after 1917, with the exceptions of the 1918 war effort *The Bond* (*Charles Chaplin in a Liberty Loan Appeal*) and his final production, *A Countess from Hong Kong* (1966), which is controlled by Universal and Cine Craft.

The majority of the early short subjects have long been available for purchase in 8mm, super-8, and 16mm film stock (see especially Blackhawk Films, Davenport, Iowa), while RBC Films has instituted a long-term leasing plan for cinema collectors. More recently, however, most of Chaplin's work has become available for rent or purchase on low-cost video tape—a development that promises to revolutionize the study of Chaplin, as well as film in general.

It is hoped that this work may be a starting point for further study of both Chaplin's art and its impact on world culture, and that it will represent one more proof of comedy's equality with the "more serious arts."

As the resources herein suggest, André Bazin was most insightful when he likened Charlie to mythical cultural heroes of the past. In this century of telecommunications magic, no other media figure has ever approached the charismatic shock waves emitted by that seemingly simple little tramp.

Today Charlie would seem to take precedence even over earlier, more self-consciously "serious" cultural heroes, for as film theorist Wylie Sypher has observed, in the context of this often absurd modern world, "The comic now is more relevant, or at least more accessible, than the tragic."[181] And Charlie continues to be the most accessibly relevant of all comedy figures, because since his cinema inception he has been the standard by which all comedians are measured. He was an economy-sized champion in a time and place when champions still won. And he remains a champion today.

NOTES

1. Richard Meryman, interviewer, "Chaplin: Ageless Master's Anatomy of Comedy," *Life*. March 10, 1967, p. 94.

2. John McCabe, *Charlie Chaplin* (Garden City, New York: Doubleday, 1978), p. ix.

3. Ibid., p. 197.

4. Gerald Mast, *The Comic Mind: Comedy and the Movies* (Indianapolis: Bobbs-Merrill, 1973), p. 83.

5. Theodore Huff, *Charlie Chaplin* (1951; rpt. New York: Henry Schuman, 1972), p. 96.

6. Raoul Sobel and David Francis, *Chaplin: Genesis of a Clown* (New York: Quartet Books Limited, 1977), p. 224.

7. John Houseman, "Charlie's Chaplin," *Nation* (October 12, 1964), p. 222; Brendan Gill, "Books," *New Yorker*, October 12, 1964, p. 238.

8. Charles Chaplin, *My Autobiography* (1964; rpt. New York: Pocket Books, 1966), p. 350.

9. McCabe, *Charlie Chaplin*, p. 91.

10. Mark Twain, *The Adventures of Huckleberry Finn* (1885; rpt. New York: Scholastic Book Services, 1967), p. xi.

11. Roger Manvell, *Chaplin* (Boston: Little, Brown, 1974), p. 229.

12. Philip G. Rosen, "The Chaplin World View," *Cinema Journal*, Fall 1969, pp. 2-12.

13. Charles Chaplin, "Creating the Role of Dr. Body in *Casey's Court Circus*," in *Focus on Chaplin*, ed. Donald W. McCaffrey (Englewood Cliffs, New Jersey: Prentice-Hall, 1971), p. 29.

14. Chaplin, *My Autobiography*, pp. 41, 72.

15. Charlie Chaplin, *My Trip Abroad* (New York: Harper & Brothers, 1922), pp. 110-111.

16. Walter E. Houghton, *The Victorian Frame of Mind* (1957; rpt. New Haven: Yale University Press, 1970), p. 305.

17. Chaplin, *My Autobiography*, p. 212.

18. Arthur Knight, "Travels with Charlie and Friends," *Saturday Review*, October 10, 1964, p. 45.

19. Chaplin, *My Autobiography*, p. 14.

20. Houghton, *The Victorian Frame of Mind*, p. 309.

21. Chaplin, *My Autobiography*, p. 7.

22. Charlie Chaplin, "A Comedian Sees the World," *Woman's Home Companion* (October 1933), p. 106.

23. Chaplin, *My Autobiography*, p. 138.

24. "Charlie Chaplin, as a Comedian, Contemplates Suicide," *Current Opinion*, February 1922, pp. 209-210.

25. Charles Chaplin, Jr., with N. and M. Rau, *My Father, Charlie Chaplin* (New York: Random House, 1960), p. 93.

26. Ibid., p. 196.

27. Ibid., p. 88.

28. Michael Chaplin, *I Couldn't Smoke the Grass on My Father's Lawn* (New York: G. P. Putnam's Sons, 1966), p. 47.

29. Chaplin, *My Autobiography*, p. 327.

30. Timothy J. Lyons, "The Idea in The Gold Rush: A Study of Chaplin's Use of the Comic Technique of Pathos-Humor," in McCaffrey, ed., *Focus on Chaplin*, pp. 113-123.

31. Chaplin, *My Autobiography*, pp. 35, 389.

32. Francis Wyndham, introduction to *My Life in Pictures*, Charles Chaplin (1974; rpt. New York: Grosset and Dunlap, 1975), p. 29.

33. Chaplin, Jr., *My Father, Charlie Chaplin*, p. 29.

34. Lita Grey Chaplin, with Morton Cooper, *My Life with Chaplin* (New York: Bernard Geis, 1966), pp. 29, 31, 33, 53.

35. Ibid., p. 31.

36. *Encyclopedia of World Art*, 1966 ed., s.v. "Sir Joshua Reynolds."

37. Lita Grey Chaplin, *My Life with Chaplin*, p. 79.

38. Chaplin, Jr., *My Father, Charlie Chaplin*, p. 181.

39. R. J. Minney, *Chaplin: The Immortal Tramp* (London: George Newnes, 1954), p. 74.

40. Chaplin, *My Autobiography*, p. 468.

41. See Gill, "Books," pp. 241-242.

42. Houghton, *The Victorian Frame of Mind*, p. 354.

43. Chaplin, *My Life in Pictures*, p. 177.

44. Chaplin, *My Autobiography*, p. 215.

45. Ibid., p. 332.

46. Stanley Kauffmann, "A Man Named Chaffin," *New Republic*, October 3, 1964, p. 19.

47. Chaplin, *My Autobiography*, p. 333.

48. Gill, "Books," p. 240.

49. Lita Grey Chaplin, *My Life with Chaplin*, cover quotations.

50. Carlotta Monti with Cy Rice, *W. C. Fields & Me* (1971; rpt. New York: Warner Paperback Library, 1973).

51. Lita Grey Chaplin, *My Life with Chaplin*, p. 32.

52. Ibid., p. 52.

53. McCabe, *Charlie Chaplin*, p. 141.

54. Lita Grey Chaplin, *My Life with Chaplin*, p. 250.

55. Chaplin, Jr., *My Father, Charlie Chaplin*, p. 14.

56. Gerald Mast, *The Comic Mind: Comedy and the Movies*, p. 69.

57. Chaplin, Jr., *My Father, Charlie Chaplin*, pp. 42, 111.

58. Charlie Chaplin, "A Rejection of the Talkies," in McCaffrey, ed., *Focus on Chaplin*, pp. 63-65. This is an excerpt from "Pantomime and Comedy," *New York Times*, January 25, 1931, sec. 8, p. 6.

59. J. D. Salinger, *The Catcher in the Rye* (Boston: Little, Brown and Company, 1951), p. 192.

60. Peter Evans, *The Mask Behind the Mask* (1968; rpt. New York: New American Library, 1980).

61. Gerith von Ulm, *Charlie Chaplin: King of Tragedy* (Caldwell, Idaho: Caxton Printers, Ltd., 1940), p. 12.

62. Ibid., 209.

63. Minney, *Chaplin: The Immortal Tramp*, p. 100.

64. Ibid., pp. 83, 145.

65. Ibid., pp. 37.39.

66. Uno Asplund, *Chaplin's Films*, trans. from Swedish by Paul Britten Austin (1971; rpt. New York: A. S. Barnes and Company, 1973), p. 114.

67. Wes D. Gehring, "Frank Capra's Harry Langdon and Jaroslav Hasek's The Good Soldier Schweik: *Not* from the Same Pattern," forthcoming from *American Classic Screen*.

68. Asplund, *Chaplin's Films*, p. 120; Gerald D. McDonald, Michael Conway, and Mark Ricci, eds., *The Films of Charlie Chaplin* (New York: Bonanza Books, 1965), p. 159.

69. Vachel Lindsay, *The Art of the Moving Pictures* (1915; revised 1922; rpt. New York: Liveright, 1970), p. 6; Carl Sandburg, "Carl Sandburg Says Chaplin

Could Play Serious Drama," in *Authors on Film*, ed. Harry M. Geduld (Blooming-ton: Indiana University Press, 1972), p. 264 (originally in *Chicago Daily News*, April 16, 1921, p. 13).

70. James Agee, "Comedy's Greatest Era," in *Agee on Film*, vol. 1 (New York: Grosset and Dunlap, 1969), p. 9 (originally appeared in *Life*, September 3, 1949).

71. Gerald Mast, Chapter 6, "Movie Czars and Movie Stars," in *A Short History of the Movies*, 2d ed. (1976; rpt. Indianapolis: Bobbs-Merrill, 1977), p. 155.

72. Mast, Chapter 5, "The Comics: Mack Sennett and the Chaplin Shorts," in *A Short History of the Movies*, pp. 100-101.

73. Gerald Mast, Chapter 6 "Chaplin: From Keystone to Mutual," in *The Comic Mind: Comedy and the Movies* (Indianapolis: Bobbs-Merrill, 1973), p. 65.

74. Walter Kerr, Chapter 9, "Chaplin: An Outline Becomes a Character," in *The Silent Clowns* (New York: Alfred A. Knopf, 1975), p. 77.

75. André Bazin, "The Virtues and Limitations of Montage," in *What Is Cinema?*, vol. 1, selected and trans. Hugh Gray (1958; rpt. Los Angeles: University of California Press, 1967), p. 52.

76. André Bazin, "Charlie Chaplin," in *What Is Cinema?*, vol. 1, p. 150.

77. André Bazin, "The Myth of Monsieur Verdoux," in *What Is Cinema?*, vol. 2, selected and trans. Hugh Gray (1958; rpt. Los Angeles: University of California Press, 1971), pp. 102-103.

78. Ibid., pp. 111-113.

79. Robert Warshow, "Monsieur Verdoux," in *The Immediate Experience* (1962; rpt. New York: Atheneum, 1972), p. 208.

80. Richard Schickel, *Movies: The History of an Art and an Institution* (New York: Basic Books, Inc., 1964), pp. 67-68.

81. Warshow, "Monsieur Verdoux," p. 211.

82. Robert Warshow, "A Feeling of Sad Dignity," in *The Immediate Experience*, p. 224.

83. Ibid., p. 229.

84. Ibid., p. 231.

85. Bazin, "The Myth of Monsieur Verdoux," pp. 110-111.

86. Huff, *Charlie Chaplin*, p. 256.

87. Charles J. Maland, Chapter 2; "The Tramp Turns Social," in *American Visions: The Films of Chaplin, Ford, Capra, and Welles, 1936-1941* (New York: Arno Press, 1977), p. 78. Originally Ph.D. diss., University of Michigan.

88. Ibid., pp. 78-79.

89. Ibid., p. 90.

90. Ibid., pp. 90-91.

91. Andrew Sarris, "Monsieur Verdoux," in *Confessions of a Cultist: On the Cinema, 1955/1969* (1970; rpt. New York: Simon and Schuster, 1971), p. 144.

92. Ibid., p. 144.

93. Ibid., p. 146.

94. Ibid., p. 145.

95. Andrew Sarris, "The Great Dictator" and "Limelight," in *Confessions of a Cultist*, pp. 127, 167.

96. Andrew Sarris, "Charles Chaplin," in *The American Cinema: Directors and Directions, 1929-1968* (New York: E. P. Dutton, 1968), p. 41.

97. Stanley Kauffmann, "Landru [and Monsieur Verdoux]," in *A World on*

Film: Criticism and Comment (New York: Harper & Row, 1966), p. 257.

98. Stanley Kauffman, "A King in New York," in *Living Images: Film Comment and Criticism* (New York: Harper & Row, 1975), p. 248.

99. Kauffmann, "The Gold Rush," in *Living Images*, p. 301.

100. Kauffmann, "Buster Keaton Festival [and Comparison with Chaplin]," in *Living Images*, p. 20.

101. Ibid., pp. 21-22.

102. Louis Delluc, *Charles Chaplin*, trans. Hamish Miles (New York: John Lane, 1922), p. 40.

103. Gilbert Seldes, " 'I Am Here Today': Charlie Chaplin," in *The 7 Lively Arts* (1924; rpt. New York: McClelland and Stewart, 1957), p. 48.

104. Iris Barry, "Comedians," in *Let's Go to the Pictures* (London: Chatto and Windus, 1926), p. 130.

105. Charlie Chaplin, "What People Laugh At," *American Magazine*, November 1918, p. 34.

106. Ibid., p. 34.

107. Charlie Chaplin, "Development of the Comic Story and the Tramp Character," in McCaffrey, ed., *Focus on Chaplin*, p. 47.

108. Chaplin, "What People Laugh At," p. 34.

109. Henri. Bergson, *Laughter* (1900), rpt. in *Comedy*, anthology ed. Wylie Sypher (Garden City, New York: Doubleday, Anchor Books, 1965), p. 141.

110. Chaplin, "What People Laugh At," p. 34.

111. Chaplin, *My Autobiography*, p. 226.

112. Chaplin, Jr., *My Father, Charlie Chaplin*, p. 113.

113. Charlie Chaplin, "Does the Public Know What It Wants?" *Adelphi*, January 1924, p. 704.

114. Chaplin, *My Autobiography*, p. 224.

115. Meryman, "Chaplin: Ageless Master's Anatomy of Comedy." p. 82.

116. Ibid., p. 83.

117. Plato, *Ion*, in *Classical and Medieval Literary Criticism*, ed. Alex Preminger, O. B. Hardison, Jr., and Kevin Kerrane (New York: Fredrick Ungar, 1974), p. 41.

118. Meryman, "Chaplin: Ageless Master's Anatomy of Comedy," pp. 83-84.

119. Ibid., p. 86.

120. Max Eastman, *Great Companions: Critical Memoirs of Some Famous Friends* (New York: Farrar, Straus and Cudahy, 1959), p. 219. Much of the Chaplin material included in *Great Companions*, pp. 207-247, appeared earlier in Eastman's *Heroes I Have Known: Twelve Who Lived Great Lives* (New York: Simon and Schuster, 1942), pp. 155-200.

121. Max Eastman, *The Sense of Humor* (New York: Charles Scribner's Sons, 1921), p. 227.

122. Gladys Hall, interviewer, "Charlie Chaplin Attacks the Talkies," *Motion Picture*, May 1929, p. 29.

123. Hall, "Charlie Chaplin Attacks the Talkies," p. 28.

124. Charlie Chaplin, "Pantomime and Comedy," *New York Times*, January 25, 1931, sec. 8, p. 6.

125. Ibid.

126. Henry King, " 'Movie' or 'Talkie'?," *New Adelphi*, March 1929, p. 249.

127. Meryman, "Chaplin: Ageless Master's Anatomy of Comedy," p. 89.

128. Lita Grey Chaplin, *My Life with Chaplin*, p. 56.
129. Chaplin, Jr., *My Father, Charlie Chaplin*, p. 79.
130. Robert Payne, *The Great God Pan: A Biography of the Tramp Played by Charles Chaplin* (New York: Hermitage House, 1952), p. 12.
131. Harry Carr, "Chaplin Explains Chaplin," *Motion Picture Magazine* (November 1925), p. 31.
132. Elsie Codd, in Chapter 5, "The Method," in *Charlie Chaplin*, general author and compiler Louis Delluc, trans. Hamish Miles (New York: John Lane, 1922), p. 45.
133. Adolphe Menjou with M. M. Musselman, Chapter 14, "A Woman of Paris," in *It Took Nine Tailors* (New York: McGraw-Hill, 1948), p. 110.
134. Timothy J. Lyons, "Roland H. Totheroh Interviewed: Chaplin Films," *Film Culture*, Spring 1972, p. 239.
135. Menjou, *It Took Nine Tailors*, p. 110.
136. Ibid., p. 111.
137. Codd, "The Method," pp. 47-48.
138. Terry Ramsaye, "Chaplin—And How He Does It," *Photoplay*, September 1917, p. 19.
139. Menjou, *It Took Nine Tailors*, p. 118.
140. Kevin Brownlow, *The Parade's Gone By . . .* (1968; rpt. New York: Ballantine Books, 1970), p. 578.
141. Chaplin, "Does the Public Know What It Wants?" p. 709.
142. Lyons, "Roland H. Totheroh Interviewed: Chaplin Films," p. 282.
143. Ibid., p. 264.
144. Mack Sennett (as told to Cameron Shipp), Chapter 16, "Poetry in Slapstick," in *King of Comedy* (1954; rpt. New York: Pinnacle Books, 1975), p. 181.
145. Ibid., pp. 178-179.
146. "Chaplin at Work: He Reveals His Movie-Making Secrets" (photographs by W. Eugene Smith), *Life*, March 17, 1952, p. 117.
147. Thomas M. Pryor, "How Mr. Chaplin Makes a Movie," *New York Times Magazine*, February 17, 1952, p. 19.
148. "Chaplin at Work," p. 122.
149. Robert Van Gelder, "Chaplin Draws a Keen Weapon," *New York Times Magazine*, September 8, 1940, p. 9.
150. Pryor, "How Mr. Chaplin Makes a Movie," p. 19.
151. "Chaplin at Work, p. 122.
152. Ibid., p. 124.
153. John Francis Lane, interviewer, "My Life as Chaplin's Leading Lady," (Dawn Addams), *Films and Filming*, August 1957, p. 15.
154. Jack Spears, "Chapter 7, Chaplin's Collaborators," in *Hollywood: The Golden Era* (New York: Castle Books, 1971), p. 226.
155. Spears, *Hollywood: The Golden Era*, p. 247.
156. Sarris, "Charles Chaplin," p. 40.
157. Ramsaye, "Chaplin—And How He Does It," p. 139.
158. Al Hirschfeld, "A Man with Both Feet in the Clouds," *New York Times Magazine*, July 26, 1942, pp. 12+ .
159. Thomas Burke, "A Comedian," in *City of Encounters* (Boston: Little, Brown, 1932), p. 133.
160. Ibid., p. 138.

161. Ibid., p. 151.

162. Ibid., p. 170.

163. Ibid., p. 168.

164. Ibid., p. 171.

165. Rosen, "The Chaplin World-View," p. 10.

166. Pryor, "How Mr. Chaplin Makes a Movie," p. 19.

167. Henry F. Pringle, "The Story of Two Mustaches," *Ladies' Home Journal*, July 1940, p. 97.

168. Adela Rogers St. Johns, "The Loves of Charlie Chaplin," *Photoplay*, February 1923, p. 29.

169. Alistair Cooke, "Charles Chaplin: The One and Only," in *Six Men* (New York: Alfred A. Knopf, 1977), p. 40.

170. Letter from Chaplin to Upton Sinclair, October 20, 1964, Manuscripts Department, Lilly Library, Indiana University, Bloomington, Indiana.

171. Franz Rottensteiner, *The Fantasy Book* (New York: Colliers Books, 1978), p. 108.

172. Lyons, "Roland H. Totheroh Interviewed: Chaplin Films," p. 285.

173. Donald Day, ed., *The Autobiography of Will Rogers* (Boston: Houghton Mifflin, 1975), p. 319.

174. Samuel Goldwyn, Chaper 13, "The Real Chaplin," in *Behind the Screen* (New York: George H. Doran, 1923), p. 159.

175. Ibid., p. 161.

176. Ibid., p. 162.

177. Chaplin, *My Autobiography*, pp. 200, 291.

178. Gill, "Books," p. 236.

179. Lyons, *Charles Chaplin: A Guide to References and Resources*, p. 209.

180. Lyons, *Charles Chaplin: A Guide to References and Resources*, p. 209.

181. Wylie Sypher, "The Meaning of Comedy," in *Comedy*, ed. Wylie Syhpher (Garden City, New York: Random House, 1975), p. 6.

5

BIBLIOGRAPHICAL CHECKLIST OF KEY CHAPLIN SOURCES

BOOKS ABOUT AND/OR BY CHAPLIN

Asplund, Uno. *Chaplin's Films.* Translated by Paul Britten Austin. 1971; rpt. New York: A. S. Barnes, 1973.

Balio, Tino. *United Artists, The Company Built by the Stars.* Madison: University of Wisconsin Press, 1976.

Chaplin, Charles. *My Autobiography.* 1964; rpt. New York: Pocket Books, 1966.

_____. *My Life in Pictures.* 1974; rpt. New York: Grosset and Dunlap, 1975.

Chaplin, Charles, Jr. *My Father, Charlie Chaplin.* New York: Random House, 1960.

Chaplin, Charlie. *Charlie Chaplin's Own Story.* Indianapolis: Bobbs-Merrill, 1916.

_____. *A Comedian Sees the World.* New York: Crowell, 1933.

_____. *My Trip Abroad.* New York: Harper & Brothers, 1922.

Chaplin, Lita Grey, with Morton Cooper. *My Life with Chaplin.* New York: Bernard Geis, 1966.

Chaplin, Michael. *I Couldn't Smoke the Grass on My Father's Lawn.* New York: G. P. Putnam's Sons, 1966.

Cotes, Peter and Thelma Niklaus. *The Little Fellow: The Life and Works of Charles Spencer Chaplin.* 1951; rpt. New York: Citadel, 1965.

Delluc, Louis. *Charlie Chaplin.* Translated by Hamish Miles. New York: John Lane, 1922.

Florey, Robert. *Charlie Chaplin.* Paris: Jean Pascal, 1927.

Gifford, Denis. *Chaplin.* Garden City, New York: Doubleday, 1974.

Hambus, Joe, comp. *Charlie Chaplin und seine Filme: eine Dokumentation.* Munich: W. Heyne, 1972.

Huff, Theodore. *Charlie Chaplin.* 1951; rpt. New York: Henry Schuman, 1972.

Leprohon, Pierre. *Charles Chaplin.* Paris: Editions Corymbe and André Bonne, 1970.

Lyons, Timothy J. "The Idea in The Gold Rush: A Study of Chaplin's Use of the Comic Technique of Pathos-Humor." In *Focus on Chaplin.* Edited by

McCabe, John. *Charlie Chaplin*. Garden City, New York: Doubleday, 1978.

McCaffrey, Donald W., ed. *Focus on Chaplin*. Englewood Cliffs, New Jersey: Prentice-Hall, 1971.

Contents: "Introduction" (Donald W. McCaffrey); "A Brief Overall View" (John Montgomery); "Creating the Role of Dr. Body in *Casey's Court Circus*" (Charles Chaplin); "Acting-Directing Apprenticeship with Mack Sennett" (Charles Chaplin); "Development of the Comic Story and the Tramp Character" (Charles Chaplin); "What People Laugh At" (Charles Chaplin); "Max Linder's and Elsie Codd's Views on the Working Method" (Louis Delluc); "A Rejection of the Talkies" (Charlie Chaplin, originally "Pantomime and Comedy," *New York Times*, January 25, 1931); "The Art of Charles Chaplin" (Minnie Maddern Fiske); "Is the Charlie Chaplin Vogue Passing?" (Harcourt Farmer); "Everybody's Language" (Winston Churchill); "A Reaction to the Praise Given Chaplin's Artistry" (George Jean Nathan); "An Evaluation of Chaplin's Silent Comedy Films, 1916-36" (Donald W. McCaffrey); "Impressions of Two Early Comedy Films" (Louis Delluc); "An Early, Detailed Account of the Action in *The Pawnshop*" (Gilbert Seldes); "The Kid" Frances Hackett; "The Pilgrim" (Robert E. Sherwood); "With the Bunk Left Out" (Charles W. Wood); "The Idea in *The Gold Rush*: A Study of Chaplin's Use of the Comic Technique of Pathos-Humor" (Timothy J. Lyons); "A Comparison of *The Gold Rush* and *The General*" (Gerald Mast); "The Circus" (Alexander Bakshy); "*City Lights* and *Modern Times*: Skirmishes with Romance, Pathos, and Social Significance" (Donald W. McCaffrey); "The Great Dictator" (Herman C. Weinberg); "Monsieur Verdoux" (Roger Manvell; "The Lineage of *Limelight*" (Walter Kerr); scenario extracts.

McCaffrey, Donald W. *4 Great Comedians: Chaplin, Lloyd, Keaton, Langdon*. New York: A. S. Barnes, 1968.

McDonald, Gerald D. *The Picture History of Charlie Chaplin*. New York: Nostalgia Press, 1965.

McDonald, Gerald D.; Michael Conway, and Mark Ricci, eds. *The Films of Charlie Chaplin*. New York: Bonanza Books, 1965.

Maland, Charles J. *American Visions: The Films of Chaplin, Ford, Capra, and Welles, 1936-1941*. New York: Arno Press, 1977. Originally Ph.D. diss., University of Michigan.

Manvell, Roger. *Chaplin*. Boston: Little, Brown, 1974.

Martin, Marcel. *Charlie Chaplin*. Paris: Seghers, 1966.

Minney, R. J. *Chaplin: The Immortal Tramp*. London: George Newnes, 1954.

Mitry, Jean. *Les films de Charlot*. 1957; rpt. as *Tout Chaplin*, Paris: Seghers, 1972.

Moss, Robert F. *Charlie Chaplin*. 1975; rpt. New York: Harcourt, Brace Jovanovich, 1977.

Payne, Robert. *The Great God Pan: A Biography of the Tramp Played by Charles Chaplin*. New York: Hermitage House, 1952.

Poulaille, Henry. *Charles Chaplin*. Paris: Bernard Grasset, 1927.

Quigly, Isabel. *Charlie Chaplin: Early Comedies*. London: Studio Vista, 1968.

Reeves, May. *Charles Chaplin Intimé*. Edited by Clair Goll. Paris: N.R.F. Gallimard, 1935.

Sobel, Raoul, and David Francis. *Chaplin: Genesis of a Clown*. London: Quartet Books, 1977.

Viazzi, Glauco. *Chaplin e la critica*. Bari, Italy: Laterza, 1955.

von Ulm, Gerith. *Charlie Chaplin: King of Tragedy*. Caldwell, Idaho: Caxton, 1940.

SHORTER WORKS ABOUT AND/OR BY CHAPLIN
Articles, Interviews, Book Chapters, and Monographs

Agee, James. "Comedy's Greatest Era" (from *Life*, September 3, 1949); "Monsieur Verdoux" (three-part analysis from *The Nation*); "Monsieur Verdoux" (from *Time*); and review of the 1942 revival of *The Gold Rush*. In *Agee on Film*, vol. 1. New York: Grosset and Dunlap, 1969.

Barry, Iris. Chapter 7, "Stars" and Chapter 8, "Comedians." In *Let's Go to the Movies*. London: Chatto & Windus, 1926.

Bazin, André. "The Myth of Monsieur Verdoux;" "*Limelight,* or the Death of Molière;" "The Grandeur of *Limelight.*" In *What Is Cinema?* vol. 2. Selected and translated by Hugh Gray. 1958; rpt. Los Angeles: University of California Press, 1971.

―――. "The Virtues and Limitations of Montage" and "Charlie Chaplin." In *What Is Cinema?* vol. 1. Selected and translated by Hugh Gray. 1958; rpt. Los Angeles: University of California Press, 1967.

Bercovici, Konrad. "Charlie Chaplin: An Authorized Interview," *Colliers*, August 15, 1925, pp. 5+.

Brownlow, Kevin. Chapter 44, "Chaplin." In *The Parade's Gone By. . . .* 1968; rpt. New York: Ballantine Books, 1970.

Burke, Thomas. "A Comedian." In *City of Encounters*. Boston: Little, Brown, 1932, pp. 129-177.

Byron, Stuart, and Elisabeth Weis, eds. *The National Society of Film Critics on Movie Comedy*. New York: Penguin Books, 1977.
  Chaplin contents: "A Chaplin Overview" (Richard Schickel); "City Lights" (Roger Ebert); "The Great Dictator" (Roger Ebert); "The Late Chaplin Films" (Bruce Williamson); "[W. C.] Fields vs. Chaplin" (Roger Ebert).

Carr, Harry. "Chaplin vs. Lloyd, A Comparison," *Motion Picture Magazine*, November 1922, pp. 55+.

―――. "How the Great Directors Work," *Motion Picture Magazine*, May 1925, pp. 52+.

Carr, Harry, interviewer. "Chaplin Explains Chaplin," *Motion Picture Magazine*, November 1925, pp. 31+.

"Chaplin at Work: He Reveals His Movie-Making Secrets" (with a large photo layout by W. Eugene Smith), *Life*, March 17, 1952, pp. 117-127.

Chaplin, Charles. "A Comedian Sees the World," *Woman's Home Companion*, September, October, November, December 1933, January 1934.

―――. "In Defense of Myself," *Colliers*, November 11, 1922, pp. 8+.

―――. Letter to Upton Sinclair, October 20, 1964. Lilly Library, Indiana University, Bloomington, Indiana.

Chaplin, Charlie. "Does the Public Know What It Wants?" *Adelphi*, January 1924, pp. 702-710.

―――. "How I Made My Success," *Theatre*, September 1915, pp. 121+.

―――. "Pantomime and Comedy," *New York Times*, January 25, 1931, sec. 8, p. 6. An excerpt appeared as "Wisdom from a Wise Man," *Theatre Guild Magazine*, March 1931, p. 7.

―――. "What People Laugh At," *American Magazine*, November 1918, pp. 34+.

Uncredited later appearances of this article: "Charlie Chaplin Says Laughs Are Produced By Rules," *Literary Digest*, May 3, 1919, pp. 80+; Louis Delluc, *Charles Chaplin* (see Books); "How Charlie Chaplin Does It: His Theory of the Comic," *World's Work*, February 1923, pp. 425-434 (credited to the Delluc book). Timothy J. Lyons, *Charles Chaplin: A Guide to References and Resources* (see Books), notes eight other foreign texts in which it was reprinted (Lyons entry #1433, p. 202).

"Charlie Chaplin, as a Comedian, Contemplates Suicide," *Current Opinion*, February 1922, pp. 209-210.

"Charlie Chaplin, Faces and Facets" (a film-by-film overview), *Film Comment*, September-October 1972, pp. 8-28.

Chaplin contents: "The Second Coming" (Charles Silvers), pp. 8-11; "The Chaplin Review" (Gilberto Perez Guillermo), pp. 11-13; "The Kid" (Gary Carey), pp. 13-15; "A Woman of Paris" (William K. Everson), pp. 15-16; "The Gold Rush" (William Paul), pp. 16-18; "City Lights" (Stanley Kauffmann), pp. 18-19; "Modern Times" (David Denby), pp. 19-20; "The Great Dictator" (Stephen Harvey), pp. 20-22; "Monsieur Verdoux" (Foster Hirsch), pp. 22-24; "Limelight" (Emily Sieger), pp. 24-25; "A King in New York" (David Robinson), pp. 25-26; "A Countess from Hong Kong" (Michael Kerbel), pp. 26-28.

Cheatham, Maude S. "A Star Who Longs for Pretty Clothes" (Edna Purviance), *Motion Picture Classic*, November 1919, pp. 54+.

Codd, Elsie. Chapter 5," The Method." In *Charlie Chaplin*, edited and compiled by Louis Delluc, translated by Hamish Miles. New York: John Lane, 1922.

Cooke, Alistair. "Charles Chaplin: The One and Only." In *Six Men*. New York: Alfred A. Knopf, 1977.

Durgnat, Raymond. Chapter 11; "Aimless Odysseus of the Alleyways." In *The Crazy Mirror: Hollywood Comedy and the American Image*. 1969; rpt. New York: Dell, 1972.

Eastman, Max. "Charlie Chaplin: Memories and Reflection." In *Great Companions: Critical Memoirs of Some Famous Friends*. New York: Farrar, Straus and Cudahy, 1959. Much of the Chaplin material in *Great Companions* originally appeared as "Actor of One Role: A Character Study of Charlie Chaplin" in Eastman's *Heroes I Have Known: Twelve Who Lived Great Lives*, New York: Simon and Schuster, 1942.

Eriksson, Lennart. "Books on/by Chaplin: A List." Västeras, Sweden: privately published, 1980.

Gehring, Wes D. "Chaplin and the Progressive Era: The Neglected Politics of a Clown," *Indiana Social Studies Quarterly*, Autumn 1981, pp. 10-18.

_____. *Charlie Chaplin's World of Comedy*. Muncie, Indiana: Ball State University Press Monograph Series, 1980.

Gill, Brendan. "Books," *New Yorker*, October 12, 1964, pp. 236-244.

Goldwyn, Samuel, Chapter 8, "The Discovery of Charlie Chaplin;" Chapter 13, "The Real Chaplin;" Chapter 14, "Jackie Coogan and 'The Kid'." In *Behind the Screen*. New York: Geroge H. Doran, 1923.

Grace, Harry A. "Charlie Chaplin's Films and American Culture Patterns," *Journal of Aesthetics and Art Criticism*, June 1952, pp. 353-363.

Hall, Gladys, interviewer. "Charlie Chaplin Attacks the Talkies," *Motion Picture*, May 1929, pp. 28-30. Also appeared as "Chaplin contre le film parlant," *Cinéa* (Paris), July 15, 1929.

Hilbert, James E. "A Day with Charlie Chaplin on Location," *Motion Picture Classic*, November 1917, pp. 59-61.

Hirschfeld, Al. "A Man with Both Feet in the Clouds," *New York Times Magazine*, July 26, 1942, pp. 12+.

Houseman, John. "Charlie's Chaplin," *Nation*, October 12, 1964, pp. 222-225.

Jacobs, Lewis. Chapter 13, "Charles Chaplin: Individualist." In *The Rise of the American Film: A Critical History*. 1939; rpt. New York: Teachers College Press, 1971.

Kauffmann, Stanley. "The Circus." In *Figures of Light: Film Criticism and Comment*. New York: Harper & Row, 1971.

————. "The Great Dictator" and "Landru." In *A World on Film: Criticism and Comment*. New York: Harper & Row, 1966.

————. "A King in New York;" "The Gold Rush;" "Buster Keaton Festival" (includes a comparison with Chaplin). In *Living Images: Film Comments and Criticism*. New York: Harper & Row, 1975.

————. "A Name Named Chaffin," *New Republic*, October 3, 1964, pp. 19-21.

Kauffmann, Stanley, ed., with Bruce Henstell. *American Film Criticism: From the Beginnings to Citizen Kane*. New York: Liveright, 1972.

Chaplin contents: "Trysting Place" (Louis Reeves Harrison); "Tillie's Punctured Romance" (George Blaisdell); "Charlie Chaplin's Art" (Harvey O'Higgins); "The Kid" (Francis Hackett); "A Woman of Paris" (Exceptional Photoplays); "The Gold Rush" (Edmund Wilson); "The Circus" (Stark Young, Alexander Bakshy); "City Lights" (Francis Fergusson); "Modern Times" (Robert Forsythe, Otis Ferguson); and "The Great Dictator" (Paul Goodman, Rudolf Arnheim).

Kerr, Walter. *The Silent Clowns*. New York: Alfred A. Knopf, 1975.

Chaplin contents: Chapter 9, "Chaplin: An Outline Becomes a Character;" Chapter 10, "Chaplin: Playfulness Unleashed;" Chapter 18, "The Risks of Length and Complexity: Chaplin Takes the Plunge;" Chapter 19, "The Chaplin Breakthrough: Making Seriousness Funny;" Chapter 20, "Chaplin Betwixt and Between;" Chapter 26, "Two Epics" (*The Gold Rush* and *The General*); Chapter 35, "The Transition, After and Just Before: A Self-Conscious Chaplin;" Chapter 36, "Chaplin Confronts Himself;" Chapter 37, "The End with an Ending: Chaplin Defines the Road."

King, Henry. " 'Movie' or 'Talkie'?" *New Adelphi*, March 1929, pp. 248-250.

Kisch, Egon Erwin. "I Work with Charlie Chaplin: Hollywood through German Eyes," *Living Age*, October 15, 1929, pp. 230+. Later appeared as "Charlie Chaplin au Studio," *Revue du Cinéma* (Paris), March 1930, pp. 21+.

Knight, Arthur. "Travels with Charlie and Friends," *Saturday Review*, October 10, 1964, p. 45.

Lane, John Francis, interviewer. "My Life as Chaplin's Leading Lady" (Dawn Addams), *Films and Filming*, August 1957, pp. 12+.

Lejeune, Caroline Alice. "Chaplin" and "Slapstick." In *Cinema*. London: Alexander Maclehose, 1931.

Lyons, Timothy J. "The Idea in The Gold Rush: A Study of Chaplin's Use of the Comic Technique of Pathos-Humor." In *Focus on Chaplin*. Edited by Donald W. McCaffrey. Englewood Cliffs, New Jersey: Prentice-Hall, 1971.

————. "An Introduction to the Literature on Chaplin," *Journal of the University Film Association*, Winter 1979, pp. 3-10.

————. "Roland H. Totheroh Interviewed: Chaplin Films," *Film Culture*, Spring 1972, pp. 230+.

Mast, Gerald. Chapter 5, "The Comics: Mack Sennett and the Chaplin Shorts;" Chapter 6, "Movie Czars and Movie Stars." In *A Short History of the Movies*, 2d ed. 1976; rpt. Indianapolis: Bobbs-Merrill, 1977.

———. Chapter 6, "Chaplin: From Keystone to Mutual;" Chapter 7, "Chaplin: First Nationals and Silent Features;" Chapter 8, "Chaplin: Sound Films." In *The Comic Mind: Comedy and the Movies*. Indianapolis: Bobbs-Merrill, 1973.

———. "The Gold Rush and The General," *Cinema Journal*, spring 1970, pp. 24-30.

McGuirk, Charles J. "Chaplinitis," *Motion Picture Magazine*, July 1915 and August 1915.

Menjou, Adolphe, with M. M. Musselman. Chapter 14, "A Woman of Paris;" Chapter 15, "Truffle Soup with Champagne" (*A Woman of Paris*); Chapter 16, "I Love That Villain" (Chaplin as director). In *It Took Nine Tailors*. New York: McGraw;Hill, 1948.

Meryman, Richard, interviewer. "Chaplin: Ageless Master's Anatomy of Comedy," *Life*, March 10, 1967, pp. 82+.

Micha, René. "Le donjuanisme dans l'oeuvre de Chaplin," *Disque Vert* (Brussels), May-June 1953. Translated into English as "Chaplin as Don Juan," *Sight and Sound*, January-March 1954, pp. 132-137.

Montgomery, John. Chapter 7, "Chaplin—The Perfect Clown." In *Comedy Films: 1894-1954*. Rev. 2d ed. 1954; rpt. London: George Allen & Unwin, 1968.

Negri, Pola. Chapter 8 (her relationship with Chaplin). In *Memoirs of a Star*. Garden City, New York: Doubleday, 1970.

Pratt, George C. *Spellbound in Darkness: A History of the Silent Film*. Rev. ed. 1966; rpt. Greenwich, Connecticut: New York Graphic Society, 1973.
    Chaplin contents: Chapter 10, "Mack Sennett and Charlie Chaplin," which includes "The Funniest Man on the Screen" (Victor Eubank), "A Day with Charlie Chaplin on Location" (James E. Hilbert), reviews of *Making a Living, His Favorite Pastime, Tillie's Punctured Romance, The Immigrant*, and *Shoulder Arms*; Chapter 15, "Chaplin in the Twenties," which includes "Dear Mr. Chaplin" (Stark Young), excerpts from "Will Charlie Kick Off His Old Shoes?" (Harry Carr), excerpt from "How the Great Directors Work" (Harry Carr), "Chaplin Explains Chaplin" (Harry Carr), "Charlot in Rome" (Stark Young), and reviews of *The Kid* and *A Woman of Paris*.

Pringle, Henry F. "The Story of Two Mustaches," *Ladies' Home Journal*, July 1940, pp. 18+.

Pryor, Thomas M. "How Mr. Chaplin Makes a Movie," *New York Times Magazine*, February 17, 1952, pp. 18+.

Ramsaye, Terry. "Chaplin—And How He Does It," *Photoplay*, September 1917, pp. 19+.

———. Chapter 64, " 'Charlie Chapman' Gets an Offer" and Chapter 74, "$670,000 for Chaplin." In *A Million and One Nights: A History of the Motion Pictures through 1925*. 2 vols. 1926; rpt. (2 vols. in 1), New York: Simon and Schuster, 1964.

Robinson, Carlyle R. "The Private Life of Charlie Chaplin." In *Great Stars of Hollywood's Golden Age*. Edited by Frank C. Platt. New York: Signet Books, 1966.

Rosen, Philip G. "The Chaplin World-View," *Cinema Journal*, Fall 1969, pp. 2-12.

St. Johns, Adela Rogers. "The Loves of Charlie Chaplin," *Photoplay*, February 1923, pp. 23+.

Sandburg, Carl. "Carl Sandburg Says Chaplin Could Play Serious Drama." In *Authors on Film*. Edited by Harry M. Geduld. Bloomington: Indiana University Press, 1972.

Sarris, Andrew. "Charles Chaplin." In *The American Cinema: Directors and Directions, 1929-1968*. New York: E. P. Dutton, 1968.

_____. "The Great Dictator"; "Monsieur Verdoux" (originally in two parts in the *Village Voice*, July 16 and 23, 1964); and On the Cinema, "Limelight." In *Confessions of a Cultist: 1955/1969*. 1970; rpt. New York: Simon and Schuster, 1971.

Schickel, Richard. "Hail Chaplin—The Early Chaplin," *New York Times Magazine*, April 2, 1972, pp. 6+.

Seldes, Gilbert. " 'I Am Here Today': Charlie Chaplin." In *The 7 Lively Arts*. 1924; rpt. New York: McClelland and Stewart, 1957.

Sennett, Mack, with Cameron Shipp. Chapter 14, "Discovering Charlie Chaplin," and Chapter 16, "Poetry in Slapstick." In *King of Comedy*. 1954; rpt. New York: Pinnacle Books, 1975.

_____. "The Psychology of Film Comedy," *Motion Picture Classic*, November 1918, pp. 70+.

Sheridan, Clare. Chapter 7, "America" (Sheridan's relationship with Chaplin). In *The Naked Truth*. New York: Blue Ribbon Books, 1928.

Spears, Jack. Chapter 7, "Chaplin's Collaborators." In *Hollywood: The Golden Era*. New York: Castle Books, 1971. This is a revised and expanded version of Spears's "Chaplin's Collaborators," *Films in Review*, January 1962, pp. 18-36.

Tyler, Parker. "Chaplin: The Myth of the Immigrant," *Western Review*, Autumn 1953, pp. 74-80.

Van Gelder, Robert. "Chaplin Draws a Keen Weapon," *New York Times Magazine*, September 8, 1940, pp. 8+.

Wallach, George, recorder. "Charlie Chaplin's 'Monsieur Verdoux's Press Conference," plus added commentary, such as an excerpt from James Agee's *Nation* review of *Verdoux*. *Film Comment*, Winter 1969, pp. 34-43.

Warshow, Robert. "Monsieur Verdoux" and "A Feeling of Sad Dignity" (originally in *Partisan Review*, November-December 1954). In *The Immediate Experience*. 1962; rpt. New York: Atheneum, 1972.

Wilson, Edmund, "The New Chaplin Comedy," *New Republic*, September 2, 1925, pp. 45-46.

Wyndham, Francis. Introduction to *My Life in Pictures*, by Charles Chaplin. 1974; rpt. New York: Grosset and Dunlap, 1975.

Young, Stark. "Dear Mr. Chaplin." In *Flower in Drama*. New York: Scribner's, 1923.

APPENDIXES

Chronological Biography

The following chronological biography draws upon time lines included in these sources: Marcel Martin's *Charlie Chaplin* (1966), Asplund's *Chaplin's Films* (1973), Sobel and Francis's *Chaplin: Genesis of a Clown* (1977), and Lyons's *Charles Chaplin: A Guide to References and Resources* (1979).

April 16 1889	Born East Lane, Walworth (London), to music hall performers Charles and Hannah Chaplin.
January 1894	First music hall performance, as unplanned substitute for his mother. By this time Charles Sr. had permanently left home.
June 1896	Young Charles and brother Sydney, with their mother, enter Lambeth Workhouse (for the poor). Within a few weeks the boys will be sent to Hanwell School for Orphans and Destitute Children.
1898	Hannah has a mental breakdown. Charles and Sydney live for a time with Charles Sr. and his mistress. Young Charles first appears with the Lancashire Lads.
December 26 1900	Young Charles is controversially comic as a cat in a production of *Cinderella* at the London Hippodrome.
May 13	Charles Sr. dies.
1901	Hannah enters Cane Hill Asylum; she never will permanently recover her sanity.
1903	Chaplin appears for the first time as Billy in *Sherlock Holmes*. He will play the part in various productions into 1906.
1906	Chaplin stars in the variety show *Casey's Circus*.
1907	Chaplin begins performing for the Karno Troupe, joining his brother Sydney, who is largely responsible for Charles's placement.

September 1910	Chaplin leaves with a Karno Troupe for a tour of the United States and Canada.
October 3 1910	He opens in the Karno production *The Wow Wows* at the Colonial Theatre in New York City.
Spring 1912	Chaplin returns to England with the Karno Troupe.
October 1912	Chaplin leaves with the Karno Troupe for a second tour of the U.S. and Canada.
May 1913	He accepts an offer from the New York office of Kessel and Bauman, the parent organization for Mack Sennett's Keystone Comedy Company. But his Karno commitment will hold him until November.
December 1913	Chaplin arrives at the Keystone Studio in California.
February 2 1914	His first film, *Making a Living*, appears. The amazing total of thirty-five films will be made in this first year.
February 7 1914	His second film, *Kid Auto Races at Venice*, opens. It marks the first appearance of a semblance of the tramp character.
November 14 1914	He stars in *Tillie's Punctured Romance*, generally considered to be the first feature-length comedy.
November 1914	He signs a contract with Essanay Films, where he will make fourteen films in the next year. Essanay will later construct a fifteenth film, *Triple Trouble* (1918), from other Chaplin works.
April 1915	*The Tramp*, the first Charlie film with real pathos, appears.
February 27 1916	Chaplin signs contract with Mutual Films, where he will make twelve celebrated short subjects in 1916 and part of 1917.
1916	Chaplin's controversial book, *Charlie Chaplin's Own Story*, comes out.
1916	After Chaplin leaves Essanay, it puts together *The Essanay-Chaplin Revue*, one of the first Chaplin film anthologies. Innumerable Chaplin cavalcades have since appeared.
January 22 1917	*Easy Street*, generally considered his best Mutual film, appears.
June 17 1917	Chaplin signs contract with First National, for which he will do eight films.
April 1918	*A Dog's Life*.
October 1918	*Shoulder Arms* is a critical and commercial success, though its World War I theme is controversial.
October 23 1918	Chaplin marries Mildred Harris.
1919	With Douglas Fairbanks, D. W. Griffith, and Mary Pickford, founds United Artists. But Chaplin will not be free of his First National contract until 1923.

June 1919	*Sunnyside.*
December 1919	*A Day's Pleasure.*
November 1920	Divorced by Mildred Harris.
February 1921	*The Kid* is the first feature he directs.
1921	Chaplin provides his mother with a California home.
September-October 1921	Triumphantly returns to Europe.
September 1921	*The Idle Class.*
1922	Chaplin's account of his 1921 trip appears as a book, *My Trip Abroad.*
April 1922	*Pay Day.*
February 1923	*The Pilgrim.*
October 1 1923	Chaplin's first United Artists production—*A Woman of Paris*—opens. Chaplin writes and directs but does not star in this critically acclaimed excursion into drama.
March 1924	Chaplin marries Lita Grey.
August 16 1925	*The Gold Rush* quickly becomes his most acclaimed film.
August 22 1927	Divorced by Lita Grey. Seemingly every stage of the proceedings has been played out in the newspapers since Grey's original filing for divorce in January.
January 1928	*The Circus* is a great, though often neglected, Chaplin feature.
August 28 1928	Hannah Chaplin dies.
May 16 1929	At the first Academy Award ceremony, Chaplin is honored with a special Oscar "for versatility and genius in writing, acting, directing and producing *The Circus.*"
February 1931	*City Lights* finds Chaplin defying the sound era with this critical and commercial success. There is a second triumphant return to England, which eventually takes him around the world.
June 1932	Chaplin returns to the United States.
1933	His account of this trip also appears in book form: *A Comedian Sees the World.*

194   Appendix

1935	Chaplin supposedly secretly marries Paulette Goddard sometime in 1935 or 1936, though mystery still surrounds the event and its verity remains in doubt.
February 5 1936	*Modern Times* sees the last appearance of the tramp. Chaplin successfully defies sound once again.
March-April 1936	Chaplin and Goddard visit the Far East.
March 16 1936	The Screenwriters and Actors Guild awards Chaplin outstanding actor honors.
October 15 1940	*The Great Dictator* sees Chaplin enter the sound era with a controversial parody of Hitler. It grosses more than any previous film by the comedian.
December 30 1940	The New York Film Critics vote Chaplin the best actor of the year award. Chaplin declines the honor.
April 18 1942	*The Gold Rush* is reissued with soundtrack and some very short deletions. Chaplin's spoken narration replaces titles.
May 1942	Chaplin, as a last-minute substitute for former ambassador to the Soviet Union Joseph E. Davies, gives a Second Front speech at an American Committee for Russian War Relief rally in San Francisco.
Summer 1942	Divorced by Paulette Goddard in Mexico. The suit is as mysterious as their supposed marriage.
July 22 1942	Gives Second Front speech, via telephone, to a Madison Square Garden rally sponsored by the CIO.
December 1942	The Joan Barry scandals begin, with damaging new twists periodically occurring through the spring of 1945.
June 16 1943	Chaplin Marries Oona O'Neill.
April 11 1947	The controversial *Monsieur Verdoux* opens.
April 12 1947	Chaplin is the victim of a witch-hunting press conference, save for support of James Agee.
1950	Successful revival of *City Lights* surprises Chaplin's critics. *Life* magazine calls the 1931 production the best picture of 1950.
September 1952	Chaplin and family leave New York by ship, bound for Europe. Chaplin will show his young family the English haunts of his youth. While at sea, Chaplin, still a British subject, has his U.S. reentry permit cancelled. If the comedian decides to return, he will have to face more witch-hunting questions on politics and morality before any possible reentry.
October 23 1952	*Limelight* will be Chaplin's last great film. Several conservative groups all but negate its American movie theater engagements.
1952	*Limelight* makes the *New York Times* annual "Ten Best" list.

January 1953	Chaplin purchases an estate, the Manoir de Ban, in the village of Corsair in Switzerland. This will be his last home.
March 1953	The Foreign Language Press Film Critics poll selects *Limelight* as its best film.
September 12 1957	*A King in New York* provides Chaplin's last starring role.
September 1959	*A Chaplin Revue* is compiled from *A Dog's Life*, *Shoulder Arms*, and *The Pilgrim*, with an added soundtrack.
September 1964	*My Autobiography* is published.
April 16 1965	Brother Sydney Chaplin dies.
1965	Chaplin's oldest child by Oona, Geraldine, becomes a film star in her own right with the release of *Doctor Zhivago*.
November 1966	*A Countess from Hong Kong* is Chaplin's final film.
April 10 1972	Chaplin is awarded a special honorary Oscar "for the incalculable effect he has had in making motion pictures the art form of this century."
September 3 1972	The Venice Film Festival awards Chaplin its Golden Lion statuette.
March 27 1973	Chaplin *wins* an Oscar (with Raymond Rasch and Larry Russell) for Best Original Dramatic Score for 1972, from *Limelight*. The 1952 film was eligible for belated consideration because a Los Angeles theater had never previously shown the film—an Academy rule.
1974	*My Life in Pictures*, Chaplin's final book, comes out.
March 4 1975	Chaplin is knighted by Elizabeth II, Queen of England.
1976	Chaplin composes music for the soundtrack of his 1923 production, *A Woman of Paris*.
December 25 1977	Chaplin dies at his estate in Switzerland.
April 16 1981	On what would have been Chaplin's ninety-second birthday, a larger-than-life statue of the comedian as Charlie is unveiled in London's Leicester Square, the heartland of the capital's cinemas. The statue stands just a few yards from one of William Shakespeare. The little tramp with the "east-west" feet has come a long way.

Filmography

The following filmography was constructed from such key listings of recent years as: McDonald, Conway, and Ricci's *The Films of Charlie Chaplin* (1965), Mitry's *Tout Chaplin* (1965/1972), Asplund's *Chapin's Films* (1973), Gifford's *Chaplin* (1974), Sobel and Francis's *Chaplin: Genesis of a Clown* (1977), McCabe's *Charlie Chaplin* (filmography by Gifford, 1978), and Lyons's definitive *Charles Chaplin: A Guide to References and Resources* (1979). When no role description follows an actor's name, it was a minor part.

KEYSTONE

1914   *Making a Living* (1 reel).*
Producer: Mack Sennett. Director: Henry Lehrman. Screenplay: Reed Huestis. Photography: E. J. Vallejo. Cast: Charles Chaplin (sneaky reporter), Virginia Kirtley (girl), Alice Davenport (her mother), Henry Lehrman (reporter), Minte Durfee (girl in bed), Chester Conklin (cop and tramp).

Kid Auto Races at Venice (split reel).
Producer: Mack Sennett. Director: Henry Lehrman. Screenplay: Henry Lehrman. Photography: Frank D. Williams. Cast: Charles Chaplin (tramp), Henry Lehrman (director), Frank Williams (cameraman), Billy Jacobs (boy), Charlotte Fitzpatrick (girl), Thelma Salter (girl), Gordon Griffith (boy).

Mabel's Strange Predicament (1 reel).
Producer: Mack Sennett. Directors: Henry Lehrman and Mack Sennett. Screenplay: Reed Huestis. Photography: Frank D. Williams. Cast: Mabel Normand (Mabel), Charles Chaplin (drunk), Chester Conklin (husband), Alice Davenport (wife), Harry McCoy (admirer), Hank Mann, Al St. John.

---

*One reel runs ten to eleven minutes.

Between Showers (1 reel).
Producer: Mack Sennett. Director: Henry Lehrman. Screenplay: depends on source, either Henry Lehrman or Reed Huestis. Photography: Frank D. Williams. Cast: Ford Sterling (masher), Charles Chaplin (masher), Emma Clifton (girl), Chester Conklin (cop), Sadie Lampe (girl).

A Film Johnny (1 reel).
Producer: Mack Sennett. Director: George Nichols. Script: Craig Hutchinson. Script: Craig Hutchinson. Photography: Frank D. Williams. Cast: Charles Chaplin (the johnny), Roscoe "Fatty" Arbuckle (Fatty), Virginia Kirtley (the Keystone girl), Minta Durfee (actress), Mabel Normand (herself), Ford Sterling (himself), Mack Sennett (himself).

Tango Tangles (1 reel).
Producer: Mack Sennett. Director: Mack Sennett. Script: Mack Sennett. Photography: Frank D. Williams. Cast: Charles Chaplin (drunk), Ford Sterling (bandleader), Roscoe "Fatty" Arbuckle (clarinetist), Minte Durfee (cloakroom girl), Chester Conklin (dancer).

His Favorite Pastime (1 reel).
Producer: Mack Sennett. Director: George Nichols. Script: Craig Hutchinson. Photography: Frank D. Williams. Cast: Charles Chaplin (drunk), Roscoe "Fatty" Arbuckle (drunk), Peggy Pearce (wife).

Cruel, Cruel Love (1 reel).
Producer: Mack Sennett. Director: George Nichols. Script: Craig Hutchinson. Photography: Frank D. Williams. Cast: Charles Chaplin (Mr. Dovey), Minta Durfee (girl), Chester Conklin (butler), Alice Davenport (maid).

The Star Boarder (1 reel).
Producer: Mack Sennett, Director: George Nichols. Screenplay: Craig Hutchinson. Photography: Frank D. Williams. Cast: Charles Chaplin (boarder), Minta Durfee (landlady), Edgar Kennedy (landlord), Gordon Griffith (son), Alice Davenport (landlady's friend).

Mabel at the Wheel (2 reels).
Producer: Mack Sennett. Directors: Mack Sennett and Mabel Normand. Screenplay: unavailable. Photography: Frank D. Williams. Cast: Mabel Normand (Mabel), Charles Chaplin (villain), Harry McCoy (racing driver boyfriend), Chester Conklin (father), Mack Sennett (rube), Al St. John, Fred Mace, Joe Bordeaux, William Seiter (henchmen).

Twenty Minutes of Love (1 reel).
Producer: Mack Sennett. Director: Joseph Madden. Story/Screenplay: Charles Chaplin. Photography: Frank D. Williams. Cast: Charles Chaplin (man), Minta Durfee (girl), Edgar Kennedy (boyfriend), Gordon Griffith (boy), Chester Conklin (thief,) Joseph Swickard (victim).

Caught in a Cabaret (2 reels).
Producer: Mack Sennett. Directors: Mabel Normand and Charles Chaplin. Story/Screenplay: Charles Chaplin. Photography: Frank D. Williams. Cast: Charles Chaplin (waiter), Mabel Normand (society girl), Harry McCoy (boyfriend), Chester Conklin (waiter), Edgar Kennedy (café owner), Minta Durfee (dancer), Alice Davenport (mother), Phyllis Allen (dancer), Joseph Swickard

(father), Gordon Griffith (boy), Alice Howell, Hank Mann, Wallace Mac-
Donald (customers and staff).

Caught in the Rain (1 reel).
Producer: Mack Sennett. Director: Charles Chaplin. Story/Screenplay:
Charles Chaplin. Photography: Frank D. Williams. Cast: Charles Chaplin
(flirt), Alice Davenport (wife), Mack Swain (husband), Alice Howell (girl).

1914   *A Busy Day* (split reel).
Producer: Mack Sennett. Director: Charles Chaplin. Story/Screenplay:
Charles Chaplin. Photography: Frank D. Williams. Cast: Charles Chaplin
(wife). Mack Swain (husband), Phyllis Allen (flirt).

The Fatal Mallet (1 reel).
Producer: Mack Sennett. Directors: disagreement, sometimes Mack Sennett
receives sole credit, other times it is shared with Mabel Normand and Charles
Chaplin. Story/Screenplay: Charles Chaplin or Mack Sennett. Photography:
Frank D. Williams. Cast: Mabel Normand (girl), Charles Chaplin (rival),
Mack Sennett (boyfriend), Mack Swain (man).

Her Friend the Bandit (1 reel).
Producer: Mack Sennett. Directors: Mabel Normand and Charles Chaplin.
Story/Screenplay: unavailable. Photography: Frank D. Williams. Cast:
Mabel Normand (Miss De Rock), Charles Chaplin (bandit), Charles Murray
(Count de Beans).

The Knockout (2 reels).
Producer: Mack Sennett. Director: Charles Avery. Story/Screenplay: Charles
Chaplin. Photography: Frank D. Williams. Cast: Roscoe "Fatty" Arbuckle
(Fatty), Minta Durfee (girlfriend), Edgar Kennedy (Cyclone Flynn), Charles
Chaplin (referee), Mack Swain (spectator), Alice Howell (spectator), Al St.
John (boxer), Hank Mann (boxer), Mack Sennett (spectator), "Slim"
Summerville (spectator), Charles Parrot (cop), Joe Bordeaux (cop), Edward
Cline (cop).

Mabel's Busy Day (1 reel).
Producer: Mack Sennett. Directors: Mabel Normand and Charles Chaplin.
Story/Screenplay: Charles Chaplin. Photography: Frank D. Williams. Cast:
Mabel Normand (Mabel), Charles Chaplin (cad), Chester Conklin (police
sergeant), Billie Bennett (girl), "Slim" Summerville (cop), Harry McCoy, Al
St. John, Charley Chase, Wallace MacDonald.

Mabel's Married Life (1 reel).
Producer: Mack Sennett. Directors: Mabel Normand and Charles Chaplin.
Story/Screenplay: Charles Chaplin. Photography: Frank D. Williams. Cast:
Mabel Normand (Mabel), Charles Chaplin (husband), Mack Swain (Mr.
Wellington, sportsman), Charles Murray (man at bar), Harry McCoy (man at
bar), Alice Howell (sportsman's wife), Hank Mann (friend), Alice Davenport
(neighbor), Al St. John (delivery man), Wallace MacDonald (delivery man).

Laughing Gas (1 reel).
Producer: Mack Sennett. Director: Charles Chaplin. Story/Screenplay:
Charles Chaplin. Photography: Frank D. Williams. Cast: Charles Chaplin

(dentist's assistant), Fritz Schade (Dr. Pain), Alice Howell (Mrs. Pain), "Slim" Summerville (patient), Joseph Swickard (patient), Joseph Sutherland (assistant).

The Property Man (2 reels).
Producer: Mack Sennett. Director: Charles Chaplin. Story/Screenplay: Charles Chaplin. Photography: Frank D. Williams. Cast: Charles Chaplin (props), Fritz Schade (Garlico), Phyllis Allen (Hamlena Fat), Alice Davenport (actress), Charles Bennett (actor), Mack Sennett (man in the audience), Joe Bordeaux (actor), Harry McCoy, Lee Morris.

The Face on the Bar-Room Floor (1 reel).
Producer: Mack Sennett. Director: Charles Chaplin. Story/Screenplay: Charles Chaplin (from a Hugh Antoine D'Arcy poem). Photography: Frank D. Williams. Cast: Charles Chaplin (artist), Cecile Arnold (Madeleine), Fritz Schade (client), Chester Conklin (man), Vivian Edwards (girl), Harry McCoy (drinker), Hank Mann (drinker), Wallace MacDonald (drinker).

Recreation (split reel).
Producer: Mack Sennett. Director: Charles Chaplin. Story/Screenplay: Charles Chaplin. Photography: Frank D. Williams. Cast: Charles Chaplin (tramp), Charlie Murray (seaman). The identity of the four other performers is in question, but the names that have been suggested include Charlie Murray, Norma Nichols, Alice Davenport, and Rhea Mitchell.

The Masquerader (1 reel).
Producer: Mack Sennett. Director: Charles Chaplin. Story/Screenplay: Charles Chaplin. Photography: Frank D. Williams. Cast: Charles Chaplin (himself), Roscoe "Fatty" Arbuckle (himself), Charles Murray (film director), Chester Conklin (himself), Fritz Schade (villain), Minta Durfee (heroine), Cecile Arnold (actress), Vivian Edward (actress), Harry McCoy (actor), Charles Parrott (actress).

His New Profession (1 reel).
Producer: Mack Sennett. Director: Charles Chaplin. Story/Screenplay: Charles Chaplin. Photography: Frank D. Williams. Cast: Charles Chaplin (Charlie), Minta Durfee (girl), Fritz Schade (uncle), Charles Parrott (nephew), Cecile Arnold (girl), Harry McCoy (cop).

The Rounders (1 reel).
Producer: Mack Sennett. Director: Charles Chaplin. Story/Screenplay: Charles Chaplin. Photography: Frank D. Williams. Cast: Charles Chaplin (Mr. Full), Roscoe "Fatty" Arbuckle (Mr. Fuller), Phyllis Allen (Mrs. Full), Minta Durfee (Mrs. Fuller), Fritz Schade (diner), Al St. John (bellhop), Charles Parrott (diner), Wallace MacDonald (diner).

The New Janitor (1 reel).
Producer: Mack Sennett. Director: Charles Chaplin. Story/Screenplay: Charles Chaplin. Photography: Frank D. Williams. Cast: Charles Chaplin (janitor), Fritz Schade (boss), Minta Durfee (stenographer), Jack Dillon (clerk), Al St. John (elevator boy).

Those Love Pangs (1 reel).
Producer: Mack Sennett. Director: Charles Chaplin. Story/Screenplay:

Charles Chaplin. Photography: Frank D. Williams. Cast: Charles Chaplin (flirt), Chester Conklin (rival), Cecile Arnold (girl), Vivian Edwards (girl), Edgar Kennedy (man), Norma Nichols (landlady), Harry McCoy (cop).

Dough and Dynamite (2 reels).
Producer: Mack Sennett. Directors: Charles Chaplin and Mack Sennett. Story/Screenplay: Charles Chaplin. Photography: Frank D. Williams. Cast: Charles Chaplin (Pierre), Chester Conklin (Jacques), Fritz Schade (Monsieur LaVie), Cecile Arnold (waitress), Vivian Edwards (waitress), Phyllis Allen (customer), Edgar Kennedy (baker), Charles Parrott (baker), "Slim" Summerville (baker), Norma Nichols (Madame LaVie), Wallace MacDonald (baker), Jack Dillon (customer).

Gentleman of Nerve (1 reel).
Producer: Mack Sennett. Director: Charles Chaplin. Story/Screenplay: Charles Chaplin. Photography: Frank D. Williams. Cast: Charles Chaplin (Mr. Wow-Wow), Mabel Normand (Mabel), Mack Swain (Ambrose), Chester Conklin (Walrus), Phyllis Allen (wife), Edgar Kennedy (cop), Charles Parrott (spectator), Alice Davenport (waitress), "Slim" Summerville (spectator).

His Musical Career (1 reel).
Producer: Mack Sennett. Director: Charles Chaplin. Story/Screenplay: Charles Chaplin. Photography: Frank D. Williams. Cast: Charles Chaplin (Tom), Mack Swain (Ambrose), Fritz Schade (Mr. Rich), Alice Howell (Mrs. Rich), Charles Parrott (manager), Joe Bordeaux (Mr. Poor), Norma Nichols (Mrs. Poor).

His Trysting Place (2 reels).
Producer: Mack Sennett. Director: Charles Chaplin. Story/Screenplay: Charles Chaplin. Photography: Frank D. Williams. Cast: Charles Chaplin (Clarence), Mabel Normand (Mabel), Mack Swain (Ambrose), Phyllis Allen (Mrs. Ambrose).

Tillie's Punctured Romance (6 reels).
Producer: Mack Sennett. Director: Mack Sennett. Screenplay: Hampton Del Ruth (from the play *Tillie's Nightmare*, by Edgar Smith). Cast: Marie Dressler (Tillie Banks), Charles Chaplin (Charlie), Mabel Normand (Mabel), Mack Swain (John Banks), Charles Bennett (Douglas Banks), Charles Murray (detective), Chester Conklin (guest), Charles Parrott (detective), Edgar Kennedy (proprietor), Harry McCoy (pianist), Minta Durfee (maid), Phyllis Allen (wardress), Alice Davenport (guest), "Slim" Summerville (cop), Al St. John (cop), Wallace MacDonald (cop), Joe Bordeaux (cop), Gordon Griffith (newsboy), Billie Bennett (girl), G. G. Ligon (cop), Rev. D. Simpson (himself).

Getting Acquainted (1 reel).
Producer: Mack Sennett. Director: Charles Chaplin. Story/Screenplay: Charles Chaplin. Photography: Frank D. Williams. Cast: Charles Chaplin (Mr. Sniffles), Mabel Normand (Mrs. Ambrose), Mack Swain (Mr. Ambrose), Phyllis Allen (Mrs. Sniffles), Harry McCoy (cop), Edgar Kennedy (Turk), Cecile Arnold (girl).

His Prehistoric Past (2 reels).
Producer: Mack Sennett. Director: Charles Chaplin. Story/Screenplay: Charles Chaplin. Photography: Frank D. Wililams. Cast: Charles Chaplin (Weakchin), Mack Swain (Kind Lowbrow), Fritz Schade (Cleo), Gene Marsh (favorite wife), Cecile Arnold (cave woman), Al St. John (caveman).

ESSANAY

1915   *His New Job* (2 reels).
Producer: Jessie J. Robbins. Director: Charles Chaplin. Story/Screenplay: Charles Chaplin. Photography: Roland H. Totheroh. Cast: Charles Chaplin (himself), Ben Turpin (himself), Charlotte Mineau (actress), Charles Insley (film director), Leo White (actor), Frank J. Coleman (manager), Gloria Swanson (stenographer), Agnes Ayars (stenographer).

1915   *A Night Out* (2 reels).
Producer: Jessie J. Robbins. Director: Charles Chaplin. Story/Screenplay: Charles Chaplin. Photography: Roland H. Totheroh and Harry Ensign. Cast: Charles Chaplin (drunk), Ben Turpin (drunk), Leo White (the Count), Bud Jamison (waiter), Edna Purviance (wife), Fred Goodwins (man).

The Champion (2 reels).
Producer: Jessie J. Robbins. Director: Charles Chaplin. Story/Screenplay: Charles Chaplin. Photography: Roland H. Totheroh and Harry Ensign. Cast: Charles Chaplin (tramp), Edna Purviance (girl), Bud Jamison (champion), Leo White (the Count), Billy Armstrong (sparring partner), Paddy McGuire (sparring partner), Carl Stockdale (sparring partner), Lloyd Bacon (Spike Dugan), Ben Turpin (salesman), G. M. Anderson (spectator).

In the Park (1 reel).
Producer: Jessie J. Robbins. Director: Charles Chaplin. Story/Screenplay: Charles Chaplin. Photography: Roland H. Totheroh and Harry Ensign. Cast: Charles Chaplin (flirt), Edna Purviance (nursemaid), Leo White (the Count), Lloyd Bacon (tramp), Bud Jamison (boyfriend), Billy Armstrong (man), Margie Reiger (girl), Ernest Van Pelt (cop).

A Jitney Elopement (2 reels).
Producer: Jessie J. Robbins. Director: Charles Chaplin. Story/Screenplay: Charles Chaplin. Photography: Roland H. Totheroh and Harry Ensign. Cast: Charles Chaplin (tramp), Edna Purviance (girl), Leo White (the Count), Fred Goodwins (father), Paddy McGuire (old servant), Lloyd Bacon (footman), Bud Jamison (cop), Ernest Van Pelt (cop).

The Tramp (2 reels).
Producer: Jessie J. Robbins. Director: Charles Chaplin. Story/Screenplay: Charles Chaplin. Photography: Roland H. Totheroh and Harry Ensign. Cast: Charles Chaplin (tramp), Edna Purviance (girl), Leo White (tramp), Fred Goodwins (farmer), Bud Jamison (tramp), Lloyd Bacon (boyfriend), Paddy McGuire (farmhand), Ernest Van Pelt (tramp), Billy Armstrong (poet).

By the Sea (1 reel).

Producer: Jessie J. Robbins. Director: Charles Chaplin. Story/Screenplay: Charles Chaplin. Photography: Roland H. Totheroh and Harry Ensign. Cast: Charles Chaplin (tramp), Edna Purviance (girl), Billy Armstrong (other man), Bud Jamison (dandy), Margie Reiger (girl), Carl Stockdale (policeman).

Work (2 reels).

Producer: Jessie J. Robbins. Director: Charles Chaplin. Story/Screenplay: Charles Chaplin. Photography: Toland H. Totheroh and Harry Ensign. Cast: Charles Chaplin (assistant), Edna Purviance (maid), Charles Insley (paperhanger), Billy Armstrong (husband), Marta Golden (wife), Leo White (lover), Paddy McGuire (hod carrier).

A Woman (2 reels).

Producer: Jessie J. Robbins. Director: Charles Chaplin. Story/Screenplay: Charles Chaplin. Photography: Roland H. Totheroh and Harry Ensign. Cast: Charles Chaplin (tramp), Edna Purviance (girl), Charles Insley (father), Marta Golden (mother), Billy Armstrong (suitor), Margie Reiger (flirt), Leo White (gentleman).

The Bank (2 reels).

Producer: Jessie J. Robbins. Director: Charles Chaplin. Story/Screenplay: Charles Chaplin. Photography: Roland H. Totheroh and Harry Ensign. Cast: Charles Chaplin (janitor), Edna Purviance (Edna), Carl Stockdale (Charlie the cashier), Billy Armstrong (janitor), Charles Insley (manager), John Rand (salesman), Leo White (officer), Fred Goodwins (thief), Frank J. Coleman (thief), Wesley Ruggles (thief), Paddy McGuire (thief), Lloyd Bacon (thief), Carrie Clarke Ward (thief).

Shanghaied (2 reels).

Producer: Jessie J. Robbins. Director: Charles Chaplin. Story/Screenplay: Charles Chaplin. Photography: Roland H. Totheroh and Harry Ensign. Cast: Charles Chaplin (tramp), Edna Purviance (Edna), Wesley Ruggles (owner), John Rand (captain), Bud Jamison (mate), Lawrence A. Bowes (cook), Billy Armstrong (seaman), Paddy McGuire (seaman), Leo White (seaman), Fred Goodwins (seaman).

A Night in the Show (2 reels).

Producer: Jessie J. Robbins. Director: Charles Chaplin. Story/Screenplay: Charles Chaplin. Photography: Roland H. Totheroh. Cast: Charles Chaplin (Mr. Pest/Mr. Rowdy), Edna Purviance (lady), Leo White (Count/Prof. Nix), John Rand (conductor), Bud Jamison (Dot), James T. Kelley (Dash), Dee Lampton (fat boy), May White (La Bella Wienerwurst), Paddy McGuire (trombonist), Fred Goodwins (tuba player), Carrie Clark Ward (woman).

1915/ *Charlie Chaplin's Burlesque on Carmen* (Chaplin's cut was 2 reels and
1916 appeared in late 1915. Essanay released a 4-reel padded version in 1916, after Chaplin had left the company).

Producer: Jessie J. Robbins. Director: Charles Chaplin. Screenplay: Charles Chaplin (from the Prosper Mérimée story and the opera by Georges Bizet, Henri Meilhac, and Ludovic Halévy). Photography: Roland H. Totheroh.

Cast: Charles Chaplin (Darn Hosiery), Edna Purviance (Carmen), Ben Turpin (Don Remendade), Jack Henderson (Lilias Pasta), May White (Frasquita), Bud Jamison (soldier), Wesley Ruggles (tramp), Lawrence A. Bowes, Frank J. Coleman.

1916 *Police* (2 reels, but somewhat altered by Essanay after Chaplin left). Producer: Jessie J. Robbins. Director: Charles Chaplin. Story: Charles Chaplin and Vincent Bryan. Screenplay: Charles Chaplin. Cast: Charles Chaplin (convict 999), Edna Purviance (girl), Wesley Ruggles (thief), Billy Armstrong (thief), John Rand (cop), Leo White (lodging house keeper/vendor/cop), James T. Kelley (drunk/tramp), Fred Goodwins (cop/pastor), Bud Jamison (cop), Frank J. Coleman (cop).

1918 *Triple Trouble* (2 reels, constructed by Essanay from already existing material Chaplin had done for them: *Police*, *Work*, and the unfinished *Life*, and released long after Chaplin's exit from the company). Producer: Jessie J. Robbins. Director: Charles Chaplin and Leo White. Story/Screenplay: Charles Chaplin and Leo White. Photography: Roland H. Totheroh. Cast: Charles Chaplin (janitor), Edna Purviance (maid), Leo White (the Count), Billy Armstrong (cook/thief), James T. Kelley (singer), Bud Jamison (tramp), Wesley Ruggles (crook), Albert Austin (man).

LONE STAR-MUTUAL

1916 *The Floorwalker* (2 reels). Producer/Director: Charles Chaplin. Story: Charles Chaplin and Vincent Bryan. Screenplay: Charles Chaplin. Photography: Roland H. Totheroh and William C. Foster. Cast: Charles Chaplin (floorwalker), Edna Purviance (secretary), Eric Campbell (George Brush), Lloyd Bacon (assistant), Albert Austin (clerk), Leo White (Count), Charlotte Mineau (detective), Tom Nelson (detective), Henry Bergman (old man), James T. Kelley (elevator operator), Bud Jamison, Stanley Sanford, Frank J. Coleman.

The Fireman (2 reels). Producer/Director: Charles Chaplin. Story: Charles Chaplin and Vincent Bryan. Screenplay: Charles Chaplin. Photography: Roland H. Totheroh and William C. Foster. Cast: Charles Chaplin (fireman), Edna Purviance (Edna), Eric Campbell (captain), Lloyd Bacon (father), Leo White (householder), John Rand (fireman), James T. Kelley (fireman), Charlotte Mineau (mother).

The Vagabond (2 reels). Producer/Director: Charles Chaplin. Story: Charles Chaplin and Vincent Bryan. Screenplay: Charles Chaplin. Photography: Roland H. Totheroh and William C. Foster. Cast: Charles Chaplin (vagabond), Edna Purviance (girl), Eric Campbell (gypsy chief), Leo White (old gypsy woman/old gypsy man), Lloyd Bacon (artist), Charlotte Mineau (mother), Phyllis Allen (woman), John Rand (trumpeter), Albert Austin (trombonist), James T. Kelley (bandsman), Frank J. Coleman (bandsman).

One A.M. (2 reels). Producer/Director: Charles Chaplin. Story/Screenplay: Charles Chaplin.

Photography: Roland H. Totheroh and William C. Foster. Cast: Charles Chaplin (drunk), Albert Austin (taxi driver).

The Count (2 reels).
Producer/Director: Charles Chaplin. Story/Screenplay: Charles Chaplin. Photography: Roland H. Totheroh and William C. Foster. Cast: Charles Chaplin (tailor's assistant), Edna Purviance (Edna Moneybags), Eric Campbell (Buttinsky-tailor), Leo White (Count Broko), Charlotte Mineau (Mrs. Moneybags), James T. Kelley (butler), Albert Austin (guest), Frank J. Coleman (cop), John Rand (guest), May White (Ima Pipp), Stanley Sanford (guest), May White (Ima Pipp), Stanley Sanford (guest), Leota Bryan (girl), Eva Thatcher (Flirtitia Doughbelle), Loyal Underwood (small man).

The Pawnshop (2 reels).
Producer/Director: Charles Chaplin. Story/Screenplay: Charles Chaplin. Photography: Roland H. Totheroh and William C. Foster. Cast: Charles Chaplin (assistant to pawnbroker), Edna Purviance (pawnbroker's daughter), Henry Bergman (pawnbroker), John Rand (clerk), Eric Campbell (thief), Albert Austin (customer), Frank J. Coleman (cop), James T. Kelley (customer), Wesley Ruggles (customer).

Behind the Screen (2 reels).
Producer/Director: Charles Chaplin. Story/Screenplay: Charles Chaplin. Photography: Roland H. Totheroh and William C. Foster. Cast: Charles Chaplin (film property assistant), Edna Purviance (country girl), Eric Campbell (film property foreman), Henry Bergman (film director), Lloyd Bacon (film director), Albert Austin (stagehand), Frank C. Coleman (assistant director), Charlotte Mineau (actress), John Rand (stagehand), James T. Kelley (cameraman), Wesley Ruggles (actor), Tom Wood (actor).

1916   *The Rink* (2 reels).
Producer/Director: Charles Chaplin. Story/Screenplay: Charles Chaplin. Photography: Roland H. Totheroh and William C. Foster. Cast: Charles Chaplin (waiter), Edna Purviance (Edna Loneleigh), Eric Campbell (Mr. Stout), Henry Bergman (Mrs. Stout), Frank J. Coleman (Mr. Loneleigh, Edna's father), Charlotte Mineau (friend), Albert Austin (cook/skater), James T. Kelley (cook), John Rand (Fritz), Lloyd Bacon (customer), Leota Bryan (friend).

1917   *Easy Street* (2 reels).
Producer/Director: Charles Chaplin. Story/Screenplay: Charles Chaplin. Photography: Roland H. Totheroh and William C. Foster. Cast: Charles Chaplin (tramp), Edna Purviance (mission worker), Eric Campbell (Big Eric), Henry Bergman (anarchist), Albert Austin (mission minister/cop), James T. Kelley (mission worker/cop), John Rand (tramp/cop), Frank J. Coleman (cop), Leo White (cop), Charlotte Mineau (wife), Lloyd Bacon (drug addict), Janet Miller Sully (mother), Loyal Underwood (police chief/father).

The Cure (2 reels).
Producer/Director: Charles Chaplin. Story/Screenplay: Charles Chaplin. Photography: Roland H. Totheroh and William C. Foster. Cast: Charles Chaplin (drunk), Edna Purviance (girl), Eric Campbell (patient), Henry

Bergman (masseur), John Rand (attendant), Albert Austin (attendant), Frank J. Coleman (proprietor), James T. Kelley (bellhop), Leota Bryan (nurse), Janet Miller Sully (woman), Loyal Underwood (patient), Tom Wood (patient).

The Immigrant (2 reels).
Producer/Director: Charles Chaplin. Story/Screenplay: Charles Chaplin. Photography: Roland H. Totheroh and William C. Foster. Cast: Charles Chaplin (immigrant), Edna Purviance (immigrant girl), Eric Campbell (head waiter), Kitty Bradbury (Edna's mother), Albert Austin (immigrant/diner), Henry Bergman (woman/artist), James T. Kelley (tramp/immigrant), Frank J. Coleman (proprietor/official), Stanley Sanford (gambler), John Rand (customer), Loyal Underwood (immigrant).

The Adventurer (2 reels).
Producer/Director: Charles Chaplin. Story/Screenplay: Charles Chaplin. Photography: Roland H. Totheroh and William C. Foster. Cast: Charles Chaplin (escaped convict), Edna Purviance (girl), Eric Campbell (suitor), Henry Bergman (father/worker), Marta Golden (mother), Albert Austin (butler), Frank J. Coleman (guard), James T. Kelley (old man), Phyllis Allen (governess), Toraichi Kono (chauffeur), John Rand (guest), May White (lady), Loyal Underwood (guest), Janet Miller Sully (Marie), Monta Bell (man).

FIRST NATIONAL

1918   *A Dog's Life* (3 reels).
Producer/Director: Charles Chaplin. Script/Screenplay: Charles Chaplin. Photography: Roland H. Totheroh. Cast: Charles Chaplin (tramp), Edna Purviance (singer), Sydney Chaplin (proprietor), Tom Wilson (cop), Albert Austin (thief), Henry Bergman (tramp/woman), James T. Kelley (thief), Charles Reisner (clerk), Billy White (café owner), Janet Miller Sully (singer), Bud Jamison (client), Loyal Underwood (client), Park Jones (waiter), Scraps (dog).

Shoulder Arms (4 reels).
Producer/Director: Charles Chaplin. Story/Screenplay: Charles Chaplin. Photography: Roland H. Totheroh. Cast: Charles Chaplin (recruit), Edna Purviance (French girl), Sydney Chaplin (Kaiser Wilhelm/soldier), Albert Austin (officer/Kaiser's driver/recruit), Tom Wilson (sergeant), John Rand (soldier), Loyal Underwood (captain), Park Jones (soldier).

Charles Chaplin in a Liberty Loan Appeal (split reel). Producer: Liberty Loan Committee. Director: Charles Chaplin. Story/Screenplay: Charles Chaplin. Photography: Roland H. Totheroh. Cast for the Four Sketches: Charles Chaplin, Edna Purviance, Albert Austin, Sydney Chaplin.

1919   *Sunnyside* (3 reels).
Producer/Director: Charles Chaplin. Story/Screenplay: Charles Chaplin. Photography: Roland H. Totheroh. Cast: Charles Chaplin (handyman), Edna Purviance (country girl), Tom Wilson (boss), Henry Bergman (father), Tom Terriss (city man), Loyal Underwood (old man), Park Jones (fat man).

A Day's Pleasure (2 reels).
Producer/Director: Charles Chaplin. Story/Screenplay: Charles Chaplin. Photography: Roland H. Totheroh. Cast: Charles Chaplin (father), Edna Purviance (mother), Tom Wilson (cop), Sydney Chaplin (father), Henry Bergman (captain), Babe London (fat girl), Albert Austin (trombonist), Loyal Underwood (musician), Raymond Lee (boy), Jackie Coogan (boy).

1921   *The Kid* (6 reels).
Producer/Director: Charles Chaplin. Story/Screenplay: Charles Chaplin. Photography: Roland H. Totheroh. Associate Director: Charles Reisner. Cast: Charles Chaplin (tramp), Edna Purviance (woman), Jackie Coogan (kid), Carl Miller (artist), Tom Wilson (cop), Charles Reisner (bully), Henry Bergman (proprietor), Albert Austin (crook), Phyllis Allen (woman), Nellie Bly Baker (neighbor), Jack Coogan (man), Monta Bell (man), Raymond Lee (boy), Lillita McMurray (angel).

The Idle Class (2 reels).
Producer/Director: Charles Chaplin. Story/Screenplay: Charles Chaplin. Photography: Roland H. Totheroh. Cast: Charles Chaplin (tramp/husband), Edna Purviance (wife), Mack Swain (father), Henry Bergman (tramp/cop), Rex Storey (robber/guest), John Rand (tramp/guest), Allen Garcia (golfer/guest), Loyal Underwood (guest), Lillian McMurray (maid), Lita Grey—formerly Lillita McMurray (maid).

1922   *Pay Day* (2 reels).
Producer/Director: Charles Chaplin. Story/Screenplay: Charles Chaplin. Photography: Roland H. Totheroh. Cast: Charles Chaplin (worker), Edna Purviance (foreman's daughter), Mack Swain (foreman), Phyllis Allen (wife), Sydney Chaplin (friend/proprietor), Henry Bergman (drinking companion), Allen Garcia (drinking companion), Albert Austin (worker), John Rand (worker), Loyal Underwood (worker).

1923   *The Pilgrim* (5 reels)
Producer/Director: Charles Chaplin. Story/Screenplay: Charles Chaplin. Photography: Roland H. Totheroh. Associate Director: Charles Reisner. Cast: Charles Chaplin (pilgrim), Edna Purviance (Edna Brown), Mack Swain (deacon), Kitty Bradbury (Mrs. Brown), "Dinky Dean" Reisner (boy), Sydney Chaplin (father), Mai Wells (mother), Charles Reisner (thief), Loyal Underwood (elder), Tom Murray (sheriff), Monta Bell (policeman), Henry Bergman (traveller), Raymond Lee (pastor), Edith Bostwick (lady), Florence Latimer (lady), Phyllis Allen (lady).

REGENT-UNITED ARTISTS

A Woman of Paris (8 reels).
Producer/Director: Charles Chaplin. Story/Screenplay: Charles Chaplin. Music: Charles Chaplin (added, 1976). Photography: Roland H. Totheroh. Cameraman: Jack Wilson. Assistant Director: Edward Sutherland. Literary Editor: Monta Bell. Art Director: Arthur Stibolt. Research: Jean de Limur and Henri d'Abbadie d'Arrast. Cast: Edna Purviance (Marie St. Clair), Adolphe Menjou (Pierre Revel), Carl Miller (Jean Millet), Lydia Knott

(Madame Millet), Charles French (Monsieur Millet), Clarence Geldert (Monsieur St. Clair), Betty Morrissey (Fifi), Malvina Polo (Paulette), Karl Guttman (conductor), Henry Bergman (maître d'hôtel), Harry Northrup (valet), Nellie Bly Baker (masseuse), Charles Chaplin (porter).

CHAPLIN–UNITED ARTISTS

1925   *The Gold Rush* (9 reels).
Producer/Director: Charles Chaplin. Story/Screenplay: Charles Chaplin. Photography: Roland H. Totheroh. Cameraman: Jack Wilson. Technical Director: Charles D. Hall. Associate Directors: Charles Reisner and Henri d'Abbadie d'Arrast. Production Manager: Alfred Reeves. Cast: Charles Chaplin (lone prospector), Georgia Hale (Georgia), Mack Swain (Big Jim McKay), Tom Murray (Black Larson), Malcolm Waite (Jack Cameron), Henry Bergman (Hank Curtis), Betty Morrissey (Betty), John Rand (prospector), Albert Austin (prospector), Heinie Conklin (prospector), Allan Garcia (prospector), Tom Wood (prospector).

1928   *The Circus* (7 reels).
Producer/Director: Charles Chaplin. Story/Screenplay: Charles Chaplin. Music: Charles Chaplin (added, 1970). Photography: Roland H. Totheroh. Cameramen: Jack Wilson and Mark Marklatt. Assistant Director: Harry Crocker. Art Director: Charles D. Hall. Editor: Charles Chaplin. Laboratory Supervisor: William E. Hinckley. Cast: Charles Chaplin (tramp), Merna Kennedy (equestrienne), Betty Morrissey (vanishing lady), Harry Crocker (Rex), Allan Garcia (proprietor), Henry Bergman (clown), Stanley J. Sanford (ringmaster), Geroge Davis (magician), John B. Rand (property man), Steve Murphy (pickpocket), Doc Stone (boxer), Albert Austin, Heinie Conklin.

1931   *City Lights* (87 minutes).
Producer/Director: Charles Chaplin. Story/Screenplay: Charles Chaplin. Photography: Roland H. Totheroh. Cameramen: Gordon Pollack and Mark Marklatt. Assistant Directors: Harry Crocker, Henry Bergman, and Albert Austin. Art Director: Charles D. Hall. Music: Charles Chaplin; José Padilla's *La Violetera*. Music Arrangements: Arthur Johnson. Music Director: Alfred Newman. Production Manager: Alfred Reeves. Cast: Charles Chaplin (tramp), Virginia Cherrill (blind girl), Harry Myers (millionaire), Hank Mann (boxer), Allan Garcia (butler), Florence Lee (grandmother), Henry Bergman (mayor/janitor), Albert Austin (sweeper/crook), John Rand (tramp), James Donnelly (foreman), James Robert Parrish (newsboy), Stanhope Wheatcroft (man in café), Jean Harlow (guest).

1936   *Modern Times* (85 minutes).
Producer/Director: Charles Chaplin. Story/Screenplay: Charles Chaplin. Photography: Roland H. Totheroh and Ira Morgan. Assistant Directors: Carter De Haven and Henry Bergman. Art Directors: Charles D. Hall and J. Russell Spencer. Music: Charles Chaplin; Leo Daniderff's *Je Cherche Après Titine*. Music Arrangements: Edward Powell and David Raskin. Music Director: Alfred Newman. Production: Alfred Reeves and Jack Wilson. Cast: Charles Chaplin (worker), Paulette Goddard (gamin), Henry Bergman

(proprietor), Stanley J. Stanford (Big Bill), Chester Conklin (mechanic), Hank Mann (burglar), Stanley Blystone (Sheriff Couler), Allan Garcia (president), Dick Alexander (convict), Cecil Reynolds (minister), Myra McKinney (minister's wife), Lloyd Ingraham (governor), Louis Netheaux (addict), Heinie Conklin (workman), Frank Moran (convict), Murdoch McQuarrie, Wilfred Lucas, Edward Le Saint, Fred Maltesta, Sam Stein, Juana Sutton, Ted Oliver, Edward Kimball, John Rand, Walter James.

1940   *The Great Dictator* (126 minutes).
Producer/Director: Charles Chaplin. Story/Screenplay: Charles Chaplin. Photography: Roland H. Totheroh and Karl Struss. Assistant Directors: Daniel James, Wheeler Dryden and Robert Meitzer. Coordinator: Henry Bergman. Art Director: J. Russell Spencer. Editor: Willard Nico. Music: Charles Chaplin, Wagner, Brahms. Music Director: Meredith Wilson. Sound: Percy Townsend and Glenn Rominger. Cast: Charles Chaplin (Adenoid Hynkel/Jewish barber), Paulette Goddard (Hannah), Jack Oakie (Benzino Napaloni), Henry Daniel (Garbitsch), Reginald Gardiner (Schultz), Billy Gilbert (Herring), Maurice Moskovich (Mr. Jaeckel), Emma Dunn (Mrs. Jaeckel), Bernard Gorcey (Mr. Mann), Paul Weigel (Mr. Agar), Grace Hayle (Madame Napoloni), Carter de Haven (Ambassador), Chester Conklin (customer), Eddie Gribbon (storm trooper), Hank Mann (storm trooper), Leo White (barber), Lucien Prival (officer), Richard Alexander (storm trooper), Esther Michelson, Florence Wright, Robert O. David, Eddie Dunn, Peter Lynd Hayes, Nita Pike, Harry Semels, Jack Perrin, Pat Flaherty.

1942   *The Gold Rush* (Chaplin reissued; with soundtrack, some very short deletions.)
Music: Charles Chaplin. Narrator: Charles Chaplin. Music Director: Max Terr. Editor: Harold McGhean.

1947   *Monsieur Verdoux* (122 minutes).
Producer/Director: Charles Chaplin. Story/Screenplay: Charles Chaplin (from an idea by Orson Welles). Photography: Roland H. Totheroh, Curt Courant, and Wallace Chewing. Associate Director: Robert Florey. Assistant Directors: Rex Bailey and Wheeler Dryden. Art Director: John Beckman. Editor: Willard Nico. Music: Charles Chaplin. Music Director: Rudolph Schrager. Sound: James T. Corrigan. Costumes: Drew Tetrick. Narrator: Charles Chaplin. Cast: Charles Chaplin (Henri Verdoux), Martha Raye (Annabelle Bonheur), Isobel Elsom (Maria Grosnay), Marilyn Nash (girl), Robert Lewis (Maurice Bottello), Mady Correll (Mona Verdoux), Allison Rodell (Peter Verdoux), Audrey Betz (Martha Bottello), Ada-May (Annette), Marjorie Bennett (maid), Helen Heigh (Yvonne), Margaret Hoffman (Lydia Floray), Irving Bacon (Pierre Couvais), Edwin Mills (Jean Couvais), Virginia Brissac (Carlotta Couvais), Almira Sessions (Lena Couvais), Eula Morgan (Phoebe Couvais), Bernard J. Nedal (police prefect), Charles Evans (Detective Morron), Arthur Hohl (estate agent), John Harmon (Joe Darwin), Vera Marshe (Mrs. Darwin), William Frawley (Jean la Salle), Fritz Lieber (priest), Barbara Slater (florist), Fred Karno, Jr. (Mr. Karno), Barry Norton (guest), Pierre Watkin (official), Cyril Delevanti (postman), Charles Wagenheim (friend), Addison Richards (manager), James Craven (friend),

Frankln Farnum (victim), Herb Virgran (reporter), Boyd Irwin (official), Paul Newland (guest), Joseph Crehan (broker), Wheaton Chambers (druggist), Frank Reicher (doctor), Wheeler Dryden (salesman), Edna Purviance (extra), Christine Ell, Lois Conklin, Tom Wilson, Philips Smalley.

CELEBRATED-UNITED ARTISTS

1952 *Limelight* (143 minutes).
Producer/Director: Charles Chaplin. Story/Screenplay: Charles Chaplin. Associate Director: Robert Aldrich. Assistant Producers: Jerome Epstein and Wheeler Dryden. Photography: Karl Struss. Photographic Consultant: Roland H. Totheroh. Art Director: Eugene Lourie. Editor: Joseph Engel. Music: Charles Chaplin. Songs: Charles Chaplin and Ray Rasch. Choreography: Charles Chaplin, Andre Eglevsky and Melissa Hayden. Cast: Charles Chaplin (Calvero), Claire Bloom (Terry-Thereza), Nigel Bruce (Postant), Buster Keaton (partner), Sydney Chaplin (Neville), Norman Lloyd (Bodalink), Andre Eglevsky (harlequin), Melissa Hayden (Columbine), Marjorie Bennett (Mrs. Alsop), Wheeler Dryden (doctor/clown), Barry Bernard (John Redfern), Leonard Mudie (doctor), Snub Pollard (musician), Charles Chaplin, Jr. (clown), Geraldine Chaplin (child), Michael Chaplin (child), Josephine Chaplin (child), Edna Purviance (woman), Loyal Underwood, Stapleton Kent, Mollie Blessing, Julian Ludwig.

ATTICA-ARCHWAY

1957 *A King in New York* (109 minutes).
Producer/Director: Charles Chaplin. Story/Screenplay: Charles Chaplin. Photography: George Perinal. Art Director:. Allan Harris. Editor: John Seabourne. Music: Charles Chaplin. Sound: Spender Reeves. Cast: Charles Chaplin (King Shadow), Dawn Addams (Ann Kay), Oliver Johnston (Jaume), Maxine Audley (Queen Irene), Jerry Desmonde (prime minister), Michael Chaplin (Rupert McAbee), Harry Green (lawyer Green), Phil Brown (headmaster), John McLaren (McAbee Sr.), Alan Gifford (school superintendent), Shani Wallis (singer), Joy Nichols (singer), Joan Ingram (Mona Cromwell), Sidney James Johnson), Robert Arden (elevator boy), Nicholas Tannar (butler), Lauri Lupino Lane (comedian), George Truzzi (comedian), George Woodbridge, MacDonald Parke.

ROY-UNITED ARTISTS

1959 *The Chaplin Revue* (117 minutes).
Compiled from *A Dog's Life*, *Shoulder Arms*, and *The Pilgrim*, with soundtrack. The opening is footage of early Hollywood and Chaplin at work, with the comedian narrating. Music: Charles Chaplin. Song: "Bound for Texas" by Charles Chaplin and sung by Matt Munro.

UNIVERSAL

1966   *A Countess from Hong Kong* (120 minutes.)
Producer: Jerome Epstein. Director: Charles Chaplin. Story/Screenplay: Charles Chaplin. Story/Screenplay: Charles Chaplin. Photography: Arthur Ibbetson. Production Supervisor: Denis Johnson. Production Designer: Don Ashton. Art Director: Robert Cartwright. Set Decorator: Vernon Dixon. Editor: Gordon Hales. Assistant Director: Jack Causey. Music: Charles Chaplin. Music Director: Lambert Williamson. Music Associate: Eric James. Sound: Michael Hopkins. Sound Recording: Bill Daniels and Ken Barker. Titles: Gordon Shedrick. Color: Technicolor. Process: Cinemascope. Cast: Marlon Brando (Ogden Mears), Sophia Loren (Countess Natascha Alexandroff), Sydney Chaplin (Harvey Crothers), Tippi Hedrin (Martha Mears), Patrick Cargill (Hudson), Margaret Rutherford (Miss Gaulswallow), Michael Medwin (John Felix), Oliver Johnston (Clark), John Paul (captain), Angela Scoular (society woman), Peter Bartlett (steward), Bill Nagy (Crawford), Dilys Lake (saleswoman), Angela Pringle (Baroness), Jenny Bridges (Countess), Arthur Gross (immigration officer), Balbina (maid), Anthony Chin (Hawaiian), Jose Sukhum Boonlve (Hawaiian), Geraldine Chaplin (girl at dance), Janine Hill (girl at dance), Burnell Tucker (receptionist), Leonard Trolley (purser), Len Lowe (electrician), Francis Dux (headwaiter), Cecil Cheng (taxi driver), Ronald Rubin (sailor), Michael Spice (sailor), Ray Marlowe (sailor), Josephine Chaplin (young girl), Victoria Chaplin (young girl), Kevin Manser (photographer), Marianne Stone (reporter), Len Luton (reporter), Larry Cross (reporter), Bill Edwards reporter), Drew Russell (reporter), John Sterland (reporter), Paul Carson (reporter), Paul Tamarin (reporter), Carol Cleveland (nurse), Charles Chaplin (old steward).

CHAPLIN APPEARANCES IN OTHER FILMS

1915   *His Regeneration* (Chaplin cameo).
Essanay film starring "Broncho Billy" Anderson, early western film hero.

1921   *The Nut* (Chaplin cameo).
United Artists film produced by and starring Douglas Fairbanks, Sr.

1922   *Nice and Friendly* (ambitious Chaplin home movie). From Accidental Film Corporation, with a cast that includes Lord and Lady Mountbatten, Jackie Coogan, and Chaplin.

1923   *Souls for Sale* (Chaplin cameo).
Goldwyn film produced, written, and directed by Rupert Hughes.

1923   *Hollywood* (Chaplin cameo).
Paramount film directed by James Cruze, which offered cameos of many stars as the "Chorus of Hollywood." Considered controversial due to its sympathetic reference to Fatty Arbuckle, whose career was curtailed by a scandal. (Cruze had directed several earlier Arbuckle films.)

1928   *Show People* (Chaplin cameo).
Cosmopolitan-MGM film directed by King Vidor and starring Marion

Davies. The Chaplin scene was later included in MGM's *Big Parade of Comedy* (1964).

1982/   In late 1982 and early 1983 Kevin Brownlow and David Gill uncovered a
1983   sizeable amount of Chaplin out-takes and other footage, the vast majority of
        which had long been in storage at the comedian's Swiss home.

Musical Compositions

1916 Songs
      "There's Always One You Can't Forget"
      "Oh! That 'Cello"
      "The Peace Patrol"

1921 From *The Kid*
      "The Kid"
      "Blue Eyes"
      "Morning Promenade"
      "Foxtrot"
      "South American"

1925 Songs
      "Sing a Song"
      "With You Dear in Bombay"

1931 *City Lights* soundtrack

1936 From *Modern Times*
      "The Factory Machine"
      "The Factory Set"
      "Charlie's Dance"
      "Charlie at the Assembly Line Belt"
      "The Ballet"
      "Visions"
      "The Gamin"
      "Charlie and the Warden"
      "Alone and Hungry"
      "Smile" (Love Theme)
      "In the City"

"Valse"
"The Sleeping Girl"
"Ten Days"
"At the Picture"
"Later That Night"
"The Toy Waltz"
"Closing Title"

1940   From *The Great Dictator*
"Napoli March"
"Falling Star"
"Zigeuner"
"Ze Boulevardier"
"Marche Militaire"

1942   From *The Gold Rush* (1925)
Original compositions with scored narration spoken by Chaplin. Late in Chaplin's career he would compose music for *Pay Day* (1922) and include it in the re-release package of *The Gold Rush*.

1947   From *Monsieur Verdoux*
"A Paris Boulevard"
"Tango Bitterness"
"Rumba"

1952   From *Limelight*
"The Theme from 'Limelight' "
    (vocal version: "Eternally")
"Ballet Introduction"
"Reunion"
"The Waltz"
"Terry's Theme"
"The Polka"

1957   From *A King in New York*
"Mandolin Serenade"
"Now That It's Ended"
"The Spring Song"
"Weeping Willows"
"Bathtub Nonsense"
"Park Avenue Waltz"
"The Paperhangers"

1959   From *The Chaplin Revue*, which is composed of:
A Dog's Life (1918)
"The Chaplin Revue Theme"
"Theme"
"Labour Exchange"
"Dog Chase"
"Green Lantern Rag"
"Coffee and Cakes"
"Flat Feet"

"The Shimmy"
"Song Triste"
"Robbers"
"Green Lantern Song"
"Progression Rag"
"Dog Diggin' "

Shoulder Arms (1918)
"Sauerkraut March"
"Shell Happy"
"Changing Guard"
"The Post"
"Over the Top"
"Blues"
"Peace"
"Tree Camouflage"
"Suspense"
"Mysterioso March"
"The Enemy"
"Agitato"
"D Minor Waltz"
"Inner March"
"Bringing Home the Bacon"

The Pilgrim (1923)
"Bound for Texas" (vocal)
"Jitters"
"Hope and Faith"
"The Deacon Presents"

1966   From *A Countess from Hong Kong*
"My Star"
"This Is My Song"
"The Ambassador Retires"
"Crossing the Dance Floor"
"The Three Ladies"
"Perdu"
"The Deb Shakes"
"Chamber Music"
"Taxi Waltz"
"A Countess from Hong Kong"
"Change Partners"
"Bonjour Madame"
"Hudson Goes to Bed"
"The Ill-Fitting Dress"
"The Countess Sleeps"
"Gypsy Caprice"
"Tango Natascha"

1970   From *The Circus* (1928)
"The Circus" (title song sung by Chaplin). The re-release package for *The Circus* also includes *A Day's Pleasure* (1919), with music by Chaplin.

1971   *The Kid* (1921) Music composed by Chaplin. The re-release package for *The Kid* also includes *The Idle Class* (1921), with music by Chaplin.

1976   *A Woman of Paris* (1923) Music composed by Chaplin. The re-release package for *A Woman of Paris* also includes *Sunnyside* (1919), with music by Chaplin.

Discography

The starting point for this section was the discography of Denis Gifford's *Chaplin*. I have expanded upon his work and arranged the material in alphabetical order. Because Chaplin's music has been, and continues to be, frequently recorded by a large and eclectic number of musicians, this list does not purport to be complete and final. But with Gifford's foundation and judicial use of a number of guides to musical recording, the following discography nicely illustrates Chaplin's ongoing musical influence.

Chaplin. Stan Butcher and his Warm Strings (Fontana SFL 13207).
The Chaplin Revue. Selection. Eric Spear (Brunswick LAT 8345).
Chaplin's Art of Comedy. Soundtrack. (Breeskin Main 6089).
Charles Chaplin's A Countess from Hong Kong. Soundtrack. Arranged and conducted by Lambert Williamson (Decca DL 1501).
Charlie Chaplin: A Legendary Performer (RCA Victor CPL1-2778).
A Countess from Hong Kong. Selection. Lambert Williamson (Brunswick AXA 4544).
Great Chaplin Film Themes. Johnny Douglas (RCA CDS 1114).
A King in New York. Selection. Norrie Paramor (Columbia SEG 7720).
Kostelanetz Plays the Music of Charlie Chaplin and Duke Ellington (Columbia PC 34660).
Limelight. Selection. Frank Chacksfield (Decca F 10106).
Living Strings Play Music from Charlie Chaplin Movies. Arranged and Conducted by Joe Douglas (RCA CASMDAN 2581).
"Mandolin Serenade"/"The Spring Song." Orchestra conducted by Charlie Chaplin, 1957 (HMV POP 370).
Modern Times. Soundtrack. Conducted by Alfred Newman (VA S 5222).

Music from the Films of Charlie Chaplin. Michael Villard (Pye NSPL 28173).

"Sing a Song"/"With You Dear in Bombay." Abe Lyman's California Orchestra, conducted by Charlie Chaplin, with a vocal by Charles Kaley, 1925 (Brunswick 2912).

These Are My Songs: Pet Clark. Contains pop singer Petula Clark's recording of Chaplin's "This Is My Song," from *A Countess from Hong Kong* (Warner Brothers-Seven Arts Records No. 1698).

INDEX

About the Author

WES D. GEHRING is Associate Professor of Film in the Department of Telecommunication at Ball State University. A lifelong aficionado of the works of Charlie Chaplin, Gehring received his Ph.D. from the University of Iowa where he studied with well-known Chaplin authorities such as Jean Mitry and Timothy Lyons. Gehring also has written *Leo McCarey and the Comic Anti-Hero in American Film* and *Charlie Chaplin's World of Comedy*.

Popular Culture Bio-Bibliographies: A Reference Series
Series Editor: M. Thomas Inge

Crockett: A Bio-Bibliography
Richard Boyd Hauck

Knute Rockne: A Bio-Bibliography
Michael R. Steele

John Henry: A Bio-Bibliography
Brett Williams

Hank Williams: A Bio-Bibliography
George William Koon

DATE DUE